OUR MOST PRICELESS HERITAGE
THE LASTING LEGACY OF THE SCOTS-IRISH IN AMERICA

Best Wishes to Dennis

Billy Kennedy

OUR MOST PRICELESS HERITAGE

THE LASTING LEGACY OF THE SCOTS-IRISH IN AMERICA

BILLY KENNEDY

AMBASSADOR INTERNATIONAL

OUR MOST PRICELESS HERITAGE
THE LASTING LEGACY OF THE SCOTS-IRISH IN AMERICA
© 2005 Billy Kennedy

Printed in the United States of America
British spellings used throughout book

Cover design & page layout by
Andrew Ramos of A&E Media

ISBN 1 932307 03 6
Published by the Ambassador Group

AMBASSADOR INTERNATIONAL
427 WADE HAMPTON BLVD.
GREENVILLE, SC 29609 USA
WWW.EMERALDHOUSE.COM

AMBASSADOR PUBLICATIONS LTD.
PROVIDENCE HOUSE, ARDENLEE STREET,
BELFAST BT6 8QJ, NORTHERN IRELAND
WWW.AMBASSADOR-PRODUCTIONS.COM

The colophon is a trademark of Ambassador International

Cover Pictures courtesy of David Wright. Main cover picture title: "Crossroads to Destiny 10." Pictured from right to left: Andrew Jackson, Sam Houston, and Davey Crockett.

There are few artists in the United States who have left such an important mark on the art of the American frontier as David Wright of Gallatin, Tennessee. Known for his exhaustive execution for authentic detail and historical accuracy, Wright has also expanded his role to that of Art Director for epic size productions in historic documentaries and films.

Wright's works can be seen at www.davidwrightart.com

THIS BOOK IS DEDICATED TO
MY WIFE SALLY, DAUGHTER JULIE AND MY PARENTS

"GOD IS OUR REFUGE AND STRENGTH, A VERY PRESENT HELP IN TROUBLE. THEREFORE WILL NOT WE FEAR, THOUGH THE EARTH BE REMOVED AND THOUGH THE MOUNTAINS BE CARRIED INTO THE MIDST OF THE SEA. THOUGH THE WATERS THEREOF ROAR AND BE TROUBLED, THOUGH THE MOUNTAINS SHAKE WITH THE SWELLING THEREOF."

PSALM 46, VERSES 1-3

Contents

BILLY KENNEDY

About the Author

This is the ninth book written by Billy Kennedy in his highly popular series of Scots-Irish Chronicles which details 18th century American frontier settlements. The books have been eagerly read by many people in both the United Kingdom and the United States, recording as they have the incredible story of a proud, dogged and determined people whose contribution to the establishment and development of the American nation has been outstanding.

Billy Kennedy, who lives in Co Armagh, has been a leading journalist in Northern Ireland for the past 35 years. He is a senior journalist with the *Belfast News Letter*, the primary morning newspaper in Northern Ireland and the oldest existing English-written newspaper in the world, having been founded in 1737. On his regular visits to the United States, Billy has lectured on the subject of the Scots-Irish diaspora at universities, colleges, historical and genealogical societies and public authorities in cities and towns of the southeastern states. His other main interests are soccer and American country music. He is married and has one daughter.

Billy Kennedy can be contacted at 49, Knockview Drive, Tandragee, Craigavon, Northern Ireland BT62 2BH. e-mail address: billykennedy@fsmail.net

JOHN RICE IRWIN

Foreword from America

When Billy Kennedy, in 1995, penned his first book on the Scots-Irish in America, I'm quite certain he had no notion that it would lead to a series of nine volumes on the subject. It may be reasonably assumed that this first volume was the result of his intense love and respect for his Scots-Irish people and incalculable contributions that they had made to the fabric and character of our country.

His skills as a researcher, his extensive experience as a writer, and his inexhaustible propensity for hard work would lead him to put together this first volume about the largely unheralded contributions which this relatively small group of stalwart people made to the character and resolve of a country that, in just a few short years, has attained a position of unparalleled stature and influence among nations of the globe.

But what about the subsequent eight books on various aspects of the same subject? Certainly the wide acceptance of the warmly embraced *The Scots-Irish in the Hills of Tennessee* was at the fore in sparking the second book *The Scots-Irish in the Shenandoah Valley*, and the third, *The Scots-Irish in the Carolinas*, and so on, through the publication of this, *Our Most Priceless Heritage*, the ninth book in this very popular series, of The Scots-Irish Chronicles.

The core reason for the acceptance of Billy's books may well be the "subject" itself—the consideration of the Scots-Irish as a people, as a group, as a national genre. We've recognised certain Scots-Irish giants of American history as individuals, the 17 Presidents, and the great military leaders, writers, inventors, etc.

However, we are not aware that these great personalities were the offspring of a distinct group—the Scots-Irish. As a group the Scots-Irish have remained largely invisible; that's the theme Billy stresses in this, as in all of his books. This emphasis is largely responsible for the interest in his works.

Billy's books have titillated countless other local and regional historians to initiate and pursue further research and writings on the phenomenal influence the Scots-Irish have had in America. Much of the publicity and exposure of these books is attributable to Billy's darting hither and yon throughout several states, speaking to innumerable historical and civic groups, making contacts with newspapers and periodicals, appearing on television and radio programs, and proclaiming the attributes and influence of these fascinating people.

I've had the honor of writing the foreword for all of Billy's nine books and, each time, I have fully anticipated that each would be the last. So, while I'm assuming that this book is indeed the last in this ongoing series, I dare not make such a prognostication.

I hope that this human dynamo—this inexhaustible, energetic, wiry and exuberant fellow—continues to inspire and inform us for years with his writings.

JOHN RICE IRWIN, FOUNDER/PRESIDENT, MUSEUM OF APPALACHIA, NORRIS, TENNESSEE.

DR. JOHN RICE IRWIN IS FOUNDER, DIRECTOR AND PRESIDENT OF THE MUSEUM OF APPALACHIA AT NORRIS, TENNESSEE, 15 MILES FROM THE CITY OF KNOXVILLE. THE EXTENSIVE EAST TENNESSEE FARM VILLAGE HAS GAINED NATIONAL INTERNATIONAL RECOGNITION FOR ITS CONCENTRATION ON THE RICH CULTURE AND FOLKLORE OF THE APPALACHIAN MOUNTAIN REGION. DR. IRWIN HAS BEEN A TEACHER, FARMER, BUSINESSMAN, HISTORIAN, AUTHOR AND HIS WIDE RANGE OF INTERESTS ALSO EXTENDS TO THE MUSIC OF HIS SOUTHEASTERN HOME REGION. HIS FAMILY IS OF SCOTS-IRISH AND WELSH EXTRACTION.

GEORGE D. HOLMES

Foreword from Northern Ireland

Someone once remarked that it is the privilege of each generation to look again at the past, sometimes with new evidence and always with new perspectives. Northern Ireland may appear to possess more "historians" than any other part of the British Isles.

However, for those of my generation and community who benefited from an otherwise excellent state education system there was little by way of formal teaching about the history of our country and we were left to our own devices to gain an insight into the history of the place where we were born.

Little wonder then that while some of our citizens drank from the fountain of historical knowledge, others merely gargled and some never found the fountain at all.

Ironically, it was while being taught the history of the United States of America that many of us became aware of the massivecontributionmadebyour18thcenturyfellowcountrymen, the "Scots-Irish", to the creation of what was to become the most powerful nation on earth.

The Alamo, San Jacinto, Kings Mountain, New Orleans, Gettysburg and Yorktown were more than just great battles on a far off continent, they became symbols of freedom and liberty with which we could easily relate.

David Crockett, J. E. B. Stuart, Kit Carson, Ulysses Simpson Grant and Thomas Jonathon "Stonewall" Jackson became more than heroes—they were the names from home and a link to our own history and heritage.

Equally the words of George Washington—"if defeated else where I will make my last stand for liberty among the Scots-Irish of my native Virginia"—is a sentiment which has a resonance this side of the Atlantic.

It was the Ulster poet Rev. W. F. Marshall, who once observed that "the average man is not a student of history, and such knowledge of it as he may be expected to acquire must come to him in handy and popular form". In his series of books on the Scots-Irish, author Billy Kennedy has admirably achieved this objective.

Through extensive research and an easy journalistic style of writing, Billy presents his readers with unique insight into the mindset and motivation of the early settlers who left these shores to escape religious and political persecution and periodic famine.

He deals fairly and uncompromisingly with this, misunderstood, misrepresented and, at times, maligned group of people.

The latest offering, the ninth in the series, from the pen of this prolific author will be eagerly awaited by his many readers and admirers.

The title *Our Most Priceless Heritage* echoes the sentiment of James Buchanan, 15th American President (1857-61)—"My Ulster blood is my most priceless heritage".

I have been privileged to attend a number of Billy Kennedy's lectures in the United States. On these occasions his knowledge, subject matter, style of delivery and pride in his home place combined to ensure his popularity.

The Scots-Irish have had few better champions and Northern Ireland no better ambassador than Billy Kennedy.

GEORGE D. HOLMES, F. I. P. C. M., F.S.A Scot, Deputy Chief Executive and Director of Culture, Ulster-Scots Agency, Belfast.

George Holmes, from Donaghadee in Co Down, has had a career in the Northern Ireland civil service dating back to 1967, and his work in various departments has brought him into direct contact with the communities in the country. His role as deputy chief executive and director of culture with the Ulster-Scots Agency, a cross-border government-funded body set of under the terms of the Belfast Agreement in 1998, allows him to extend his considerable knowledge on history, culture and music. He is a highly accomplished musician, playing banjo, guitar, mandolin, bouzouki, dulcimer, flute and percussion (mainly the Lambeg drum, bodhran and Latin American instrument). He also has very extensive knowledge of the traditional music of Scotland, Ulster and Ireland and was for nine years a guest soloist with the Grammy-award-winning Belfast Harp Orchestra, which is highly regarded as a cross-cultural ensemble, performing the music of Ireland, both North and South.

PRESIDENT ULYSSES S. GRANT, COMMANDER OF THE
UNION ARMY IN THE CIVIL WAR.

1

RAW COURAGE OF THE SCOTS-IRISH ON THE AMERICAN FRONTIER

Heroism was a distinct characteristic of the Scots-Irish immigrants who settled on the American frontier in the 18th century. The raw courage shown by this dogged, determined people in very difficult circumstances helped shape the fabric of the United States as an embryonic nation and, ultimately, as the world power that it is today.

Forging a civilisation out of a wilderness was a real challenge for the tens of thousands of Ulster Presbyterians who landed on American shores in different waves 200-250 years ago, and how well they succeeded in moulding a decent, law-abiding society, from the eastern New England seaboard states, into the Appalachian region, south to Texas and Mississippi and west towards California on the Pacific coastline.

The Scots-Irish heroes, and the heroines (the wonderful womenfolk who made the family, the home and Christianity the cornerstone of frontier life!) have become enshrined in American history—not just United States Presidents, statesmen, soldiers and churchmen, but the many plain ordinary citizens whose quiet, unselfish deeds were worthy of note and a shining example to others.

The outstandingly high level of achievement by so many luminaries from the Scots-Irish diaspora in states like Tennessee, Virginia, Pennsylvania, Kentucky, North Carolina, Georgia, South Carolina and Texas must be measured against the great suffering and pain first families endured during early formative years on the frontier.

Faith and *Freedom* were the cherished watchwords of the doughty Scots-Irish Presbyterians. These ideals kept them going as they moved during the 17th century plantation years over the short sea journey from Scotland to Ulster, and then trekked arduously across the Atlantic on the adventure into the great unknown of the frontier lands of the 'New World'.

God-fearing Scots-Irish, or Ulster-Scots, combined in their ideals: a total reverence for the Almighty, a deep devotion to their families, sincere love of country and passionate belief in their liberty. Generally, as a people the Scots-Irish stayed true to the four main cornerstones of life: God, country, family and liberty, although there were some, as in every community, who did not attain these standards.

The Scots-Irish were well-prepared for establishing settlements on the American frontier. They had endured, for more than a century, life in the harsh, rugged and, in parts, hostile countryside of the north of Ireland, and by the time they reached America they had survived wars, sieges, famines, drought and religious persecution. They were a people certainly not deterred by the dangers they faced in their new environment, and most found the wide open spaces to their liking.

Indeed, largely due to past experiences in lowland Scotland and the north of Ireland, Scots-Irish fared much better than other white ethnic groups like the English, Germans, Welsh, Dutch, Scottish highlanders and Scandinavians in resisting hostilities of the native American tribes; in fending off English, French and Spanish colonial predators and oppressors and in pushing the frontier south and west to its outer limits.

The Scots-Irish effectively set parameters of life in many cities and towns along the western frontier of 18th century America, and with close identification to church, school and home they were able to lay foundations for a civilised society, which placed total emphasis on a belief in God and in the liberty of conscience and democracy.

Celebrated Northern Ireland historian-folklorist Rev. W. F. Marshall summed up their work ethic and commitment to a cause: "The Scots-Irish were the first to start and the last to quit. The vigour and grit of the race were seen in their pioneering instinct."

The early Scots-Irish settlers were willing, even eager, to go beyond the "outer fringe of civilisation" and establish settlements on the frontier. Their experience as colonists in Ireland had made them adaptable and assimilative of the best traits needed for survival on the frontier, and their farming methods—the slash-and-burn clearing of farms, corn-based cropping and the running of livestock in open woods—were techniques ideally suited for the southern Appalachian backcountry.

Three hundred years have elapsed since the first Scots-Irish immigrants landed on American soil, and in that time the enormous landscape they inhabited has changed beyond all recognition, with political, social and cultural perspectives of the population now increasingly diverse in what has become a great melting pot of humanity.

Fundamentals of faith and freedom, so profound, meaningful and enriching to the proud pioneering people from Ulster and lowland Scotland, were permanently enshrined in the constitutional imperatives of the American nation. Today they are testimony to all that was achieved in early formative years of struggle and supreme sacrifice on the frontier.

The Declaration of Independence of July 4, 1776, which Ulstermen helped draw up, contained fine Christian sentiments: "We hold these truths to be self-evident, that men are created equal, that they are endowed by their creator, with certain inalienable rights, that among them are life, liberty, and the pursuit of happiness."

John Patterson MacLean, noted 19th century historian, said of the Scots-Irish: "They practiced strict discipline in morals and gave instruction to the youth in their schools and in teaching Biblical scriptures. To all this combined in a remarkable degree, acuteness of intellect, firmness of purpose and conscientiousness to duty."

From Pennsylvania through the Shenandoah Valley of Virginia to the Carolinas along the Great Wagon Road they came; to Tennessee, Georgia, Kentucky, on to the territories of Mississippi, Louisiana, Texas, Oklahoma,

Kansas, Colorado and California. The Scots-Irish blazed the pioneering trail in America for others to follow. They were a durable, determined people with the special personal stamp needed to tame the wilds of the frontier and to make it a place for civilised family life.

The Scots-Irish, who settled on the American frontier through the 18th century, were of the people who moved across from lowland Scotland from 1610 in the Ulster Plantation. They made the short sea journey from settle Ayrshire, Argyllshire, Renfrewshire, Lanarkshire, Dunfrieshire to principally counties Antrim, Down, Londonderry, Tyrone and Donegal. In the passage of time, many of them, because of religious persecution and economic deprivation, faced the long arduous trek across the Atlantic.

North Carolina academic James G. Leyburn, in a social history of the Scotch-Irish, described the Scots who moved to Ulster as humble folk with ambition and qualities of character that made good pioneers. "Even Presbyterian ministers who worked among them in Ulster were usually from humbler walks of Scottish life, for the Kirk offered no sinecures for younger sons of the gentry," he said.

The Scots-Irish were a unique people and the extent of their influence in the establishment of the USA after the Revolutionary War was considerable. Scots-Irish are described as clannish, contentious, hard to get on with and set in their ways. A Scots-Irish prayer ran, "Lord grant that I may always be right, for Thou knowest I am hard to turn."

As Presbyterians, this independent spirited people were non-conformist to the established church of the day, the Anglican or Episcopalian code, and during their 17th century settlement in Ulster they found great obstacles raised to the means of propagating and witnessing for their Calvinist doctrine and faith.

For about 100 years from 1610, the Scots worked the farms and the textile industry with French Huguenots. They erected meeting houses for Presbyterian form of worship and schools for their children's education. In Presbyterian mindset, the church and the school are inter-twinned, and this was the case when the Scots-Irish arrived in Ireland, and subsequently in America.

During the reign of Queen Anne, from about 1702, a High Anglican Church faction became dominant in government circles in London, enacting laws which weighed heavily on the minds and consciences of the Ulster

Presbyterians. These laws required all officer-holders under the Crown in Ireland to take sacraments of the established Episcopal church, and as many Presbyterians were magistrates and civil servants in towns like Belfast, Londonderry, Lisburn and Carrickfergus, they were automatically disqualified unless they renounced the Calvinist faith of their forefathers in Scotland.

Members of the Roman Catholic faith, who in the main constituted the native Irish population in Ireland, also bore the brunt of the discriminatory Test Act. However, in the administering of religion Roman Catholic priests were at least recognised by the High Churchmen as being lawfully ordained.

This was not so Presbyterian ministers, and right across the north of Ireland they were turned out of their pulpits and threatened with legal proceedings should they defy the Episcopal edict from London. Ministers had no official standing; they were unable to sanctify marriage, to officiate at the burial of members of their congregations, to confer baptism and were prevented from teaching on any aspect of Presbyterian doctrine.

This was a narrow ill-thought-out piece of legislation which left the Presbyterian population of Ulster, by then a highly significant section of the community, deeply resentful and almost totally alienated from political masters in the English established church. It had the effect of making the Presbyterian people speak increasingly of starting a new life in America. Their protests were ignored and there was, from the pulpit to the pew, the feeling that this might be the only way to ease the suffering.

The harsh economics of life in the north of Ireland in the early 18th century was another salient factor which made immigration more appealing. Four years of drought made life almost unbearable for the small peasant farmers on the hillsides of Ulster, and with the High Church landlords staking claims to exorbitant rents (evictions were commonplace in Ulster at the time!) and the textile industry in recession, movement of the Scots-Irish to America began in earnest.

Between 1717 and the American Revolutionary War period, an estimated quarter of a million people left the north of Ireland for the New World, most of them Presbyterian stock. They sailed, in simple wooden sailing ships, from Belfast, Larne, Londonderry, Portrush and Newry, arriving at Philadelphia, New Castle (Delaware), New York and Charleston. The hazardous journey across the Atlantic took an enormous toll on some, but despite health perils faced through over-crowding and lack of food and water, most reached their destination to start a new life in more amenable surroundings.

In 1717, the first year the ships were chartered for 5,000 men and women to head to Pennsylvania, drought completely ruined crops on the Ulster farmlands. Poverty in the homeland, and restrictions placed on dissenting faith by the ruling British Establishment of the day, made the promise of a better life irresistible.

There were five great waves of Ulster Presbyterian emigration to America: in 1717-18, 1725-29, 1740-41, 1754-55 and 1771-75. The Irish famine of 1739-41 had resulted in the death of 400,000 people, and when the Ulster settlers arrived in America in those years they set their sights beyond the borders of Pennsylvania—along the path of the Great Wagon Road down through the Valley of Virginia, the Shenandoah and on to South and North Carolina.

Next to the English, the Scots-Irish became by the end of the 18th century the most influential of the white population in America, which by 1790, numbered 3,173,444. At the time, the Scots-Irish segment of the population totalled about 14 percent and this figure was much higher in the Appalachian states.

The Scots-Irish totally assimilated into the mainstream of American society. They were, of course, first Americans, and pioneered new townships after cutting their way through dense forests and crossing formidable river and mountain barriers.

The Revolutionary War was a watershed for the contribution the Scots-Irish made to American life, and it is estimated that up to 75 percent of this diaspora backed the patriot cause against the Crown. As many as 10 of the 56 signatories of the Declaration of Independence of July 4, 1776 were of Ulster origin. John Hancock, President of Congress, was the best known-he had family ties to Co Down. John Dunlap, who moved to America from Strabane, Co Tyrone, printed the first copies of the Declaration, while Colonel John Nixon, of Ulster grandparents, gave the first public reading of the document in Philadelphia on July 8, 1776.

Seventeen of the 43 U.S. Presidents have Scots-Irish ancestry: Andrew Jackson, James Knox Polk, Andrew Johnson, James Buchanan, Ulysses Simpson Grant, Chester Alan Arthur, Grover Cleveland, Benjamin Harrison, William McKinley, Theodore Roosevelt, Woodrow Wilson, Harry Truman, Richard Millhouse Nixon, James Earl Carter, George Bush Sr., William Jefferson Clinton and George W. Bush.

James Buchanan, whose family came from Co Tyrone, said, "My Ulster blood is my most priceless heritage."

John C. Calhoun, eminent 19th century South Carolina statesman, was Vice-President for two terms; his father Patrick was a Co Donegal Presbyterian. Charles Thomson, Continental Congress Secretary for 15 years until 1789, left his Maghera, Co Londonderry homeland at the age of 10. He was a close associate of George Washington and designed the first Great Seal of America.

Statesmen, politicians, soldiers and frontiersmen—there was Davy Crockett, born at Limestone, East Tennessee, grandson of an Ulster emigrant from East Donegal/North Tyrone, while Sam Houston, born at Lexington, Virginia, was of an East Antrim family. Their lifestyles and exploits centered on Tennessee and Texas are legendary.

The men who founded Nashville in 1780—John Donelson (Andrew Jackson's father-in-law!) and James Robertson—were of Co Antrim roots, while the founding fathers of Knoxville were also of Ulster vintage—James White, his grandfather was from Londonderry, and John Adair and George McNutt, born Ballymena, Co Antrim.

There were illustrious churchman: Rev. Samuel Doak, who raised the standard for the Overmountain Men at the battle of Kings Mountain in 1780 by taking inspiration from the deeds of Gideon; Rev. Joseph Rhea; Rev. John Craig (his Shenandoah Valley parish in the 1740s extended to thousands of miles!); Rev. William Martin, outspoken fiery Covenanter; and Rev. William Tennant, of the Princeton log cabin theological college.

Nine of the 189 men, mostly Texans and Tennesseans who died at The Alamo in March, 1836, fighting for the freedom and liberty of Texas, were born in Ireland, mostly in Ulster. Many others in this gallant number, like Davy Crockett, were one, two or three generations away from 18th century Scots-Irish pioneering settlers who crossed the Atlantic on the emigrant ships. Irish-born soldiers who died at the Alamo were: Samuel Burns,

Andrew Duvalt, Robert Evans, Joseph Mark Hawkins, Thomas Jackson, James McGee, Jackson J. Rusk, Burke Trammel and William B. Ward

Many Civil War soldiers of distinction on the Confederate and Union sides were of Ulster-Scots origin. They included Thomas Jonathan 'Stonewall' Jackson, whose great grandfather John Jackson came from the Birches in Co Armagh; J. E. B. Stuart, a great-great grandson of Archibald Stuart from Londonderry; Ulysses Simpson Grant; George Brinton McClellan and Ambrose Everett Burnside.

Others of Scots-Irish roots were: Samuel Lanthorn Clements (the author Mark Twain!); poet-playwright Edgar Allen Poe; 19th century farm machine inventor Cyrus McCormick; Pittsburgh banker Andrew Mellon; songwriter Stephen Collins Foster; Co Antrim-born James Adair, who in the mid-18th century wrote the first authoritative book on native American tribes; James Maitland Stewart, the Hollywood film actor; frontier mountain man Kit Carson and William Clark, who, with Meriwether Lewis, led the great expedition in 1804-06 from Mississippi over the Rocky Mountains to the Pacific.

The Clark-Lewis expedition, initiated by President Thomas Jefferson, was remarkable in its exploration of soil, climate, plant and animal life. Clark's Virginian family was of Ulster origin. The wealthy Hearst publishing dynasty also traces its roots back to John Hearst, a Co Monaghan Presbyterian who, along with 300 kinsfolk, sailed from Newry, Co Down in 1764 for a fare of six shillings and eight-pence each.

In the United States today an estimated 44 million people claim Irish extraction. Of these, 56 percent can trace their roots back to the Scots-Irish Presbyterians who moved in the 18th century. There were many daring exploits by this people who tamed the American frontier. They were a people undeterred, God-fearing with a sterling work ethic and a stake in life which unrelentingly pushed them towards new horizons.

The Twain Whom God Made One

They were Twain when they crossed the sea,
And often their folk had warred,
But side by side, on the ramparts wide,
They cheered as the gates were barred.
And they cheered as they passed the king,
To the ford that daunted none,
For field or wall, it was each for all,
When the Lord had made them one.

Thistle and Rose, they twinned them close,
When their fathers cross the sea,
And they dyed them red, the live and the dead,
Where the blue starred-lint grows free;
Where the blue starred-link grows free,
Here in the northern sun,
Till his way was plain, he led the Twain,
And he forged them into one.

They were one when they crossed the sea,
To the land of hope and dream,
Salute them now, whom none can cow,
Nor hold in light esteem!
Whose footsteps far in peace in war,
Still sought the setting sun!
With a dauntless word and a long, bright sword,
The Twain whom God made One!

W. F. Marshall (Rev),
Co Tyrone.

A SIMPLE INSCRIPTION AT GREENVILLE
PRESBYTERIAN CHURCH IN THE SOUTH
CAROLINA PIEDMONT REGION SUMS UP
THE CONTRIBUTION OF THE SCOTS-IRISH
IN AMERICA:

"SACRED TO THE MEMORY OF THE SCOTS-IRISH
PIONEERS. FROM THE HOME LAND THEY
BROUGHT THEIR FAITH TO ENRICH THE SOUTH.
THEIR BRAVE HEARTS AND STRONG ARMS TO
SUBDUE THE WILDERNESS."

President Woodrow Wilson, Whose
Grandfather Came from Strabane, Co Tyrone

2

WHAT THEY SAID ABOUT THE SCOTS-IRISH

GENERAL GEORGE WASHINGTON: "If defeated everywhere else, I will make my stand for liberty among the Scots-Irish in my native Virginia."

Confederacy leader GENERAL ROBERT E. LEE was once asked: "What race of people do you believe make the best soldiers?" He replied: "The Scots who came to this country by way of Ireland."

PRESIDENT WOODROW WILSON: "The beauty about a Scotch-Irishman is that he not only thinks he is right, but he knows he is right."

Historian J. A FROUDE: "The Scots-Irish had a system of religious faith which has ever borne an inflexible front to illusion and mendacity, and has preferred to be ground like flint than to bend before violence or melt under enervating temptation."

American historian the REV. JETHRO RUMPLE: "We have good reason to be proud of the early pioneers from Ireland and Germany, others of English, Welsh and Scottish descent. They laid the foundations of their homes. They were men and women who suffered from conscience sake, or fled from despotism to seek liberty unrestrained by the shackles of a worn-out civilisation."

19th century American historian GEORGE BANCROFT: "They brought to America no submissive love for England; and their experience and their religion alike bade them meet opposition with prompt resistance. The first voice publicly raised in America to dissolve all connection with Great Britain came not from the Puritans of New England or the Dutch of New York or the planters of Virginia, but Scots-Irish Presbyterians. A paradoxical fact regarding the Scotch-Irish is that they are very little Scotch and much less Irish. They do not belong mainly to the so-called Celtic race, but they are the most composite of all of the people of the British Isles. They are called Scots - because they lived in Scotia and they are called Irish because they moved to Ireland. Geography and ethnology has given them their name."

Historian CHARLES WILLIAM DABNEY: "Wherever the Scotch-Irish settled in America they started schools. As the parsons were the best educated men they taught the youth as part of their ministry. In time, the schools they started in their frontier congregations grew to be common schools for all. Later some of them became academies and a few became colleges and universities. In this way, Ulster Presbyterians did more to start schools in the South and West than any other people."

JAMES LOGAN, Ulster-born Provincial Secretary in Pennsylvania in the early 18th century, wrote: "A settlement of five families from the north of Ireland give, me more trouble than 50 of any other people." Logan admitted the Scots-Irish were "troublesome settlers and hard neighbours to the Indians". Many settled on lands without bothering to secure legal rights for it—they started the practice of squatting.

PRESIDENT THOMAS JEFFERSON: "The Scots-Irish held the valley between the Blue Ridge and the North Mountain and they formed a barrier which none could venture to leap."

Scotch-Irish Congress of Tennessee declaration 1889: "An overwhelming majority of the early settlers of Tennessee were Scotch-Irish. Every Tennessean descending from our first settlers is to be put down as of this people if they cannot prove his descent to be otherwise. No church other than theirs, the Presbyterian Church, was founded in East Tennessee for 60 years after the first settlement."

3

Origins of the Scots-Irish

Scottish lowlanders who left Scotland for Ulster between 1610 and 1690 were biologically compounded of many ancestral strains. While the Gaelic highlanders of that period were (as they still are) overwhelmingly Celtic in ancestry, this was not the case with the lowland inhabitants.

The Lowlander had long since become a biological mix, in which nine strains had met and mingled in different proportions. Three of the nine were present in Scotland in pre-Roman days: the Stone Age aborigines; the Gaels, a Celtic people who overran the western part of the British Isles; and the Britons, another Celtic folk whose arrival pushed the Gaels north into Scotland and west to Wales.

Roman, Teutonic, Scots, Norse, Norman and Flemish influences were also brought to bear over a period of 1,000 years on the biological mix of a people that were to become known as the Scots-Irish.

Dourness was the most obvious characteristic of the lowland Scots. The word derives from the Latin "durus" and the French "dur"; which literally means hardness and durability, having the qualities of iron. Men and women who survive centuries of living in a harsh environment, both physical and social, learn how to endure the worst that life can inflict on them. Such were the lowland Scots.

The Scots knew famine, and plague, thin soil, insecurity of life and poverty, raids and aggression. They learned to fight back, to give blow for blow, and, when they had done their best, to endure. From the beginning of man, the Scots had a reputation of not being prepared to submit to any authority except their own. And this was shown in the Scottish homeland, in Ulster and on the American frontier lands.

Lowland Scots lived for their freedom, the freedom to live life as traditional Scots, with no man saying nay to their familiar rights. They did not tolerate subservience. There was nothing automatic about the loyalty a Scot showed to his chief although pragmatism and canniness were the attributes of both. The Scottish lowlander has long been regarded as notoriously argumentative.

This trait developed after the Protestant Reformation as theological points were debated over for hours in the Presbyterian Kirk. The educational system which the Presbyterian Kirk introduced became the cornerstone of life in Scotland, and the twin pillars of church and school were to lay the foundations of society for the Scots-Irish when they moved to Ulster and thence to America.

The Presbyterian tradition of church and school dates back to the teachings of Scottish reformer John Knox, who in his first *Book of Discipline* in 1560, instructed that "everie severall churche have a school maister," and that each father (minister or elder) in a congregation be compelled no matter what his "estair or condition," to bring up his children in "learnying and virtue."

Renowned Anglican bishop the Rev. Gilbert Burnet while on a tour of Scotland in the late 17th century was much impressed by the Presbyterian regard for education. He was surprised to find even "a poor communality" was able to dispute fine points of secular and sacred government and was even more surprised to find knowledge "among the lowest of them, their cottagers and servants." So it was in Scotland, in Ulster and in America where the Presbyterians settled.

Economic deprivation, caused by tighter landlord control on the leases of their tenant farmers, forced many Scottish lowlanders to participate in the Plantation of Ulster from 1610. This came about against a background of poverty, lawlessness and insecurity in Scotland, and after the first 30 years of the Plantation, an estimated 40,000 lowland Scots were located in the various counties of Ulster, with the figure multiplying in the years that followed.

Religious upheaval continued in Scotland for 100 years after the Reformation, and tensions increased when the Scottish Stuart kings moved to Westminster to also embrace the English throne. James VI of Scotland, the son of Mary Queen of Scots and later to be known as James I, was not enamoured by the Presbyterian form of worship. He believed the teachings of the Kirk, by its authority and freedom of speech, was a menace to the monarchical principle. England, he felt, had ordered its Protestant Reformation better by retaining bishops and a church hierarchy.

Throughout his reign, James I tried to impose Anglican guidelines on Presbyterians, without success. He undertook even to "correct" John Knox's hallowed *Book of Common Prayer*, so that it might be brought nearer the English *Book of Common Prayer*. His son Charles I, who ruled from 1625-49, shared his father's ideas about imposing English form of worship on the Scots, but he was just as frustrated in his attempts. On Charles's execution in 1649, Oliver Cromwell tried to impose his Commonwealth form of government on the Scots, but they remained opposed and some paid for it with their lives when the Cromwellian forces headed north.

Charles II was an even more ruthless monarch as far as the Scots were concerned. He was determined to bring the Presbyterian Scots to heel, and within two years of ascending the throne, he had begun a campaign to drive from their pulpits those ministers who would not conform to the ways of the episcopacy. There followed in Scotland what was known as "the killing times" when the resolute and fierce Covenanters of the western lowlands fought guerrilla warfare against Charles's men.

Refusing to accept episcopacy and, determined to worship God after their own accord, they left the towns to hold their meetings on hillsides and in secluded valleys.

They carried arms to defend themselves against the soldiers sent to hunt them down. Many were killed on the moors, hundreds were cast into prison, others tortured and some were hanged. But nothing could tame their spirit—their Reformed dissenting beliefs remained.

Events like the Battle of Bothwell Bridge in 1679, where the Covenanters were beaten, but not totally vanquished, stirred the nation, and the Covenanters found an honoured place in Scottish history.

Many Covenanters fled to America, settling in South and North Carolina, while others joined their fellow countrymen in Ulster with their numbers greatly strengthening the Presbyterian elements in the Province. Presbyterians about the middle of the 17th century became dominant in five Ulster counties—Antrim, Down, Tyrone, Donegal and Londonderry—and they far outnumbered the English Anglicans settled there.

Population movements in both directions between Scotland and Ulster have gone on for most of 2,000 years. The sea journey between the Ulster coastline and western parts of Scotland is at its shortest 15 miles and longest 50 miles, and at most, the peoples of the two countries are never more than a few hours sailing away from each other.

Scholars confirm the name Scotland was never applied to that country before the 10th century. It was called Alban or Albion, and in that period, the geographical and territorial term for Ireland was *Scotia*. *Scotus* was the race/generic term.

From about 500AD, Dalriadic Scots, operating in the north eastern part of Ireland around Co Antrim under the leadership of Fergus McErc and his brothers Lorne and Angus, left Ireland to settle in Argyllshire and the western isles of Scotland.

From Fergus was derived the line of Scoto-Irish kings and for centuries the inhabitants of the highlands of Scotland shared a common bond and language similarities.

THE JOURNEY ACROSS THE ATLANTIC TO AMERICA
WAS AN ENORMOUS ORDEAL.

4

Crossing the Atlantic

The journey across the Atlantic from Ulster to America in the 18th century took an average span of six to eight weeks, depending on the weather and the sea worthiness of the vessel. However, the arrival at an American port did not automatically mean that passengers could embark ship immediately. The quarantine laws had to be strictly observed and passengers were often forced to remain on board for weeks until the danger from disease and infection had passed.

Serious overcrowding and lack of food and fresh water were the main complaints of those who travelled on the immigrant ships, both paying passengers and indentured servants. The weather forced many passengers to remain below deck for long periods, and it was there, in the steamy atmosphere of the confined spaces, that exposure to the fatal diseases lay.

Child mortality was common on the journey, but illness also took its toll on adults. When death came the bodies were thrown overboard, after the appropriate burial rights were observed. It is remarkable, however, that of the hundreds of thousands of 18th century Ulster immigrants who set out for America in the numerous wooden sailing ships, only a small percentage perished before completion of the journey.

A large proportion of Atlantic journeys were completed with the minimum of fuss. Indeed, the greatest hardships of the passengers on board some ships were said to be boredom and discomfort. But such was the harshness of conditions for many people on the Ulster hillsides in the 18th century that they were happy to put up with some short deprivation and suffering to obtain freedom and a better deal in the New World.

The immigrant ships normally sailed in the spring, summer and autumn. A mid-winter journey across the Atlantic was not advisable. Weather predictions in those days were somewhat hazy and very often ship captains threw caution to the wind in venturing out into the unknown.

Heavy trans-Atlantic storms caused shipwreck for some vessels, but those which did not reach their destinations were the exception rather than the rule. It was generally accepted that Ulster ship-owners and captains had a better safety and success record than their counterparts from German, Dutch and French ports who ferried German Palatine Lutheran immigrants to America.

Ships carrying German immigrants in the early part of the 18th century were often ravaged by typhus, a deadly disease that became commonly known at the time as the "Palatine fever". On one German ship eighty people died before the journey began, and on another, 330 were afflicted by typhus over the duration of the journey.

Ulster emigration agents always presented a positive opinion on the trans-Atlantic voyage, and accounts rarely mentioned sickness. Fever thrived on overcrowding, and during the years of heavy immigration sickness was prevalent.

Thousands emigrated in 1740-41 at the time of the great famine in Ireland, and in Pennsylvania a hospital or rest house was set up to accommodate the sick. Irish and German immigrants, in that order, were specified as being most in need of attention. Smallpox was reported on two ships that sailed from Larne in 1772, and passengers on two Newry ships Charleston-bound were reported "remarkably sick." Some died on the crossing.

On arrival in America—at the eastern seaboard ports of Philadelphia, New York, Boston, Charleston, New Castle (Delaware)—it took a few days for the settlers to get their bearings. Finding land to erect a home was a priority for those who had paid their ship's fare and had still a few pounds left from their meagre savings raised by selling their small farms back home.

Those who had come as indentured servants worked for up to two years to pay off their debts, but such was the vastness of the country and opportunity that it was not long before they too were able to procure land settlement. Accounts of early Pennsylvanian settlements speak of great hardships.

The Rev. David McClure in Pennsylvania records thus: "The people are mainly Scots-Irish Presbyterians. On this journey we overtook several families from the older settlements in the East to the West. I remember one in particular, a family of about 12. The man carried a gun and an axe on his shoulders, the wife had the rim of a spinning wheel in one hand and a loaf of bread in the other. The little boys and girls carried a bundle according to their age. Two poor horses were loaded with some of the bare necessities of life. On top of the baggage of one was a sort of wicker cage in which a baby lay, rocked to sleep by the motion of the horse. A cow was one of the company, and she was destined to bear part of the family's belongings. A bed cord was strapped around her horns and a bag of meal was on her back. The family was not only patient, but cheerful, pleased at the prospect of finding a happy home in one of the valleys which stretched from the mountains on to Pittsburgh."

It was said that the conduct of the Scots-Irish frontier inhabitants demonstrated their faith, their patriotism and their spirit of mutual helpfulness. The early pioneer was not a philosopher and a thinker in the academic sense. In the rigorous struggle for survival in a virtual wilderness there was not the time to develop these interests.

The average Scots-Irish frontiersman was a doer whose values and beliefs were reflected in his everyday behaviour. He was a man who was high-principled and narrow, strong and violent, as tenacious of his own rights as he was blinded often to the rights of others; acquisitive, yet self-sacrificing; but most of all fearless, confident of his own power, determined to have and to hold.

In the Carolinas in the mid-18th century, most of the settlers worked subsistence-type farms that produced barely enough wheat to feed one family. These settlers enjoyed good crops when the weather was favourable, but they went hungry when frost, drought, flood and hail struck.

The houses of many of the settlers, Scots-Irish and Germans in the Piedmont area of South Carolina and Western North Carolina, were one or two-roomed log cabins with dirt floors and wood shutters for windows. It was common for the settlers to barter wheat for salt, bushel for bushel, and from the little money they acquired to buy sugar, coffee and tea or requirements for their holdings like a gun, an axe, a spinning wheel and iron pots for cooking.

Wages were low, with two shillings a day standard wages in 1762 for killing hogs, threshing or carpentering. Mowing grain paid a little more. One day's labour would buy a bushel of corn, half bushel of wheat, half bushel of dried beans, half pound of sugar, half pound of coffee, fifth pound of tea and a pound of wool or a pound of nails.

The belongings of the small farming and labouring settlers were few. Furniture was made by hand—a few stools, a table, shelves and a chest or cupboard of sorts containing the usual cooking utensils of the day.

Beds were mattresses made with leaves or straw. Cornbread, pork, vegetables and fruit were the basic foods and the horse and cow were proud possessions. Chickens and hogs, of the "razor back" or "wind splitter" species, were also kept. The animals were branded and turned loose to fend for themselves most of the year and were generally poor and scrawny.

Adults and their older children worked from dawn to dusk to eke out a living in the harsh conditions.

PRESIDENT ANDREW JACKSON—PIONEER,
SOLDIER AND STATESMAN.

5

THE SCOTS-IRISH PRESIDENTS

PRESIDENT ANDREW JACKSON:

Andrew Jackson, son of Co Antrim-born parents, more than anyone else guided the enormous explosion of the American nation during the first four decades of the 19th century. His pivotal role in the war of 1812 ensured that the expansive territories on the south-eastern frontier did not fall back into British and Spanish hands.

Jackson's great triumphs as a soldier climaxed at the Battle of New Orleans, and of this encounter, he observed with considerable satisfaction, "This morning of January 8, 1815, will be recollected by the British nation and always hailed by every true American."

In the American mindset, the victory over the British at New Orleans was all down to Andrew Jackson's sterling leadership, and he remained a popular hero across the nation for the rest of his life.

Old Hickory—Hero of New Orleans—had restored the confidence of the nation, and he provided reassurance in its ability to maintain its freedom and independence against heavy odds.

From his days growing up in the Waxhaw region of the Carolinas during the Revolutionary War period, Andrew Jackson, developed a loathing for British colonial interests on American soil. His two brothers, Hugh and Robert, were casualties during the War and his widowed mother Elizabeth, a woman of extraordinary courage and determination, died from cholera fever in 1780 while attending sick nephews on a British prison ship in Charleston harbour.

Andrew, who as a 12-year-old received a facial wound from the sword of a British soldier during an affray in the Waxhaws, was embittered by these deaths and, alone in the world at the age of 14, he vowed his revenge. More than 30 years later, just before the Battle of New Orleans, he told his wife Rachel that "retaliation and vengeance characterised his attitude to the British and their Spanish and Creek Indian allies."

His personal experiences during the Revolutionary War shaped Andrew Jackson's character and purpose in life. He emerged with deep patriot and nationalistic convictions, perceiving himself to be in a struggle for the liberties of his people and not forgetting the price that others had paid to secure them.

"I owe to the British a debt of retaliatory vengeance. Should our forces meet, I trust I shall pay the debt—she is in conjunction with Spain arming the hostile Indians to butcher our women and children," said Jackson, whose parents, Andrew and Elizabeth, had left their home at Boneybefore near Carrickfergus in Ulster in 1765 for Charleston, South Carolina, sailing from the Co Antrim port of Larne.

The Jackson family were Scottish lowland Presbyterian stock who had been in the north of Ireland from the mid-17th century. Andrew was born in the Waxhaws on March 15, 1767, a few weeks after the death of his father.

His youthful years were spent in the rough, tough world of the late 18th century Carolina frontier, and this prepared him for the rigours of life as a soldier, lawyer, politician and statesman. He moved from being an apprentice saddler to become a teacher at 17, and eventually a lawyer at 20. He practiced law in Monroe, Anson County, and was public prosecutor of North Carolina's western district.

Jackson moved to the Tennessee country with others in 1788 trekking along the Wilderness Road over the Allegheny Mountains and arriving in Nashville, which was starting to expand out from its original Fort Nashborough log cabined frontier station. He opened a law office and met his wife Rachel Donelson, daughter of the settlement founder Colonel John Donelson, while staying as a boarder guest in her widowed mother's home.

Rachel had been married before to Kentuckian Lewis Robards, who started divorce proceedings but dropped these without telling his estranged wife. This meant that Rachel unwittingly committed bigamy when she married Andrew in 1791, but when Robards later was granted a divorce, the couple remarried, and although they had no children, they had a very happy 27-year marriage. Rachel and, even Andrew had to endure much slander and insults over the impropriety of their marriage, and it became an issue during election time.

Andrew even fought a duel in Kentucky in 1806 with a Charles Dickinson, who spoke harshly of Rachel. Dickinson died from bullet wounds in the pistol shoot-out, while Jackson had rib and chest wounds, but survived. Duels were commonplace on the American frontier at the time, but the Dickinson incident was an unfortunate chapter in Jackson's life, and it took him several years to live it down.

Rachel, even though she was of a family of ten, inherited a substantial amount of property and money from her father's estate, and Andrew, until then not a man of great means, benefited and his influence in Nashville expanded considerably.

By 1804, the couple were living at The Hermitage outside Nashville, then a plantation house and farm, and by 1819 this homestead had made way for a luxury brick house and expansive estate. Jackson's political career began in the constitutional convention of Tennessee in the mid-1790s, and he was the first Congressman for the state, and later elected a U.S. Senator. In between, however, his military prowess came to the fore, and this established him as a household name across America.

Jackson was appointed major-general of the Tennessee militia in 1802, and for the next 20 years he was seen as essentially a military man. His first major assignment in the regular army came in 1812 when the war department in Washington ordered his Tennessee soldiers to Natchez and there dismissed them. Jackson refused to obey orders and he marched his men back to Tennessee, earning for himself in that episode the title of "Old Hickory". A year on, he engaged his men against the Creek Indians at Talladega, and went on to triumph in other battles against the tribes. The treaty of Fort Jackson, concluded in 1814, led to the transfer of most of the Creek lands in Alabama and southern Georgia to white settlers.

In May, 1814, Jackson was ordered to defend the Gulf coast against an expected British invasion, and, after leading his troops into Florida and seizing the key port of Pensacola, he marched to New Orleans, where on the morning of January 8, 1815, he routed the British in a battle that has become immortalised in the annals of American history.

Jackson's army consisted of Tennesseans, Kentuckians, Blacks, Indians, and Creoles, and, when heavy British artillery fire failed to dislodge them from their location at the dried-up Rodriguez River, British commander Edward Packenham ordered 6,500 Crown soldiers to attack head-on. Within 30 minutes, 2,000 British soldiers were killed or wounded, while only 13 American fatalities were reported.

Theodore Roosevelt, in his book Naval War of 1812, said that American soldiers deserved great credit for doing so well. He added: "Greater credit still belongs to Andrew Jackson, who, with his cool head and quick eye, his stout heart and strong hand, stands out in history as the ablest general the United States had produced from the outbreak of the Revolution down to the beginning of the Great Rebellion."

While Jackson may have had his critics over the manner of his victory at New Orleans through the imposition of martial law, suspension of habeas corpus and the execution of mutinous militia-men, he won acclaim throughout the nation, and, to many, he was second only to General George Washington in service to the fledgling American republic. Interestingly, Jackson earned 5,000 dollars a year plus expenses as U.S. Army general, the same salary he received as governor of Florida.

Over the next few years Jackson successfully negotiated land treaties in Georgia, Alabama, Mississippi, Tennessee and Kentucky, with the Cherokees, Choctaw and Chickasaw Indian tribes. In 1818, he led troops into Florida, this time to suppress the Seminole Indians and again seized Pensacola and caused an international crisis by ordering the execution of two British subjects suspected of arming the Seminole tribes.

Jackson's hardline stance was vindicated in 1819 when he supervised the transfer of Florida from the Spanish to the United States, and later he served as territorial governor there for three months during the establishment of state government. His remit extended to captain-general of Cuba, which meant complete military command throughout the highly volatile region.

Jackson resigned his Army commission on June 1, 1821. In November of that year, he and Rachel left Florida for their Hermitage home in Tennessee, where he set about resuming his political career with a vigor which eventually led him to the White House in 1828 for the start of two Presidential terms.

His war service and spell in the swamp heat of Florida took serious toll of Jackson's health. He had two bullets lodged in his body, which regularly formed abscesses and produced coughing spasms leading to massive hemorrhages. He also contracted dysentery and malaria and developed bronchitis which was to plague him for the rest of his life.

Despite his health strictures, Jackson managed to soldier on and for the next two decades as a national politician and statesman he articulated the doctrine of Jacksonian democracy. This argued that it was the obligation of the United States government to grant no privilege that assist one class over another, to act as honest broker between classes and to protect the weak and defenceless against the abuses of the rich and powerful.

It was said Andrew Jackson looked beyond the overarching institutions of American life, linked as they were to inherited wealth. To the dismay of Virginia and new England dynasties that had held the Presidency since the country's founding, Jackson was the first President whose name meant only what he himself could make it mean.

He challenged the power of Eastern banks, making credit available to the West, and resisted threats of secession from the South. By promoting the West and by holding America together, Jackson set a course for the common man within the nation. After his presidency, candidates running for office searched in their backgrounds, not for degrees from the universities of Virginia or Harvard, but for a log cabin to incorporate in their election manifesto.

Tragically, Rachel Jackson died a few weeks after Andrew was elected for his first four-year term as president. After just recovering from the shock of the death of their 16-year-old adopted Indian son Lyncoya, Rachel was devastated by the public accusations during the presidential election campaign of "adultery and bigamy" resulting from her marriage to Jackson before a divorce from her first husband Lewis Robards was sanctioned.

Heartbroken, that she was targeted in this way, Rachel's physical and mental condition rapidly deteriorated, and although Andrew tried frantically to rally her, she died on December 22, 1828 and was buried in the garden of the Hermitage on Christmas Eve. One of the pall bearers at the funeral was Sam Houston, then governor of Tennessee and a close aide of Jackson.

For several days the new president was inconsolable, and he told his aides, "A loss so great can be compensated by no earthly God."

He had to prepare for the trip to Washington to begin his presidency, but until the day he died in 1845, Andrew grieved for a wife who was so dear to him.

For most of his life Andrew Jackson had never been a particularly religious man, but things changed for him on Sunday July 15, 1838, when he joined the Presbyterian church. Both his mother Elizabeth and wife Rachel both devoted church members until their deaths. He promised Rachel he would join, but had postponed a decision because he felt a that as a politician a public display of his religion might be regarded as "hypocritical."

Now retired, Jackson consulted the Rev. James Smith, who ministered at the Hermitage church which had been built for Rachel in 1823, and admitted he felt more identified with the Presbyterian Church than with any other denomination.

During the service, Jackson rose in his pew to announce that he wanted to join the church, and further declared belief in its doctrines and resolved to obey the Presbyterian precepts. For the rest of his life, it was said Andrew Jackson conducted himself as a true believer, and his faith was described more uniquely his own than what might be organised with the Presbyterian church. He could never accept the idea of an "elect" chosen by God, because it offended his democratic soul.

It would have been most uncharacteristic of him to have submitted totally to all the precise teachings of the church, but he attended services regularly, and he read a portion of the Bible each day along with other Biblical commentaries and the hymnbook. He led family and servants in prayers at the Hermitage each night.

Jackson died of chronic tuberculosis on June 8, 1845, aged 78. His final words were: "Oh, do not cry. Be good children and we shall all meet in heaven."

Andrew Jackson said on a visit to Boston in 1833: "I have always been proud of my ancestry and being descended from that noble race. Would to God, Sir, that Irishmen on the other side of the great water enjoyed the comforts, happiness, contentment and liberty that they enjoy here."

PRESIDENT JAMES BUCHANAN:

President James Buchanan once declared with firm conviction, "My Ulster blood is my most priceless heritage." This was a definitive statement of identity made by a man whose father James had left Co Tyrone in 1783 with his wife Elizabeth Speer and whose family remained intensely proud of their Ulster Presbyterian roots.

The Buchanan family lived at Deroran near Omagh, Co Tyrone before they moved to America and settled in eastern Pennsylvania. James was of merchant stock and his wife Elizabeth—a well-read and highly intelligent woman—was the daughter of an immigrant farmer from Ulster.

James, the 15th United States president, was strongly influenced by his father, and in later years, he wrote: "My father was a man of practical judgment, and of great industry and perseverance. He was a kind father, sincere friend and an honest and religious man."

President Buchanan's mother was also a devout Christian, one who provided the intellect which allowed her son to develop successful legal and political careers.

Of his mother, he wrote: "I attribute my little distinction which I have acquired in life in this world to the blessing which He (God) confided upon me in granting me such a mother."

James Buchanan was born in a log cabin at Stone Batter in Cove Gap, Franklin County, Pennsylvania in 1791. When the family moved to Mercersburg, he studied Greek and Latin at the Old Stone Academy, a Presbyterian-run institution, in between working at his father's trading store. James later studied law in Lancaster, then the Pennsylvanian state capital, and he was admitted to the bar in 1812.

Like his father, James was a federalist and a Jacksonian Democrat, and was nominated for the Pennsylvanian assembly on August 4, 1814, the same day as British troops burnt the White House during their occupation of Washington.

James had a brief military career, but he was essentially a politician, and by the time he was President in 1857, he had completed 42 years in public life as a Democratic state assembly man, U.S. Representative, minister to Russia, secretary of state and minister to Britain.

He was a close associate of President Andrew Jackson, also of Ulster Presbyterian stock. It was Jackson who appointed him minister to Russia in 1832, and later in 1844, President James Knox Polk, another of Ulster Presbyterian lineage, had him as secretary of state, a role overseeing expansion of the United States through acquisition of south-western Mexican lands and populating the Oregon territory.

James Buchanan, an imposing six-foot figure, was the only bachelor president, and his orphaned niece Harriet Lane served as official White House hostess during his 1857-61 term. James was engaged to Ann Coleman, daughter of a wealthy Pennsylvanian ironmonger, but sadly Ann died after terminating the engagement.

In his presidency, James Buchanan was confronted with the acute dilemmas resulting from the slavery issue, and he also had to contend with urban expansion across the states, a dramatic increase in immigration and economic problems of a nation which was steadily extending its borders. He was elected with 45 percent of the popular vote and 59 percent of the electoral college vote.

Buchanan was 70 when he stood down from the Presidency in 1861, greatly dismayed by the bitter wrangle over slavery and the ominous threatening clouds of civil war. His successor at the White House was Republican Abraham Lincoln.

On slavery, Buchanan said as far back as 1826 that it was a great political and moral evil. "I thank God that my lot has been cast in a state where it does not exist," he said.

President Buchanan retired to his residence at Wheatland, Lancaster, Pennsylvania, worn out by the rigours of high office, but he continued as a member of the House of Representatives until he was 77, serving 47 years. He died on June 1, 1868, and 20,000 people attended his funeral.

James Buchanan was a strict Sabbatarian, reciting daily prayers and being very conversant with the Bible. He was of the Presbyterian tradition, but he did not formally belong to a church in Washington. When he retired from the Presidency, he re-joined the congregation at Lancaster.

A younger brother, the Rev. Edward Young Buchanan, was rector of Trinity Episcopal Church in Philadelphia and married Ann Eliza Foster, sister of the famous composer Stephen Collins Foster, whose family also emigrated from Ulster.

In a unique tribute to President James Buchanan, Republican President Ulysses S. Grant said: "In 1856, I preferred the success of a presidential candidate whose election would prevent or postpone secessation of states to seeing the country plunge into a war, the end of which no man could foretell. With a democrat elected by the unanimous vote of the slave states there could no pretext for secession for four years. I therefore voted for James Buchanan as President".

The name *Buchanan* is of Scottish origin, territorial from the district of Buchanan in Stirlingshire, from the Gaelic/Gallic name of *Chanain* which means "house of the canon." In Ulster, the name is most common in Co Tyrone, where President James Buchanan's family originated .

PRESIDENT ANDREW JOHNSON:

Andrew Johnson, who rose to the United States Presidency with little or no education, came of Co Antrim Presbyterian stock. His grandfather and namesake emigrated to America from the port of Larne about 1750, and Andrew was born at Raleigh in North Carolina in 1808.

The 17th President of the United States was reared on the wrong side of the tracks in a Carolina community which was known as "the poor Protestants." He literally managed to lift himself up by his bootlaces to became the third Tennessean to reach the White House. The rags to riches story began for Andrew Johnson at the age of three when his janitor father died; the little boy and his older brother were eventually bound out to a tailor, to be fed and clothed for their work until they became 21.

The apprenticeship was not served to the full and when both boys ran away to South Carolina, a reward of 10 dollars was put up for their capture. They returned to Raleigh for a time and young Andrew secured journey work at Laurens courthouse in South Carolina. He remained there for 20 months, before deciding in September, 1826 to head in the direction of East Tennessee.

On the journey across the Appalachian Mountains Andrew was joined by his mother Mary McDonagh Dougherty, her second husband Turner Dougherty and his older brother. It was said they travelled the road by which Andrew Jackson had entered Tennessee 40 years earlier, their sparse belongings packed on a little one-horse wagon.

Greeneville was a strong Scot-Irish village settlement nestled in the foot-hills of the Great Smoky Mountains, and as Andrew and his family were of this kith they were warmly welcomed.

The postmaster in Greeneville was William Dixon (Dickson), a Covenanter of Ulster stock, and with John A. Brown, a clerk at the Dixon store, they persuaded Andrew to stay and pursue his tailor's trade.

There he met his wife Eliza McArdle, only daughter of a Scots-Irish shoemaker, and it was her ambition and drive which helped push Andrew up the social scale.

Johnson ran his tailor's shop at Main Street, Greeneville, where he made coats for $3.50, pants for $1.50, vests for $3.50 and suits for $10.

Increasingly, however, he interested himself in the affairs of the region, took part in debates in the village square or at Greeneville College and Tusculum Academy, which was founded by Scots-Irish pioneering pastor the Rev Samuel Doak. He became an alderman and eventually rose to the Mayorship of Greeneville in 1834 and Governorship of Tennessee for two terms, taking office in 1853.

Andrew Johnson became a senator in 1857 and in the White House was much involved in the moves to abolish slavery. His Union tendencies were disliked in the South. He was labelled "a home-made Yankee," "white trash," "a traitor," but he still maintained a solid support base in the Greeneville area of East Tennessee.

Johnson, however, was not a typical Southern Democrat, and when elected to the United States Senate, he stood apart from the 21 other senators from the South in opposing the secession from the Union on the abolition of the slavery issue.

Abraham Lincoln, the then president, saw in Andrew Johnson a man who could help him bring the South along in his bid to abolish slavery, but Johnson made himself a figure of ridicule with many of his own people.

During the Civil War, Andrew left the Senate at Abraham Lincoln's request to become military governor of Tennessee and, it was while serving in this post, that he was nominated Vice-President in 1865. On President Lincoln's assassination on April 14, 1865, Johnson was elevated to the presidency and he served almost four years until 1869.

While president, Johnson increased his unpopularity in the South by insisting on personally punishing the Confederate leaders and economically penalising the Southern states. Colleagues managed to get him to soften his line and a Proclamation of Amnesty was issued which gave a general pardon to all in the Confederate rebellion, provided they took an oath of allegiance to the Union. A total of 14,000 Southerners received pardons.

The Civil War had created immense political and economic problems, none the least making the Southern states bankrupt and having four million slaves freed, all of them badly needing education, housing and work.

Johnson became increasingly more conciliatory towards the South, and he tried to rally the east and mid-west of the country against demands for severe punishment of the Southern states. Joining him in this was General Ulysses S. Grant, the triumphant commander of the Union Army, and, ominously, it was Johnson who got the jeers, Grant the cheers.

Later, Johnson suffered more humiliation when impeachment charges were levelled against him for "high crimes and misdemeanours." This led to difficulties between Johnson and his Secretary of State Edwin M. Stanton, a radical Republican.

The full Senate met for the trial on May 26, 1868 and voted 35 in favour of conviction and 19 against. It was just one vote short of the necessary two-thirds—by the slimmest of margins, Johnson was acquitted. Soon after his Presidential term ended, but he was to return to Washington in 1875 when the people of Tennessee elected him to the Senate.

He was the only president to serve as a senator, and in the same year Johnson died suddenly at the home of his daughter at Carter Station, Tennessee. He had a stroke which mainly affected his left side. He was 67.

Johnson was a man of solid build, black hair, deep-set dark eyes and an expression of grim determination which personified his Scots-Irish characteristic.

His wife Eliza's health had deteriorated by the time he reached the White House, and she was so weakened by tuberculosis that she made only one public appearance during her four years' residence there. A married daughter, Martha Johnson Patterson, carried out the First Lady duties.

Eliza Johnson survived her husband by only six months and both are buried in Greeneville, Tennessee.

President Ulysses Simpson Grant

Ulysses Simpson Grant, heroic and successful commander of the Union Army in the American Civil War and the 18th United States President, is of Co Tyrone farming stock. His great-grandfather on his mother Hannah's side John Simpson left Ulster for Pennsylvania in 1760, and after moving through the Shenandoah Valley of Virginia, the Simpson family eventually settled in Ohio.

The Simpson family homestead at Dergenagh is situated about five miles west of the town of Dungannon, Co Tyrone, Northern Ireland. The family was Presbyterian, although Ulysses Grant was a nominal Methodist, who, although he did not attend church regularly, spoke often about his belief in God, the Bible and the afterlife.

On his father's side, Grant's original immigrant father, Matthew Grant, emigrated from Plymouth, England to Dorchester, Massachusetts in 1630 shortly after the movement of the Pilgrim fathers.

His great-great grandfather, Captain Noah Grant, was killed in action in 1756 during the French-Indian War, and his grandfather, also Captain Noah Grant, served on the revolutionary side during the War of Independence and fought at Bunker Hill.

Ulysses, the rugged soldier-politician, was born on a farm at Mount Pleasant, Ohio in 1822, and after he graduated from West Point military college in 1843, standing 21st in a class of 39, he was involved as a captain in army assignments in Missouri, Louisiana and Mexico, where he earned a citation for bravery.

After the Mexican War, Grant resigned his commission in 1854 because of loneliness, depression and a desperate need to be with his wife Julia and young family. Julia was a tower of strength to him when he was in depressive moods, very often brought on by an over-indulgence of alcohol, and it was her steadying influence that pushed him eventually to the pinnacles of his military and political careers.

By the start of the Civil War in 1861, Ulysses Grant returned to service as a colonel in the Illinois volunteer infantry regiment of the Union Army and within a short time he graduated to brigadier general. His leadership qualities were evident in the Kentucky-Tennessee campaigns of 1862, which lead to the capture of Forts Henry and Donelson from the Confederates. Raised on a farm, Grant had a great love of horses and he seemed to be always at his best on horse-back.

At Shiloh in April of that year, his regiment sustained a lot of casualties, but they recovered and eventually overcame the Confederates. Grant's unconventional tactics in the field and his uncharacteristic manner and shabby appearance for a senior officer brought criticism, but Abraham Lincoln rejected calls for his dismissal, stating: "I can't spare this man. He fights."

Lincoln's belief in Grant, untutored and a shy retiring man of changing moods, paid off. With systematic authority and unflinching calculation, he skilfully turned things around for the Northern forces, with significant successes at Vicksburg on the Mississippi River and at Chattanooga in Tennessee. In March 1864, Lincoln appointed him commander-in-chief.

The war was in its final phase with the Confederates losing men and resources, and Grant moved on to Virginia where General Robert E. Lee was based, while his successor in Tennessee, General W. T. Sherman marched into Georgia towards Atlanta.

The summer of 1864 saw Grant and Lee engaging in some of the most bloody battles of the war at the Wilderness, Spotsylvania, Cold Harbour and Petersburg, with tens of thousands of men lost on both sides. The most decisive battle for Grant came in the spring of 1865, when, backed with up by General Philip Sheridan, he managed to outflank Lee's Confederate troops in the Shenandoah Valley.

Grant offered Lee generous terms of surrender, with the assurance that Confederate soldiers would be paroled and allowed home to their various southern states. Lee signed the surrender document at Appomattox Court House on April 9, and, over the summer, General Grant supervised the dismantling of the Union Army.

In a fulsome tribute to Grant, Robert E. Lee said: "I have carefully searched the military records of both ancient and modern history and I have never found Grant's superior as a general."

President William McKinley said of Grant: "Faithful and fearless as a volunteer soldier, intrepid and invincible as commander-in chief of the armies of the Union and confident as president of a reunited and strengthened nation, which his genius had been instrumental in achieving."

After the War, Grant was nominated for secretary of state by President Andrew Johnson, but he was never approved for that office in Congress. He did, however, make it to the presidency in 1868 after accepting the Republican nomination.

Grant's reputation, as a victorious war general, made him a popular figure in the North, and, without much electioneering and a simple poll theme—"Let us have peace"—he won an overwhelming mandate, defeating New York Democrat Horatio Seymour.

In his inaugural presidential speech, he said: "I ask patient forbearance one toward another throughout the land, a determined effort on the part of every citizen to do his share toward cementing a happy Union."

In 1872, Grant's presidential success over another New Yorker Horace Greeley was even more convincing.

Grant, however, fully realised his shortcomings as a politician and he never enjoyed high rating as an American president. At the end of his two terms in the White House, he said: "It was my fortune or misfortune to be called to the office of chief executive without any previous political training."

And on his Army career, Ulysses Grant modestly commented: "The truth is I am more of a farmer than a soldier. I never went into the army without regret and never retired without pleasure." His military prowess spoke for itself and in war he operated with the simple formula—"find the enemy, hit them hard and move on."

The American Civil War was very costly for both sides in terms of lives lost, but it is widely acknowledged that Grant's triumphs were down to his commonsensical approach to generalship, emphasis on co-ordination and co-operation, calmness under pressure, determination to achieve his goals, energy in action, and a resourcefulness, perseverance and decisiveness in the heat of battle.

Ulysses Simpson Grant died in July, 1885, after suffering from painful throat cancer. An estimated million people turned out for his funeral in New York.

In 1878 Ulysses S. Grant was made a freeman of Londonderry, today Northern Ireland's second city, and from where many Scots-Irish emigrants left for America in the 18th century. The honour recognised both Grant's gallantry as a soldier and his service as an American statesman, not forgetting his 18th century Ulster family roots.

In July, 1878, Grant travelled to Ireland as a part of a world tour to receive the Londonderry freemanship, arriving in Dublin and travelling by train to Londonderry via Omagh and Strabane. He stopped off for a time at Ballygawley, Co Tyrone to see the Grant family homestead, and he also visited Coleraine.

During his stay in Londonderry, President Grant, who was accompanied by a number of American friends and aides, was keenly interested in the full story of the famous Siege in the city in 1688-89, and he was given a full tour of the walls of Derry, remarking on their remarkable thickness.

In his inaugural address as president on March 4, 1869, Ulysses S. Grant said: "The country having just emerged from a great rebellion, many questions will come before it for settlement in the next four years which preceding Administrations have never had to deal with. In meeting these it is desirable that they should be approached calmly, without prejudice, hate or sectional pride, remembering that the greatest good to the greatest number is the object to be achieved. This requires security of persons, property and free religious and political opinion in every part of our common country. Without regard to local prejudices. All laws to secure these ends will receive my best efforts for their enforcement."

PRESIDENT WOODROW WILSON:

Thomas Woodrow Wilson, United States president at the early part of the 20th century when America was emerging as a world super power, had very strong Ulster and Scottish roots which he spoke often about.

This son of a Presbyterian minister, born in Staunton in the Shenandoah Valley of Virginia in 1856, guided the United States through the First World War and was awarded the Nobel Peace Prize for his contribution.

President Wilson's paternal grandfather, James Wilson, emigrated from Strabane in North Tyrone in 1807, while his maternal grandfather, the Rev. Thomas Woodrow was a native of Paisley in Scotland who moved to America in 1835 to take up a Presbyterian congregational charge in Ohio.

James Wilson was 20 when he sailed from Londonderry to Philadelphia, having grown up in the rural hamlet of Dergelt, about two miles from Strabane town and in the picturesque foothills of the Sperrin Mountains. He had just completed his apprenticeship as a printer at Gray's Shop at Bridge Street, Strabane when he moved. Remains of the humble Wilson homestead at Dergelt are still preserved to this day and descendants of the original family reside in the area.

A previous employee at Gray's print shop was John Dunlap, who printed the first copies of the July 4, 1776 Declaration of Independence and founded the first American daily newspaper *The Pennsylvania Packet*. There was a close connection between Gray's and America, and when James Wilson arrived in Philadelphia, John Dunlap was still alive and the Ulster link was sustained.

James Wilson worked at the Democratic newspaper *The Aurora* and within five years he was the owner of the paper. He was a Democratic in the Benjamin Franklin mould and when he moved to Ohio becoming editor of the *Western Herald* and *Gazette* in Steubenville. He was a Democratic representative in the state legislature and was assistant judge at the Court of Common Pleas.

Wilson's wife, Anne Adams—they married in Fourth Philadelphia Presbyterian Church in 1808—was a Co Down woman and the couple had 10 children, seven sons and three daughters. The youngest and seventh son, Joseph Ruggles Wilson, became a scholarly Presbyterian minister and his third child was President Woodrow Wilson. The president's mother was Jessie Woodrow, from Carlisle in England, who had emigrated to America with her family when she was four.

President Wilson often spoke of his Scots-Irish background, claiming with great pride that he had inherited the stern, strongly independent characteristics of the Scottish Covenanters. Speaking at a St. Patrick's Day rally in New York in 1909, when he was President of Princeton University, he said: "I myself am happy that there runs in my veins a very considerable strain of Irish blood."

In 1913, a year after he was elected to his first term as a Democrat, President Wilson said: "I am sorry that my information about my father's family is very meagre. My father's father was born in the north of Ireland; he had no brothers on this side of the water. The family came from the neighbourhood of Londonderry."

Woodrow Wilson actually visited Ireland in August 1899, taking in both the North and South of the island. He is understood to have made it to Belfast, and the only evidence of his trip is in a letter located amongst his personal papers. This was written on August 20 from the White Horse Inn, Drogheda in Co Louth, about 25 miles south of the present Irish border.

Wilson at the time was professor of jurisprudence and political economy at Princeton University, and, apart from academic friends, few in Ireland would have been aroused by his 1899 visit. He knew little about the geography and certainly did not reach North Tyrone to trace his grandfather's roots.

President Wilson's 1913-21 Presidential term coincided with the years of bitter political struggle in Ireland, but despite intense pressure on him from Irish American elements within the Democratic Party to intervene on behalf of the Irish nationalist cause, the president wisely did not get involved.

He saw the Irish situation purely as an internal British matter and did not perceive the dispute and the unrest in Ireland as comparable to the plight of the various nationalities in Europe as a fall-out from the First World War. He ignored a letter from Irish nationalist leaders in Dublin in 1918 calling on the United States to back moves for the disengagement of British interests in Ireland. The nationalist letter was countered by a communique from Ulster Unionist leaders in the North, including Lord Edward Carson, but the President was unmoved that American involvement was required.

Woodrow Wilson was an emotionally complex man, one who craved affection and demanded unquestioned loyalty. He once described his nature as a struggle between his Irish blood—"quick, generous, impulsive, passionate, always anxious to help and to sympathise with those in distress" and his Scotch blood—"canny, tenacious and perhaps a little exclusive."

Paradoxically, before large crowds, he was supremely self-confident and a gifted moving orator; with small groups of strangers he was often shy and awkward.

He was married twice—first, to Belle Louise Axson, daughter of a Presbyterian minister from Savannah, Georgia, and, after her death 29 years into the marriage, he wed widower, Mrs. Edith Bolling Galt, who survived him by 37 years.

Religion was Woodrow Wilson's driving force, and he said his life would not be worth living were it not for faith, pure and simple. He asserted: "I have seen all my life the arguments against it without ever having been moved by them. Never for a moment have I one doubt about my religious beliefs."

Wilson read his Bible daily in the White House, said grace before meals and prayed on his knees each morning and night. He belonged to Central Presbyterian Church in Washington and regularly attended the midweek prayer meetings. He firmly believed in providence and predestination and that God had pre-ordained him as president. His Calvinistic upbringing remained with him throughout his life.

Woodrow Wilson was a college lecturer in the years up to the end of the 19th century, teaching in Pennsylvania and Connecticut before taking the chair in jurisprudence and political economy at Princeton. In 1902, he became the first laymen to head Princeton, an institution founded by Scots-Irish Presbyterian clerics from Ulster. He held this position until 1910.

Wilson became governor of New Jersey in 1911 and the following year he was elected president with a 42 percent popular vote (6,286,820) over Theodore Roosevelt, who had 27 percent (4,126,020) and the outgoing Republican President William Howard Taft on 23 percent (3,483,922). Wilson carried the electoral vote in 40 states.

Four years later he had a 49 percent poll (9,129,606) over Republican Charles Evans Hughes, who had 46 percent (8,538,221). On this occasion his electoral college majority was slimmer—277-254.

Woodrow Wilson, at the outset of war in 1914, advised that the United States should remain strictly neutral, but American opinion gradually changed after incidents of German brutality, including the sinking of the British liner *Lusitania* off the southern coast of Ireland, which claimed,

1,200 lives including 120 American passengers. However, it was not until 1917 that the United States was officially engaged.

America's intervention secured victory for the Allied command, yet when the armistice was signed on November 11, 1918, more than 300,000 Americans had been killed. Woodrow Wilson led the American delegation at the Paris Peace Convention, and he played a leading part in drawing up the Treaty of Versailles of 1919, which placed full blame for the war on Germany. The League of Nations was formed as a result of the deliberations.

For his efforts in achieving world peace, President Wilson was awarded the Nobel Peace Prize, but by the end of 1919 he suffered a stroke, from which he never fully recovered. Under Wilson's leadership, the United States became a world power—industry and commerce flourished across the states and the nation's stability was maintained until the Great Depression emerged a decade later.

Woodrow Wilson bowed out as President on March 4, 1921, but his retirement lasted only three years. He died on February 3, 1924, aged 67. He had no state funeral, preferring to be buried at home.

The quiet God-fearing academic ranks among the presidential greats. President Herbert Hoover, in a tribute to Woodrow Wilson, said: "Three qualities stood out for Woodrow Wilson. He was more than just an idealist; he was the personification of the heritage of idealism of the American people. He brought spiritual concepts to the peace table; he was a born crusader."

Woodrow Wilson, in the highest tradition of Ulster-Scots, advanced American prestige and honour throughout the world. His patriotism, idealism and Christian faith were inspiring to the free world.

Wilson is one of the most common surnames in the English-speaking world, particularly in the United States and Scotland. In Ulster, where Woodrow Wilson's folks originated, it is the third most common name. It is lowland Scottish in origin, traceable to the Clan Gunn, of Caithness.

THE OTHER SCOTS-IRISH PRESIDENTS:

JAMES KNOX POLK: (Democrat 1845-49). The 11th American President, James Knox Polk was born in 1795 near Charlotte, North Carolina. His Scottish-born great-grandfather, Robert Bruce Polk (Pollok) of Lifford (East Donegal), arrived in the American colonies about 1680, settling in Maryland with descendants moving on North Carolina. James Knox Polk was governor of Tennessee before becoming president and he and his wife Sarah are buried in Nashville. Both were Presbyterians. Polk served seven terms in the U.S. Congress and was speaker of the house, the only president ever to hold this office. A great uncle Thomas Polk signed, with other Scots-Irish citizens in North Carolina, the Mecklenburg Declaration of May, 1775, a very significant document which preceded the Declaration of Independence of July 4, 1776.

CHESTER ALAN ARTHUR: (Republican 1881-85). The 21st American President was born at Fairfield, Vermont in 1830. Arthur's grandfather and his father, Baptist pastor Rev. William Arthur, emigrated to Dunham, Quebec, Canada from Dreen near Cullybackey, Co Antrim in 1801, and the family settled in the neighbouring American state of Vermont. Arthur, a graduate of Princeton College and a lawyer who later became a teacher, was an officer in the New York state militia during the Civil War. He was Vice-President for six months to President James A. Garfield, becoming President on Garfield's assassination in September, 1881. Although of Presbyterian/Baptist family roots, Arthur became an Episcopalian.

GROVER CLEVELAND: (Democrat 1885-89 and 1893-97). The 22nd and 24th President was born 1837 in Caldwell, New Jersey. His maternal grandfather, Abner Neal, left Co Antrim in the late 18th century. Grover was the son of Presbyterian minister Rev. Richard Falley Cleveland, who ministered in Connecticut, New York and New Jersey. His mother Ann Neal Cleveland was the daughter of a Baltimore book publisher. Grover Cleveland, a lawyer, was mayor of Buffalo, New York and governor of New York before rising to the presidency. He served two terms in the White House, winning the first and third elections (1884 and 1892) and losing the second (1888) to Benjamin Harrison. Cleveland, a man who weighed 250 pounds, retained a deep faith in God and always upheld his strict religious upbringing in a Presbyterian manse.

BENJAMIN HARRISON: (Republican 1889-93). The 23rd American president was born in 1833 at North Bend, Ohio. Harrison, grandson of the ninth President William Henry Harrison, was related to Ulster immigrants James Irwin and William McDowell. His mother Elizabeth Irwin Harrison was born and raised in Mercersburg, Pennsylvania, a strong Scots-Irish settlement, and his father was a member of the U.S. House of Representatives. President Harrison was a devout Presbyterian, and he chartered a career as a lawyer and brigadier-general soldier in the Civil War. Harrison served in the U.S. Senate for six years (1881-87) and, although he narrowly lost the popular vote in the 1888 presidential election, he reached the White House by having a sizeable majority of the electoral vote.

WILLIAM MCKINLEY: (Republican 1897-1901), Born 1843 in Niles, Ohio. A Presbyterian, he was great grandson of James McKinley, who emigrated to America from Conagher near Ballymoney, Co Antrim about 1743. The Presbyterian McKinleys were originally from Perthshire, Scotland and they moved to Ulster in the 17th century Plantation years. McKinley's grandparents fought in the Revolutionary War and the family was involved in iron manufacturing. William McKinley, was a U.S. Representative for 12 years and Governor of Ohio for four. He was assassinated at Buffalo, New York on September 6, 1901. President McKinley married his wife Ida Saxton in a Presbyterian church, but he was a Methodist. He was intensely proud that the Scots-Irish were the first to proclaim for liberty in the United States.

THEODORE ROOSEVELT: (Republican 1905-09). The 26th American president was born 1858 in New York City. 26th President Roosevelt, who wrote admiringly of the courage and exploits of the Scots-Irish on the American frontier, is claimed to have Presbyterian ancestors on his maternal side from Larne, Co Antrim. Folklore in East Antrim link him to the Irvines of Carneac near Larne and the Bullochs from the same area. Roosevelt, a distinguished U.S. Cavalry officer in the Spanish-American War and New York governor and politician before becoming president in 1904, belonged to the Dutch Reformed Church. He described the Scots-Irish as "a stern, virile, bold and hardy people who formed the kernel of that American stock who were the pioneers of our people in the march westwards."

HARRY TRUMAN: (Democrat 1949-53). The 33rd president was born 1884 at Lamar, Missouri. His maternal grandfather, Solomon Young, was of Scots-Irish settler stock and moved from Kentucky to Kansas City, Missouri in 1840. President Truman, who also had English and German ancestry, was a popular straight-talking American President after the Second World War. He had been a United States Senator for 10 years from 1935. Truman was a Baptist, but attended the Presbyterian church as a youth.

RICHARD MILLHOUSE NIXON: (Republican 1969-74). The 37th president was born in 1913 at Yorba Linda, California and had Ulster connections on two sides of his family. His Nixon Presbyterian ancestors left Co Antrim for America around 1753, while the Millhouses came from Carrickfergus and Ballymoney, also in Co Antrim. Richard Nixon, himself, was a Quaker and his wife Thelma Catherine "Pat" Ryan, had Irish Roman Catholic family connections. Nixon, a lawyer and controversial president, served as vice-president during the two presidential terms of Dwight D. Eisenhower.

JAMES EARL CARTER: (Democrat 1977-81). The 39th president was born 1924 in Plains, Georgia. Scots-Irish settler Andrew Cowan, believed to come from Co Antrim, was President Carter's great grandfather on his mother's side. Cowan, a Presbyterian, was in 1772 one of the first residents of Boonesborough, a frontier buffer zone in the South Carolina Piedmont region. Jimmy Carter, who also has English ancestry, is a Baptist and, since ending his Presidential term, he has been noted for his humanitarian work.

GEORGE BUSH: (Republican 1989-93). The 41st president was born 1924 at Milton, Massachusetts. The Bush family came mainly of English stock, but an ancestor on George Bush's mother's side was William Gault, who was born in Ulster (very probably Co Antrim!) and with his wife Margaret were first settlers of Tennessee, living in Blount County in 1796, the year Tennessee became a state. The Gaults were identified by the Bush family as being first families of Tenneseee in the research carried out by the East Tennessee Historical Society George Bush is an Episcopalian.

WILLIAM JEFFERSON CLINTON: (Democrat - 1993-2001). The 42nd president was born in 1946 in Hope, Hempstead County, Arkansas. Bill Clinton claims to be a relative of Lucas Cassidy, who left Co Fermanagh for America around 1750. Lucas Cassidy was of Presbyterian stock; President Clinton is a Baptist. During his eight-year period as President, Bill Clinton made three visits to Northern Ireland to publicly express his full support for the peace process in the Province.

GEORGE W. BUSH: (Republican 2001-). Born in 1946 in Texas, President Bush, son of President George Walker Bush, is descended on his father's maternal side from the late 18th century East Tennessee settler William Gault, who was born in the north of Ireland (very probably Co Antrim). Like Bill Clinton, President George W. Bush has expressed a strong interest in the affairs of Northern Ireland. He is a Methodist.

VICE-PRESIDENT:

JOHN C. CALHOUN (Democrat 1825-32 Democrat). Son of a Co Donegal Presbyterian father Patrick Calhoun and mother Margaret Caldwell, who was Virginia-born of Co Antrim immigrant parents, this South Carolina statesman was Vice-President to President John Quincy Adams and President Andrew Jackson. Calhoun, a Covenanting Presbyterian, was the leading South Carolina politician of the early 19th century and was secretary of state for war under President James Monroe.

Two other American Presidents can claim Irish lineage: JOHN FITZGERALD KENNEDY, whose paternal great-grandfather came from Dunganstown, Co Wexford and maternal grandfather was also Irish, and RONALD REAGAN, whose paternal line can be traced back to Ballyporeen, Co Tipperary. Both were of Irish Roman Catholic stock, but on his mother's side President Reagan had Presbyterian ancestry.

President William McKinley on the Scots-Irish (Scotch-Irish)—Ohio May, 1893

"We can for the most part determine where we live, the people among who we will dwell, our occupation or profession but we cannot select either our ancestors or our birthplace; these we must accept for good or ill. It is fortunate where both are favorable and helpful bringing blessings rather than bight.

"The Scotch-Irish would not change either ancestry or birthplace if they could. They were proud of both; but they are prouder yet of their new home they helped to create under the Stars and Stripes, the best and freest under the sun. The Scotch-Irish were not only well born, but they have improved upon their beginning, have progressed with their opportunities and have made opportunities where none seemed present.

"While he is distinctive as a type, the Scotch-Irishman is a racial evolution—the result of a slow fusion of diverse characteristics. It is said of the Scotch-Irish that they are doers rather than talkers or writers. True, they have been builders, and their foundations were deep and strong and enduring. They have builded for the ages, but they write and talk quite as well as other races. Their deeds in behalf of American Independence should ever be cherished in patriotic remembrance; and it is a remarkable fact, as observed by those who have taken the trouble to examine the matter, that it is only within the past few years that recorded history has given just credit to the sturdy race, to whom Washington looked as his never-failing support and as his forlorn hope when all others should have left him, when defeat should have encompassed him.

"Representatives of the Scotch-Irish are among the highest names in American history. They have shone in every great epoch of national life. So long as there is a struggle for human liberty, so long as patriotism has a place in the American heart, that long will the name and fame of your ancestors be embraced and enshrined. The roll-call is a large one: I can pick out only a name here and there: Patrick Henry, Andrew Jackson, James Knox Polk, James Buchanan, the heroic Ulysses S. Grant and the immortal Lincoln. Not only in state-craft and war have Scotch-Irish distinguished themselves in American annals. There was Fulton, McCormick and Morse in invention.

"The Scotch-Irish came of mighty stock—that we know, descending from those who would fight, who would die, but never surrender. Celt and Saxon are in him combined, after each has been tempered and refined. The Celt made his final stand as a racial individuality after each in the extremities of western Europe. Hence he issued forth, both as a coloniser and missionary. Taking up his abode in the lowlands of Scotland, he became subject to Anglo-Saxon influence. The blood of the North Britons mingled with that of the Celt from the Green Isle. The result of this commingling of blood and of local environment was the Lowland Scotch, even then possessing characteristics distinct from the Highlander and the Irish Celt.

"The Lowlander re-crossed the narrow sea to Ulster. His going marked an epoch in the history of civilisation. The tragic history of Ireland has been for centuries food for racial hate. In this land at least, however, the irremediable past should not be matter of quarrel for who of us, of whatever blood, that naught of wrong tarnishes the history of his race? Scot through the Ulsterman is proud to call himself, yet he is also re-transplanted Celt.

"The Americanised Scotch-Irishman is the perfection of a type which is the development of the commingling and assimilating process of centuries; even before Lexington, Scotch-Irish blood had been shed on behalf of American freedom. In the forefront of every battle was seen their burnished mail, and in the gloomy rear of retreat was heard their voice of constancy and courage. Of no race or people can John Milton's words be applied in juster eulogy: "Inflamed with the study of learning and the admiration of virtue; stirred up with high hope of living to be brave men and worthy patriots, dear to God and famous to all ages."

"Next to their intense patriotism, the distinguishing characteristics of the Scotch-Irish are their loving of learning and of religion. The Scotch-Irishman is the idea educator and he is a natural theologian. It would be difficult to find a college or university without a Scotch-Irishman on its faculty. And he was the early schoolmaster of Ohio, whose manual training was with the birch rod. Another marked characteristic of the Scotch-Irish is the love of home and family, and wherever this prevails there are found manly virtue, and high integrity, and good citizenship. The home and the schoolhouse have been mighty forces, marking the progress of the Scotch-Irish race.

"In the American Scotch-Irishman we behold the personification of liberty and law. His thoughts have been 'widened with the process of the suns' and the civilisation which he has helped to secure has added light and sweetness to the stern faith of his fathers. To the distinctive qualities of his type has been added the humanising and fraternal influence of the American spirit of toleration and equality.

"Here in Ohio, this true American spirit of toleration and equality prevails—perhaps as nowhere else. Here the Puritan and Cavalier, the Protestant and Catholic, the Englishman and Irishman, the Scotch-Irish and the pure Celt live together in harmony and fraternity as American citizens, struggling together to secure the highest destiny for mankind, and vying with each other in their love for our free institutions and in their devotion to liberty."

The Scotch-Irish by Charles A. Hanna. Published by Genealogical Publishing Company, New York. 1902

PRESIDENT THEODORE ROOSEVELT ON THE SCOTCH-IRISH

"Along the western frontier of the colonies that were so soon to be the United States, among the foothills of the Alleghenies on the slopes of the wooded mountains, and in the long trough-like valleys that lay between the ranges, dwelt a peculiar and characteristically American people.

"The backwoods mountaineers were all cast in the same mould and resembled each other much more than any of them did their immediate neighbours of the plains. The backwoodsmen of Pennsylvania had little in common with the peaceful population of Quakers and Germans who lived between the Delaware and Susquehanna rivers; and their near kinsmen of the Blue Ridge and the Great Smoky Mountains were separated by the equally wide gulf from the aristocratic planter communities that flourished in the Tidewater regions of Virginia and the Carolinas.

"The backwoodsmen were American by birth and parentage, and of mixed race; but the dominant strain in their blood was that of Presbyterian Irish—the Scotch-Irish as they were often called. Full credit has been awarded the Roundhead and the Cavalier for their leadership in our history; nor have we been altogether blind to the deeds of the Hollander and the Huguenot; but it is doubtful if we have wholly realised the importance of the part played by that stern and virile people, the Irish whose preachers taught the creed of Knox and Calvin. These Irish representatives of the Covenanters were in the West almost what the Puritans were in the North-East, and more than the Cavaliers were in the South. Mingled with the descendants of many other races, they nevertheless formed the kernel of the distinctively and intensely American stock who were the pioneers of our people in the march Westwards.

"They were a truculent and obstinate people and gloried in the warlike renown of their forefathers, the men who had followed Olive Cromwell and who had shared the defence of Derry and in the victories of the Boyne and Aughrim. The West was won by those who have been rightly called the Roundheads of the South, the same men who before any other declared for American independence.

"That those Irish Presbyterians were a bold and hardy race is proved by their at once pushing past the settled regions and plunging into the wilderness as the leaders of the white advance. They were the first and last set of immigrants to do this; all others have merely followed in the wake other predecessors. But indeed they were fitted to be Americans from the very start; they were kinsfolk of the Covenanters; they deemed it a religious duty to interpret their own Bible, and held for a divine right the election of their own clergy. For generations their whole ecclesiastic and scholastic systems had been fundamentally democratic."

Winning of the West by Theodore Roosevelt. Published New York 1889.

The Scotch-Irish by Charles A. Hanna. Published by Genealogical Publishing Company, New York, 1902

HEREDITY BY THOMAS HARDY

I am the family face;
Flesh perishes, I live on,
Projecting trait and trace
Through time to times anon,
And leaping from place to place
Over oblivion.

The years—heired feature that can
In curve and voice and eye
Despise the human span
Of durance—that is I;
The eternal thing in man,
That heeds no call to die.

MUSIC AND DANCE WAS PART OF AMERICAN
FRONTIER CULTURE.

·6·

THE MUSIC OF THE SCOTS-IRISH

The distinctive styles of many modern-day American country, bluegrass and folk music performers can be traced directly back to the 18th century Ulster-Scots or Scots-Irish settlers. And the dance tradition of the Appalachian region in the south eastern part of the United States has also very strong Ulster-Scots roots.

This is music and dance which crossed the Atlantic during the great waves of emigration and in the modern idiom. It is a rich cultural expression which is being taken back to the homeland.

The Ulster-Scots sound of drone notes, associated with the pipes and fiddles, are very pronounced, and the story-telling balladry of the Scots-Irish diaspora remains deeply rooted in what is American country and folk music today.

These were a people who brought with them to North America the old Scottish, Irish and English folk songs and ballads, and in remote communities in the Appalachian, Cumberland and Great Smoky Mountains, the songs stayed unaltered until the 20th century.

Music lightened toil for early Scots-Irish pioneers, with the fiddle giving the lift at weddings, and Jew's Harp providing accompaniment along the wagon roads to the new settlements. Dulcimer, banjo and mandolin were other favoured instruments on the frontier, traditional backing for the nasal-vocals of the hardy settler people.

The fiddle, distinctively Scottish and Irish, was the main instrument for playing the tunes and providing the backing for the traditional songs. It was the first musical instrument in the Appalachian region 200/250 years ago. There might just have been one fiddle in a whole community and one player.

The Appalachian mountain people, where Scots-Irish culture is so strong, have maintained a folk-song culture for several centuries. Leading balladeer and folk historian from the early 20th century Cecil Sharpe related how he discovered that nearly every one he met in the mountain region, young and old, could either sing or play an instrument.

The ballads which Sharp collected in Kentucky, Tennessee, Virginia, the Carolinas and North Georgia were in the traditional vein, with Scots-Irish influences a very dominant strain. Popular Appalachian folk songs and tunes like the "Girl from Knoxville," "Barbara Allen," "The Irish Washerwoman," "Haste to the Wedding," "The Virginia Reel," "The Green River March" and "Turkey in the Straw" are in that tradition.

The music of the American frontier was primarily vocal, through the singing of hymns and folk songs. In the very early settlements in Pennsylvania from the 1720s, the fiddle provided the musical background for the reels and jigs which the Ulster-Scots enjoyed. In the austere and, at times lonely sur-roundings of the frontier, music was the source which brightened the lives of the settlers.

Fiddle styles varied from state to state, even within states. Individual fid-dlers differed in the way they held the instrument, the emphasis which they devoted to noting and the manner in which they bowed.

Some fiddlers stuck resolutely to the melody, while others improvised freely or employed their own prepared techniques—all a very Scots-Irish trait!

Richard Nevins, in his book *Old-Time Fiddle Classics*, notes that since fiddling was a Celtic art, modern aficionados strain to establish a direct link between Celtic styles and Appalachian renditions. Nevins maintained it is likely all the countless variations in southern fiddling are traceable to seven or eight different styles brought over to America by the predominantly

Celtic-cultured immigrants from various sections of the north of Ireland, southern Scotland and, to a lesser degree, parts of England.

While yodelling has its origins in the Swiss mountains, many performers of a Scots-Irish background in states like Kentucky, Tennessee, North Carolina, Virginia and Georgia were adept at raising the tone to a falsetto head voice.

Gospel music was very dear the to the God-fearing Scots-Irish and many colloquial hymns, later adopted in mainstream Christianity, had origins in the Appalachian region. Methodist evangelical hymns of Isaac Watts, John Newton and John and Charles Wesley struck a chord with those moving along the Great Wagon Road to the frontier.

Bluegrass music is strongly linked to the Scots-Irish folk of Kentucky, Virginia and Tennessee and top Nashville performer Ricky Skaggs is very proud of his roots.

"My family on my mother's side were Scots-Irish—they were the Fergusons, who left Limavady and East Donegal in the early part of the 18th century. They eventually moved to Kentucky, where I grew up with a real taste for bluegrass music, which has its origins in the north of Ireland and Scotland. To me, traditional country music has a value in it, a wholesomeness and warmth that some of the other kinds of music don't have. It's our heritage, our roots, it's everything that we're about," says Ricky.

Dolly Parton, Nashville's first lady of country music, also has strong Scots-Irish family links—her late father Robert Lee Parton could trace his roots back to the early settlers.

At Dolly's theme park at Pigeon Forge in the Great Smoky Mountains of East Tennessee, the musical documentary "Fire on the Mountain" tells the fascinating story of American country music and its historical roots, particularly the Scots-Irish theme.

The musical narration confirms the link: "And so they came… a strong-willed people who forged their homes out of this region and brought their love and beauty with them. The deeds of our Scots-Irish ancestors are blended with the skills of the musicians who seized the Smokies' fiery spirit, and this heritage has been passed on from generation to generation…!"

Other American country stars with Scots-Irish family connections include bluegrass performers the late Bill Monroe and Jim and Jesse McReynolds; as well as the Everly Brothers; Loretta Lynn and her sister Crystal Gayle; Jean

Shepherd; Emmylou Harris; George Hamilton IV, Billy Walker; the late Roy Acuff, presenter at the Grand Old Opry in Nashville; not forgetting, Clayton McMichen, a noted old-tyme early 20th century musician from Georgia, whose family left Ulster in the late 18th century.

The dance tradition in America is very ethnically-based. Irish, Scottish and English "clogging" form of dancing blended over the years in the Appalachians, although there were slight variants from region to region, hill and holler and one to another. The cultural roots in a community could be detected by the dances they did. There was a lot of instrument backing for the Scots-Irish forms of dancing, with dancers operating quite a bit on their toes, from a very erect still upper and body movement.

Celebrated American songwriter Stephen Collins Foster was a second generation Ulster-Scot whose family emigrated from Londonderry to Pennsylvania in the late 18th century.

Foster, born near Pittsburgh in 1826, wrote 200 classic songs, among them "Beautiful Dreamer," "Jeannie With the Light Brown Hair," "My Old Kentucky Home" and "Campton Races." Foster wrote both the words and the music of most of his songs.

Jimmy Kennedy, a songwriter born in Omagh, Co Tyrone in the early part of the 20th century, became a renowned name in American popular music, writing classic songs such as "South of the Border Down Mexico Way" and "Red Sails in the Sunset."

IN THE VANGUARD FOR AMERICAN INDEPENDENCE
WERE THE SCOTS-IRISH.

7

SCOTS-IRISH INFLUENCES ON AMERICAN INDEPENDENCE

The Scots-Irish during the Revolutionary War were acknowledged as the most effective element in George Washington's patriot army. They were also highly influential in the Continental Congress which ran America during the War from its Pennsylvania base, and in the various colonial assemblies, from the eastern seaboard region to the Appalachian frontier lands.

The Scots-Irish—in the Continental Congress, the army and in the colonies—were indeed the activists, the intelligencia, and, in the ranks of the backwoods militias, resolute and uncompromising champions of the movement for independence in America.

A minority of the Scots-Irish settlers in the American colonies remained loyal to the British Crown, but up to 75 percent of these people were persuaded that their interests were best served by breaking the constitutional link with the old country and forging independence for their new homeland.

Bitter experience of religious discrimination and economic deprivation were major factors for many after their movement from the north of Ireland to America through the 18th century.

The Revolutionary War was fought over three fronts—along the eastern coastal states where the patriots came into direct conflict with the British army and naval forces; in the middle country of the Carolinas where rebels and loyalists fought it out and along the outer frontier where the settler militia units took on the Indian tribes who were on the side of the British.

On all three fronts, the Scots-Irish were in the vanguard of patriot involvement, but it was in the frontier lands that they made their most significant contribution. Quite uniquely, as a people they rose to the awesome challenge of the American frontier—its danger, its impenetrability and sheer enormity.

At the outbreak of the Revolutionary War in 1775, up to 20 percent of the white population in the 13 American colonies was Scots and Scots-Irish, next to persons of English ancestry, and with such numbers the influence was considerable.

The challenge for the frontier settlers to provide their own protection came to a head in the French-Indian War of 1754-63. Until then, everything west of the Appalachians was French and the French were using the Indians to keep the English and kindred settler groups on the eastern side of the mountains.

Pennsylvania was a main battlefield in the French-Indian War, and it was there that the Scotch-Irish made their initial appearance on American soil as a cohesive fighting unit. Of the 13 American colonies then, Pennsylvania was the least prepared for war, ruled as it was from Philadelphia by the pacifist Quakers. The Scots-Irish settlers on its frontiers were left peculiarly vulnerable to attack from the Indian tribes of the Shawnee and Delaware nations.

The Quakers had been in Pennsylvania since 1681 and by 1715 they represented the largest single element in the white population, administering the colonial system on behalf of the Crown. However, as the 18th century progressed and the tens of thousands of immigrants arrived from the north of Ireland, England and Scotland arrived, Quaker control of affairs began to wane.

In 1766, Benjamin Franklin, the leading Quaker politician, estimated the population of Pennsylvania at 160,000, with about one-third of them Quakers. Others felt this was an exaggeration, stating the number of Quakers in 1775 at around 25,000. By this time, the Scots-Irish and German settlements could each muster higher proportions of the population.

Indian attacks on the Scots-Irish settlements reached a climax in September and October, 1755, with the log cabins burned and many of the settlers either massacred or captured and held for torture. As lives were taken, and the Scots-Irish settlers forced to flee from their frontier outposts, the placid Quaker assembly in Philadelphia ignored the danger, with somewhat indifference and a large degree of incompetence.

The Quaker assembly recoiled in horror at the prospect of declaring war against the French-backed Indians as Scots-Irish anger at the ineptitude of their political masters rose to boiling point. Finally, realising the danger, Pennsylvania Governor Robert Hunter Morris seized the initiative and proclaimed war against the Shawnees and the Delawares, offering bounties for their scalps.

The Quakers were aghast at the measures, but they soon found that the general Pennsylvania populace would no longer tolerate their neglect in providing defence for the colony. The struggle between the Quakers and the Scots-Irish had also intensified by Quaker attempts to change Pennsylvania from a proprietary to a royal colony. The Quakers wanted Pennsylvania to be placed under the authority of a King who was "justly celebrated for his tender regard to the constitutional rights of Englishmen."

Quaker politicians in Philadelphia were inclined to frown disdainfully on the Scots-Irish, with leading theorist John Dickinson proclaiming they were "strangers to our laws and customs."

By 1756, the Quakers were beginning to effectively lose control of Pennsylvania—power they were never to regain in America after it fell completely from their grasp in the 1770s. American historian Wayland Dunaway said the fundamental issue between the Scots-Irish and the Quakers was whether Pennsylvania should be a democracy or an obligarchy.

Inevitably, steps were taken to properly arm the Pennsylvania province for an engagement that was to evolve over a decade and a half to the Revolutionary War.

Two hundred forts were erected on the frontier with money raised to buy arms. The Scots-Irish settlements of farmers, craftsmen and traders had now stretched extensively from Philadelphia down the south east of the province through Chester, York, Lancaster and Bucks counties and were heading west towards Fort Pitt (Pittsburgh). They were an increasingly vocal lobby for change!

They organised voluntary bands of frontiersmen, known as rangers, to defend their homes against the Indians, and they provided the manpower for the militia units. At this precise point in American history, the Scots-Irish set down a marker that when it came to attacks on their hearth and home, and in the engagements of war, they were a people not to be trifled with.

Isaac Sharples, noted Quaker scholar and historian, paid tribute to the contribution of the Scots-Irish in the ranks of the Pennsylvania Line, referred to by General Henry Lee as "The Line of Ireland." Sharples wrote: "The Scotch-Irishman did not waver, he now had the chance for which he was waiting. The Revolution was at least three-fourths a Presbyterian (Scotch-Irish) movement."

Throughout the colonies generally the Scots-Irish rallied strongly to the patriot cause, especially in Pennsylvania, Virginia and the Carolinas. In Pennsylvania they provided more officers and soldiers than any other racial strain.

The Scots-Irish, numbering about a quarter of the Pennsylvania population, suffered severely during the French-Indian War, but it was they who provided the leadership and the backbone of the successful resistance in the fierce conflict.

The Scots-Irish battles with the Indian tribes in the years leading up to, during and after the Revolutionary War were quite decisive in creating the American nation. Indeed, the major events from 1755 to 1790 centered around the Appalachian territory and the gaps in them where the frontier settlers had to enter to progress towards the new lands.

The Mohawk was the largest of the Appalachian gaps, and the only one essentially at sea level. The gap that linked Philadelphia and Pittsburgh in Pennsylvania was very high and not as easily accessible in the early years of settlement, while the Cumberland Gap was the main entry to the Kentucky and Tennessee lands and beyond the Ohio River towards the Mississippi.

There was also a fourth passage of movement for the settlers, around the Appalachians by going south via Georgia and Alabama. Of course, the frontier settlers were forbidden in a decree from King George III (the Proclamation Line of 1763) to go across the mountain, but there was a common and very apt saying of the stubborn Scots-Irish at the time—"It's a long way to London."

The first chink of defiance to the King's edict came in 1772 at Watauga in a part of North Carolina of what today is in the state of Tennessee. But after leasing two large tracts of land from the Cherokees, the settlers were not for moving, and eventually they managed to purchase the land deeds from the Indians.

The Wataugans (the first batch 16 families from North Carolina, mostly Scots-Irish led by Colonel John Sevier and Colonel James Robertson) moved on to lands officially designated Cherokee country, much to the consternation of Lord Dunmore, the royal governor of Virginia. Dunmore reported back to London that there were "a set of people in the back country of the colony, bordering on Cherokee country, who, finding they could not obtain the land they fancied here, have set up a separate state."

Under the colonial laws of King George III, the Wataugans were squatters on Indians lands, but finding possession nine-tenths of the law they steadfastly stood their ground and ignored all the enforcements from Dunmore and the other colonial leaders.

The Wataugans set up their own militia and entered into negotiations with the Indians, first to lease the lands from the Cherokees and then to make a permanent purchase. They were 100 years later described by President Theodore Roosevelt as "a people who bid defiance to outsiders."

The Watauga Presbyterian settlers used the theology of manifest destiny to define their attitudes to far-off London rule, maintaining: "If God did not want us to have this land, we would not be out here." As was the case in Ulster during the 17th century Scottish Plantation there, so it was in the 18th century settlements of the Appalachian backcountry, as God had intended.

This was meant to be, and, with such a mindset, the Scots-Irish found the courage, determination and feeling that they were doing God's will in settling along the frontier and pushing civilisation to the outer limits.

Of course, the official response to Scots-Irish demands for frontier land was documented in the 1720s by Ulster-born Quaker James Logan, the provincial secretary of Pennsylvania, who declared: "The Scotch-Irish maintain that it is against the laws of God and nature, that so much land should be idle, while so many Christians wanted it to labor on and to raise their bread."

Professor George Schweitzer, of the University of Tennessee in Knoxville, attributes, almost exclusively, to the Scots-Irish the American frontier action against British colonial interests for 40 years up to 1790.

"They were the frontiersmen; they did it, they penetrated the Appalachians; they fought the Revolution on the frontier. It is important to realise the immigrant settlers, particularly the Scots-Irish, did not bring all of their problems with them from the homelands.

"A great deal of it was engendered by the environment in which they were put. The Scots-Irish obviously left Ulster with many grievances, but their actions were quickened by their experiences on the ground when they arrived in America and tasted freedom, far removed from the diktats of monarchy and established church. They seized the opportunity and their whole social scene and outlook changed in the clamour for independence," said Professor Schweitzer.

In context, it was observed that the Scots-Irish were long accustomed, from both ancient memories and from their recent experiences in the north of Ireland, to an attitude of hostility towards the English. Being a politically-minded people, they were highly sensitive to any wrongs or fancied wrongs inflicted upon them by the government in London, or by colonial governors in America carrying out its instructions.

The separation of church from state was fundamental to the thinking of Scots-Irish Presbyterians in America. One of their leaders during the Revolutionary War period—Scottish-born Rev. John Witherspoon, the only clergyman among the 56 signatories of the Declaration of Independence—justified opposition to the link-up between church and state with the words—"God alone is the Lord of the conscience."

Witherspoon, who before he moved from Scotland to America had been involved in the revolt against the established Anglican Church, was a prolific pamphleteer and in his sermons he used every opportunity to advocate a disengagement of church from state.

The terminology of Witherspoon was clear and unequivocal: "No compulsion ought to be used to constrain men's choice in the matter of religion" and "Has not every man a natural right, to judge for himself in matters of religion?" He promised students at his College of New Jersey that "every denomination may have free and equal advantages of education… any different sentiments in religion, notwithstanding."

The Witherspoon theory can be summarised in three clauses: that God alone is Lord of the conscience; that freedom of conscience is an inalienable right and that the state has no authority either to grant or deny religious liberty.

Historian J. A. Froude very accurately summed up the situation of the Scots-Irish Presbyterians at the time of the Revolutionary War, thus: "The resentment which they carried with them continued to burn in their new home, and in the War of Independence England had no fiercer enemies than the grandsons and great grandsons of the Presbyterians who held Ulster for the Crown."

Colonel A. K. McClure, the distinguished Philadelphia writer, went even further: "It was the Scotch-Irish people of the colonies that made the Declaration of 1776. Without them it would not have been thought of except as a fancy. The actions of the Continental Congress voiced the teachings of the Scotch-Irish people of the land.

"They did not falter, they did not dissemble, they did not temporise. It was not the Quaker, not the Puritan, not the Cavalier, not even the Huguenot or the German; it was the Scotch-Irish of the land whose voice was first heard in Virginia.

"In the valley of Virginia, in North Carolina, in Cumberland and Westmoreland counties of Pennsylvania, the Scotch-Irish had declared that these colonies are, and of right, ought to be free and independent. They had taught this not only in their public speeches, but at their altars, in their pulpits, at their firesides, and it was from these that came that outburst of rugged and determined people that made the Declaration of 1776 possible.

"They were its authors, and they were ready to maintain it by all the moral and physical power they possessed. They meant that Scotch-Irish blood was ready to flow on the battlefield, and come weal or woe, they would maintain it with their lives."

The 1776 Pennsylvania Constitution, which had as its cornerstone the Declaration of Independence, is looked upon as the "high-water mark" of radicalism during the American Revolution. It was the product of the victory by western Scots-Irish farmers and Philadelphia artisans over the Quaker ruling class.

Historian John C. Miller recounts that it was majority rule in Pennsylvania under the constitution of 1776, and the privileged Quaker class was stripped of its power as the centre of gravity shifted from "the polite and genteel of Philadelphia to the rough Scots-Irish farmers of the west and the plebeians of the metropolis."

"It is a fact that the Irish immigrants and their children are now in possession of the government of Pennsylvania, by their majority in the Assembly, as well as a great part of the territory; and I remember the first ship that brought them over," wrote Benjamin Franklin in 1784.

The very substantial role which the Scots-Irish played in heralding in the new American nation is not as widely known in modern-day United States society as it should be. As visionary leaders and brave foot soldiers of the Revolution, the Scots-Irish moved on to patiently fashion with others of like mind a political dynasty and confederation of states that was to evolve in the space of 200 years as the most prosperous and powerful nation in the world.

In the making of America, and in perpetuating the union of states from the Atlantic coastline to the Pacific, the efforts of the Scots-Irish were certainly considerable!

In addition to supplying their considerable soldiering prowess in the Revolutionary War, American citizens of Ulster stock provided the necessary finance in 1780 to help sustain the fight for freedom. Blair McClenaghan, from Co Antrim gave $50,000; John Murray, from Belfast, and three others from Scots-Irish families—John Nixon, Thomas Barclay and John Nesbitt each donated $30,000. James Mease, from Strabane in Co Tyrone, gave $25,000, while his uncle John, and John Dunlap, from the same town, both raised $20,000 each. John Donelson, the Tennessee-North Carolina frontiersman, weighed in with $10,000. Even by today's standards the contribution from these sources was huge.

PATRIOT MILITIA ENCOUNTER BRITISH REDCOATS
DURING THE BATTLE OF KINGS MOUNTAIN IN
OCTOBER 1780.

Picture courtesy of Robert Windsor Wilson, Woodruff, SC

8

THE REVOLUTIONARY WAR AND SCOTS-IRISH ACTIVISTS

HENRY KNOX—GEORGE WASHINGTON'S NO 2 IN THE REVOLUTIONARY WAR

General Henry Knox, commander of the Continental Army and chief of artillery in the Revolutionary War, was a second generation Ulster-Scot, in that his father William emigrated from Londonderry to Boston in 1729 as part of the flow across the Atlantic at the time by Presbyterian families.

The Knoxes were Scottish lairds of Gifford near Edinburgh and William Knox's branch of the family settled in Londonderry and Co Down during the 17th century Scottish Plantation of Ulster. They would have been involved in defending Londonderry from the Irish Roman Catholic forces under King James II during the 1688-89 siege.

William Knox, who became a wealthy shipmaster and wharf owner, married Mary Campbell in a Boston Presbyterian church in 1729. They had 10 sons, with Henry the seventh, born in 1750.

Henry Knox joined the militia at 18, and after witnessing the Boston "massacre" in 1770, he got involved full-time in the patriot struggle. He was a volunteer at the Battle of Bunker Hill and at the Boston Siege, and his courage and commitment to the patriot cause impressed George Washington, who appointed him colonel of the still-fledgling Continental Regiment of Artillery.

Knox's artillery, when they got properly up and running, dealt a damaging blow to the British, leading to the evacuation of Boston, and they fought at the battles of Trenton and Princeton.

By 1777, the Continental artillery had developed from a poorly armed and inexperienced force to a well-organised and disciplined unit, and Henry Knox and his men performed well at the battle of Brandywine. Washington's high approval of Knox continued for the duration of the war, with commendations at the battles of Monmouth and Yorktown.

He was appointed major-general in March, 1782, and six months later he assumed central command at West Point U.S. Army base, and succeeded George Washington as commander-in-chief during the period December 1783-June 1784.

In 1785 Knox became America's first secretary of state for war, an office approved by the Continental Congress, and held the post during George Washington's Presidency until 1794. He pressed for a strong navy, and Fort Knox was named in his honour.

Historians describe Henry Knox as being a man with outstanding administrative abilities, a loyalty to his chief and the patriot cause, and a sanguine outlook that made him a major figure in the winning of independence.

This father of 12 children died at the age of 56, peculiarly, when a chicken bone lodged in his intestines.

A Covenanting Presbyterian family of Knoxes emigrated from Co Antrim to Charleston, South Carolina, sailing on the Earl of Hillsborough from Belfast in March, 1767. James and Elizabeth Craig Knox and their young family settled on 450 acres of land at Boonesborough or Belfast township in the Carolina Piedmont and four of their sons John, James, Robert and Samuel fought with the South Carolina Continental line.

They were also at Charleston when the British attack came in May, 1780 and later fought at Kings Mountain. James Knox Jr. was killed a year later by loyalists avenging the defeat at Kings Mountain. A cousin, Captain Hugh Knox led the patriot militia in battles at Rocky Mountain, Hanging Rock, Congaree Fort and Kings Mountain

UNCOMPROMISING SCOTS-IRISH IN THE "HORNET'S NEST"

Charlotte, a North Carolina town settled largely by Scots-Irish Presbyterian families in the mid-18th century and ironically named for the wife of George III, was described by Lord Charles Cornwallis, British commander in the Revolutionary War, as the "Hornet's Nest."

The ferocity of the Charlotte militia and the passion generated for the American patriot cause by the Ulster Presbyterian settlers was a factor which influenced the British in paying more than a passing attention to this rather troublesome region in the Carolina backcountry.

It was quite significant that far more Presbyterian churches were burned to the ground then than places of worship, for other denominations and Charlotte, with its strong Presbyterian influences, became an irritation for Cornwallis and his colonial associates.

Hawkins Historical Notices of the period recount that the Presbyterian Church suffered severely during the War of Independence—"its ministers and elders went into the struggle for constitutional liberty with all their strength. Churches were destroyed, ministers and elders slain, congregations scattered."

The American colonial congress had long been worried by the anti-establishment feeling that was spreading through the Carolinas in the late 1760s and early 1770s. They prevailed on Philadelphia Presbyterian ministers to appeal to their North Carolina brethren to bear in mind that the dispute was over taxation without representation, and there was no question of disloyalty or separation from the Crown.

A direct appeal evoked the proud memories of the Ulster Protestant stock: "If we are now wrong in our conduct, our forefathers that fought for liberty at Londonderry and Enniskillen in King James's time were wrong. But we hope that such language will never be heard from the mouth of a Protestant, or from an English subject, and much less from anyone of our denomination, that have ever maintained the revolution principles, and are firmly devoted to the present reigning family as the asserters of the British privileges and English liberty."

This appeal had a measure of success over a large part of the Carolina up-country, but not in Charlotte, principal township for Mecklenburg County, where anti-British feeling was very strong. This was fuelled in 1773 by the refusal of the English Privy Council to grant a charter to the local Queen's College because of its Presbyterian ethos.

The undercurrent of patriotism in the Carolinas led to a declaration of independence drawn up by community leaders in Charlotte fourteen months before the appearance of the July 4, 1776 document, which confirmed the legitimacy and authority of the United States.

The conflict that erupted at Lexington and Concord in April, 1775 was also a factor in the hardening of opinion at Mecklenburg county, and there was swifter reaction by the patriot class in this area there than anywhere else in the 13 American colonies.

The radicalism that surfaced in Charlotte and Mecklenburg County was to a large degree influenced by the Scots-Irish Presbyterian clerics, such as the Rev. Alexander Craighead, the Rev. David Caldwell and the Rev. Hezekiah Balch.

Craighead, a nephew of leading Irish Presbyterian minister of the 18th century the Rev. Robert Craighead, had long been in militant opposition to the establishment in the colonies, while his son-in-law, Caldwell, was in the vanguard of the struggle with his congregation.

Caldwell, born in the Scots-Irish stronghold of Lancaster County, Pennsylvania, absolved his flock from their path of allegiance, and closely studied the taxation problem and the charter of the North Carolina colony so that he could instruct them in their rights.

The Scots-Irish had been in the North Carolina territory from the early 1740s, when lands were opened up on behalf of the Crown by Lord Granville, and, it was through the colonialisation a decade later by Carrickfergus, Co Antrim man Arthur Dobbs and Granville's agent Henry McCulloch, that this ethnic influence became more pronounced.

Some historians claim there is not a document to confirm the existence of the Mecklenburg Declaration, and even Thomas Jefferson disputed its authenticity. However, a set of anti-British resolutions were drawn up by a Charlotte committee of leading citizens and militia men in May 1775, calling for the nullification of the authority of all Crown officials in the region, and swearing allegiance to the American Continental Congress.

Details of these resolutions appeared in the *Raleigh Register* and *North Carolina Gazette* in April, 1819 as part of an article by Dr. Joseph McKnitt Alexander, whose father John was clerk of the Mecklenburg assembly. Dr. Alexander insisted his version was a "true copy" of the papers on the subject.

It was said that the minutes of the Charlotte meeting approving the resolutions were destroyed in a fire in April, 1800 after being kept in storage for 25 years. However, not until 1847 was the precise narrative of the resolutions published, in a Charleston newspaper.

The 20 Mecklenburg resolutions stated, among other things, that all laws and commissions derived from British Royal or Parliamentary authority be suspended and that all legislative or executive power henceforth should come from the Provincial Congress of each colony under the Continental Congress. Phrases used, including the term "a free and independent people," later turned up in the text of the American Declaration of Independence.

The Mecklenburg Declaration resolved:

• "That whomsoever or indirectly abetted, in any way, form or manner countenances the unchartered and dangerous invasion of our rights, claimed by Great Britain, is an enemy of this county, to America and to the inherent and inalienable rights of men.

• "That we the citizens of Mecklenburg County do hereby dissolve the political bonds which have connected us to the mother country, and hereby absolve themselves from all allegiance to the British Crown, and abjure all political connections, contact or association with that nation, who have wantonly trampled on our rights and liberties and inhumanly shed the blood of American patriots at Lexington.

• "That we do hereby declare ourselves a free and independent people, and, by right ought to be, a sovereign and self-governing association, under the control of no power, other than that of our God and the general government of Congress; to the maintenance of which we solemnly pledge to each other our mutual co-operation, our lives, our fortunes and our most sacred honour."

Similar sentiments were expressed four months earlier—on January 20, 1775—by Scots-Irish Presbyterian settlers at Abingdon in south west Virginia, close to the present state line with Tennessee.

In a memorial to the Virginia legislature the Abingdon settlers stated: "We are willing to contribute all in our power if applied to constitutionally, but cannot think of submitting our liberty and property to a venal British Parliament or a corrupt ministry.

"We are deliberately and resolutely determined never to surrender our inestimable privileges to any power on earth, but at the expense of our lives. These are our real and unpolished sentiments of liberty and loyalty, and in them we are resolved to live or die."

Another such resolution was the Pine Creek Declaration, drafted by a group of Scots-Irish settlers in a western part of Pennsylvania, 200 miles north of Philadelphia. This was issued simultaneously with the July 4, 1776 Declaration of Independence. Although the log cabin settlers were unaware of what Continental Congress politicians were doing in Philadelphia, the Pine Creek resolution was seen as an expression of support for the main document.

The hardy Pine Creek settlers squatted illegally on lands on the west bank of the Susquehanna River, outside the terms of the Land Purchase of 1768 and beyond the laws dictated from Philadelphia. Despite being "seated on doubtful territory," the settlers were not for moving and they formed a compact among themselves and established a tribunal known as the "Fair Play System."

Early in the summer of 1776, news reached this remote settlement that the Continental Congress might be about to declare for independence and the "fair play" advocates readily voiced their approval for a formal endorsement of their own. Thus, on July 4, 1776, they gathered on the banks of Pine Creek and, after lively discussion, they enthusiastically framed their local declaration.

The set of resolutions absolved the settlers from all allegiance to Great Britain and declared that they were henceforth free and independent. The Pine Creek declaration is viewed as a singular coincidence, action taken in the backwoods of Pennsylvania by a body of Scots-Irishmen, who, while not knowing precisely what was in the minds of the politicians and academics in Philadelphia, were of similar attitude.

The Pine Creek men went on to bravely serve on the battlefields of the Revolution and on December 21, 1784, the legislature of Pennsylvania recognised this service by granting the settlers the right to pre-emption to the lands they had squatted on before titles could be legally granted.

More than a year earlier, Scots-Irish settlers at Hanna's Town (Hannastown), Westmoreland county in south-western Pennsylvania had declared, on May 16, 1775, themselves publicly for the American patriot cause. They signified in the Westmoreland Declaration "a readiness to use armed resistance should our country be invaded by a foreign army or should troops be sent from Great Britain to enforce the arbitrary acts of its parliament."

Two Westmoreland battalions of militia were set up under the command of Colonel John Proctor and Colonel John Carnigan and took in the various battles.

Meanwhile, the Bill of Rights for the state of Virginia, heavily influenced at its drafting in 1776 by the Scots-Irish, declared that one of the inalienable rights of man is his right to worship God, according to the dictates of his conscience.

This bill led to the separation of church and state in Virginia and throughout the Union, but while religious liberty was a core ideal, Scots-Irish Presbyterian dissenters, particularly in the Shenandoah Valley, still laboured under the laws of toleration rather than being able to enjoy full religious freedom.

Under the legislation, dissenters were exempted from the tithe or tax paid to the Episcopal (Anglican) church, but it was not until the end of the War that Presbyterian ministers were given a limited right to perform marriages. The Presbyterian settlers, well versed in the separation of church and state by their ministers, were not a people easily staved off with mere toleration ahead of total liberty.

The 27 signators to the Mecklenburg Declaration in North Carolina, most of them Scots-Irish, were: Dr. Ephraim Brevard, Rev. Hezekiah Balch, James Phifer, Colonel James Harris, William Kennon, John Ford, Richard Barry, Henry Downs, Ezra Alexander, William Graham, John Queary, Hezekiah Alexander, Colonel Adam Alexander, Charles Alexander, Captain Zaccheus Wilson, Weightstill Avery, Benjamin Patton, Matthew McClure, Neil Morrison, General Robert Irwin, John Flennigin, David Reese, Major

John Davidson, Richard Harris, Colonel Thomas Polk, Colonel Abraham Alexander and John McKnitt Alexander ("the clerk.")

The reputed author of the Declaration was Dr. Ephraim Brevard, of French Huguenot stock, with a grandfather who emigrated from Ulster with the McKnitt family.

David Reese's Welsh-born father, the Rev. David Reese, was a Presbyterian chaplain at the Siege of Londonderry in 1688-89 and who later returned to Wales. David Jr. emigrated to America as a 15-year-old and married Susan Polk, of the family of President James Knox Polk. He was magistrate, and a county court judge and a main purchaser of firearms for the Mecklenburg militia.

Although adopted by the Charlotte committee, the resolutions were never presented to the Continental Congress, thus their non-appearance in official manuscripts. But the flag and the Great Seal of the state of North Carolina carries to this day the legend "May 20, 1775," reputed date of the drawing up of the Charlotte resolutions. May 31, 1775 has also been recorded as the date of the resolutions, but the difference can be explained in terms of the old and new calendar.

Colonel Abraham Alexander and Colonel Thomas Polk, of first generation Ulster immigrant families from Londonderry-Donegal, led the debate for the declaration as representatives of Mecklenburg County to the North Carolina legislature.

Abraham Alexander presided at the Mecklenburg Convention which started on May 20, 1775 (the resolutions were signed at midnight on this date!), and he was active throughout the Revolutionary War as a magistrate and militia leader.

Thomas Polk, a great uncle of American President of 1845-49 James Knox Polk, was joined in the militia by his younger brother Ezekiel, the president's grandfather, and, like Abraham Alexander, they became a thorn in the flesh of Cornwallis and his Redcoat army.

Other leading citizens of Scots-Irish lineage prominent in Mecklenburg County in the decisive mid-1770s period were Captain James Jack, the Rev Charles Cummings and General George Graham.

The Scots-Irish Presbyterian clan in the Charlotte region was solid in its support of the American patriot cause, and this uncompromising stance caused ire with the British forces, thus Lord Cornwallis's intemperate remark about the "Hornet's Nest."

Cornwallis found the North Carolina region around Charlotte, Waxhaws and Salisbury a much tougher nut to crack than South Carolina, which he secured in 1780. Defeat for his forces at Kings Mountain in October of that year forced Cornwallis to abandon his plans for North Carolina, and this signalled the beginning of the end for British interests in the south eastern Appalachians.

The crown position worsened at Guilford Courthouse, North Carolina in March, 1781, one of the bloodiest battles of the War. The patriots withdrew after losing 261 men, but Cornwallis paid a heavy price for a questionable victory, with 532 of his men reported killed, wounded or missing. Six months later the game was up when Lord Cornwallis's army surrendered at Yorktown.

In 1834, a North Carolina historian J. S. Jones wrote that the original Whig party of North Carolina comprised the wealth, virtue, and the intelligence of the province. This party, he said, carried with it the support of the Carolina back-country Presbyterian clergy, elders and people.

AMERICAN SETTLERS WHO STAYED LOYAL TO THE CROWN

While the great majority of the Scots-Irish committed themselves to the American patriot cause in the American War of Independence, a significant number remained loyal to the Crown, particularly in the Carolina back-country.

The dividing lines were not so clear in some areas of the Carolinas with instances of frontier militia men changing sides. While the Scots-Irish Presbyterians gained a high profile for declaring for different sides more than once over the duration of war. Members of the same family fought on opposite sides in the war, with father pitted against son, brother against brother and neighbour against neighbour, with hostilities on some fronts taking on the mantra of a civil war.

The Scots-Irish, whether patriot or loyalist, could easily identify the native American tribes as their enemy, but it was much more difficult to come to terms with fighting men from their own ethnic immigrant strain.

It is generally reckoned that more than three-quarters of the Scots-Irish settlers were sympathetic in varying degrees to the clamour for American independence, but those who fought for the Crown and the maintenance of the link with Britain were not an inconsiderable number. Indeed, some historians estimate there were as many as 25,000 Carolina loyalists who bore arms against the American patriots.

Support for loyalism (or Toryism!) was ironically strongest in areas of the Carolinas where the regulation movements had operated in the years leading up the war. Regulators—local vigilantes—were pledged to take action, even outside the law, against exorbitant taxes and fees set by landlords and officials acting on behalf of the colonial authorities.

The Scots-Irish outnumbered the other ethnic strains in the militant Regulation movements, but English and German backcountry farmers also participated, and by the late 1760s up to eight Carolina backcountry countries were in Regulatory control.

The Regulatory activities lasted about five years, and in 1771 things came to a head in bloody exchanges at Alamance in North Carolina where Irish-born Governor William Tyron broke up the movement. A number of Regulators were hanged by the provincial authorities for crimes committed.

The South Carolina Regulators may have violently railed against the colonial establishment in the years before the war, but by 1775 they would have been considered half-hearted patriots. The hostilities provided Regulators and ex-Regulators, who had secured forgiveness for their past illegal actions by taking the oath of loyalty to the Crown, with the opportunity of paying off old sores.

All around them in the Carolina backcountry the Regulators found their former enemies in control of government affairs and the view was taken that it was better to remain under British colonial rule than change to a government run by easterners from the gentry class, albeit from the Scots-Irish diaspora, who had never shown any sympathy for them, and effectively surpressed their movement.

The Continental Congress, aware of the dissenting voices in the Carolinas against their independence call, sent two Presbyterian ministers to North Carolina, at a salary of forty dollars a month, to try to win backing for the patriot cause.

Joseph Hewes and William Hooper, North Carolina delegates to the Continental Congress, persuaded Presbyterian ministers in Pennsylvania to write to fellow church members in the Carolinas to persuade them on the merits of the revolution. But, set against the strong patriotic feelings in Mecklenburg and the Waxhaws areas, this call resulted in at best only lukewarm support in other parts of the Carolinas backcountry.

Alexander Chesney, who was born in Dunclug near Ballymena in Co Antrim in 1756, is probably the best known of the Scots-Irish loyalists in the Carolina Piedmont. It is remarkable that when the war ended in 1782, he returned home to spend the last years of his life in Ulster.

Interestingly, Chesney and a local Scots-Irish compatriot Moses Kirkland in the Carolina backcountry, bore arms against the Crown in situations where they were compelled to, but tactically switched sides when the opportunity arose.

Chesney's father was Robert McChesney—the "Mc" was dropped when the family moved to Charleston in 1772—and they were given 100 acres of land on backcountry territory reserved for incoming Irish Protestant settlers. The Chesneys were married into the Ulster immigrant families of Purdy, Gillespey, Archbold, Wilson, Symonton, Cook, Nisbit, Grier, Wylie, McCleland, Barclay, Pogue, Phillips and Brandon and their influence extended widely in the frontier settlements.

The Chesneys were only a few years on the Carolina frontier when hostilities commenced and the agitation for independence began to be felt. The backcountry Scots-Irish settlers were isolated from the political wrangling that took place in Pennsylvania, Virginia and Charleston, but the seeds of dissension were still being sown and the clamour for independence was heard more stridently.

Alexander Chesney, Moses Kirkland, John Philips, Joshua English and Andrew Williamson were men who were exerting a large degree of influence on the Scots-Irish families in the Carolina backcountry townships of Belfast, Londonderry (Londonborough) and Williamsburg.

However, when attempts were made in July, 1775 by the revolutionary council to persuade the frontier settlers to sign a document refusing to import or buy British goods and withholding an allegiance to the Crown, Chesney, Kirkland, Philips and the others resolved not to get involved.

Alexander Chesney and his neighbours chose instead to remain faithful to King George III, who—they perceived as being a benevolent benefactor, and they organised themselves into defence groups.

In November, 1775 these South Carolina backcountry loyalists engaged in the first military battle with the patriot militia—at Ninety Six, where, after emerging victorious, they dispersed on learning that a superior force was on its way from the coastal areas.

Alexander Chesney led many of the loyalists to his father's lands, and they hid in caves until the danger was averted. The loyalist faction among the Scots-Irish settlers joined on the side of the Redcoat army under Patrick Ferguson at Kings Mountain and Banastre Tarleton at Cowpens.

Among those of Scots-Irish vintage who fought under Chesney were John Adams, William Atkins, Charles Brandon, Christopher Brandon, Robert Chesney (father), William Chesney (brother), William Cunningham, Hugh Cook, Jonathan Frost, Matthew Gillespey, John Heron (brother-in-law), Robert McWhorter and James Millar.

Alexander Chesney was captured several times by the patriots, once after the battle of King Mountain.

When the War ended, some of the Scot-Irish loyalists evacuated with the British from Charleston in December, 1782. They went first to Florida or islands in the Caribbean and from there to Nova Scotia. Others went to England, or like Alexander Chesney, returned directly to Ireland.

They settled chiefly in Belfast, Larne, Ballymena, Lisburn and Bangor and obtained posts with the British goverment mainly in customs. Chesney was given a civil service appointment in Bangor, an area with a strong Presbyterian presence.

The majority, however, of the Scots-Irish loyalists chose to remain in South Carolina and returned to their homes and land on the frontier. There, provided they had not committed what were regarded as war crimes against their fellow South Carolinians, they were permitted to melt back into society.

Some were imprisoned, a number were burnt out of their homes, but a large number managed to satisfactorily mend fences with their neighbours and were able to live together thereafter in harmony.

Alexander Chesney, who is buried in Kilkeel, Co Down, left behind a very detailed account of his experiences on the loyalist side in the Revolutionary War, and his original diary is preserved for posterity in the Northern Ireland Public Records Office in Belfast.

EXPLORATIONS AND SOLDIERING OF GEORGE ROGERS CLARK

General George Rogers Clark, celebrated conquerer of the old North West trail on the upper reaches of the Ohio River, was a Virginian of Ulster Presbyterian family stock whose exploits as a surveyor, explorer and soldier give him an honoured place in the annals of the Revolutionary War.

This red-haired frontiersmen with penetrating black eyes first came to prominence as a 20-year-old in the summer of 1772 when he explored down the Ohio River from Pittsburgh to the mouth of the Kanawha River with a group of adventurers.

In the following spring, Clark went on another expedition 130 miles below Pittsburgh which led to his involvement with the Ohio company in opening up lands in Kentucky for settlement.

When the war started, George Rogers Clark distinguished himself for the patriots in a number of battles, and particularly significant, in 1778, was his role in rescuing Kentucky frontier settlements under attack from British-backed Cherokee Indians.

After running to the gauntlet of Indian ambushes over 400 miles of frontier territory, Clark and his comrades managed to get fresh gunpowder supplies to the settlers. He later led a force of 175 men from Virginia through 18 miles of swamp and forest in Illinois to capture Kaskasakia, Cahokia and Vincennes forts.

As a result of this campaign, the United States, through the Treaty of Paris, obtained the lands northwest of the Ohio River and Clark's sterling efforts considerably eased the pressures on settlers in the upper Ohio River region.

After the war, Clark, born in Charlottsville, Virginia, served on a board which supervised the allocation of 150,000 acres of land in the Louisville area of mid-Kentucky which the state of Virginia had granted for Revolutionary War veterans.

Along with Benjamin Logan, another Scots-Irishman, Clark conducted a campaign against the Wabash Indians and Shawnee tribes who were harassing the white settlers in northern Kentucky.

Clark's adventurous militarism in the north-west campaigns of the Revolutionary War was not entirely approved by the American establishment and in some ways this made him sympathetically inclined in his later years towards French interests in North America.

In 1793, he wrote to France's United States representative Edmond Charles Genet: "My country has proved notoriously ungrateful for my services, but I still have much influence in the West." This led to Clark accepting a commission in the French army, with the objective of attacking Spanish interests west of the Mississippi.

An attempt by Clark to found a colony in Louisiana failed because the Spanish Roman Catholic authorities there would not accept his demand for political and religious freedom. A planned expedition in 1793-94 to take possession of disputed lands between the Yazoo River and the Natchez region in French Louisiana, with the help of 1,500 Kentucky and Tennessee troops, was halted on the instructions of President George Washington.

The United States demanded that he surrender this commission, and he was forced to take refuge in St Louis. Out of favour with his own government, Clark built a cabin at Clarksville on the Indiana side of the Ohio River, and from there he ran a gristmill and served as chairman of the local commission for apportioning land to veterans of his Illinois regiment.

By this time his health had deteriorated and, after moving to Louisville, Kentucky, he died in 1818.

Brigadier-General William Clark, younger brother of George Rogers Clark, was involved with Captain Meriwether Lewis in the celebrated overland expedition of 1804-06 from the Mississippi over the Rocky Mountains to the northwest Pacific coast region, ordered by President Thomas Jefferson, after the United States government had purchased the Louisiana lands from the French Government for 15 million dollars in 1803.

The heroism of the Clarks—George Rogers and William—was aptly summed up by American author James Alexander Thom when he said:

"In one generation the Clark family of Virginia fought for our nation's independence and explored, conquered and settled the continent from sea to shining sea."

CONTRASTING VIEWS FROM IRELAND ON THE WAR

During the American Revolutionary War, Sir John de Blacquire presented, on behalf of Roman Catholics in Ireland, an address to King George III in London "abhorring the unnatural rebellion which has lately broken out among some of his American subjects."

This may seem odd to many in the Ireland of today, for it is somewhat of a paradox that generally Irish Protestant and Roman Catholic attitudes to Britain during the American Revolutionary War were so different from what currently prevails, with almost all the Protestants (unionists) now backing the maintenance of the Union and the majority of Roman Catholics (nationalist) seeking separation and the setting up of an all-Ireland republic.

Interestingly, a large swathe of middle class Roman Catholic opinion in Ireland, in both the clerical and lay sectors, publicly supported the British war effort in America in the 1770s. When the war broke out in 1775, a group of influential Roman Catholics in Dublin sent memorials to the British authorities, stating their abhorrence of the Presbyterian rebellion in America and offering to encourage recruitment, even though Roman Catholic enlistment at the time was barred.

In Limerick, Roman Catholic leaders raised half a guinea per volunteer for the first two hundred men to enlist in the British army. In the Co Down town of Newry, Roman Catholic merchants publicly aligned themselves with British interests in quelling the Presbyterian uprising in America. Loyal addresses were also sent to London from Cork.

This attitude by Irish Roman Catholics was entirely in line with that taken by the Vatican, where the then pope in 1760 gave full recognition to British monarch King George III, a High-Church Anglican. The fall-out from the aborted Roman Catholic-supported rebellions against the Crown in Scotland in 1715 and 1745 had run its course, and both the Irish and

Scottish Church hierarchies were broadly on track with the established order in the British Isles.

In return for their support in the American War, the British government provided legal relief for the Roman Catholics in Ireland and Scotland, legislation which effectively freed the Roman Catholics from educational, marital and professional disabilities.

Anglicans or members of the Church of Ireland, many of whom held civil positions under the Crown in the administration run from Dublin Castle, were also generally agreeable to the continuance of British interests in the American colonies.

However, in these Irish cities and towns there was a significant measure of Protestant Whig support for the American revolution, as was evidenced by referenda conducted among its citizens. Roman Catholics were disenfranchised at the time.

Ulster Presbyterians were warmly sympathetic with the fight for independence on the other side of the Atlantic, not surprising since their kinsmen who had emigrated in large numbers over a period of half a century were in the vanguard of the struggle in Pennsylvania and the Appalachian frontier backcountry.

In 1775, 250 leading citizens of Belfast, almost to a man Presbyterian, called on King George III in London to "dismiss his Ministers and sheath his sword."

Historian George Bancroft observed Protestant attitudes in the north of Ireland to fight across the Atlantic: "The Oak Boys and the Hearts of Steel with their other relatives were being well and favourably heard from in George Washington's army, and Ulster's sympathy and best wishes were with them and the cause they were fighting."

At the end the war in 1783, the Presbyterian-influenced Yankee Club of Stewartstown in Co Tyrone sent a message of congratulations to George Washington at his Mount Vernon home in Virginia. Washington acknowledged the Stewartstown message with appreciative sentiments.

Armagh Presbyterian minister, the Rev. Dr. William Campbell, as moderator of the Synod of Ulster in the 1770s/1780s, said the Presbyterians of Ulster condemned the American War of Independence as "unjust, cruel and detestable."

Newry-born Campbell, minister of First Armagh congregation and chaplain to Lord Charlemont's regiment of volunteers in Ulster, declared: "The Presbyterians of Ulster beheld the war with anguish and with horror, as the most wanton unprovoked despotism. Their friends and relations abounded in the different provinces of America, and they heard with pride that they composed the flower of Washington's army, being carried on by a native love of liberty, to encounter every danger for the safety of their adopted country."

W. E. Lecky, late 19th century author of the American Revolution (1763-1783) wrote: "Protestant Ireland in 1776 was indeed far more earnestly enlisted on the side of the Americans than any other portion of the Empire."

"Emigrants from Ulster formed a great part of the American army, and the constitutional question of independence of the Irish Parliament was closely connected with the American question," said Lecky.

THE WAXHAWS AND ANDREW JACKSON FAMILY'S REVOLUTIONARY WAR EFFORT

Scots-Irish settlements of the Waxhaws region close to Charlotte in North Carolina where President Andrew Jackson grew up became a hotbed of American patriotic feeling during the Revolutionary War with much of the passion raised by the excesses of British cavalrymen led by Colonel Banastre Tarleton.

The defining moment for many backcountry Scots-Irish farmers, who, until then, had not taken sides between American and British interests in the war, came on May 29, 1780 in an incident known as Buford's Massacre.

The 350-strong 11th Virginia Regiment, led by Colonel Abraham Buford, was retreating back to their home state when they were ambushed at Waxhaws by the Tarleton-led Redcoats, numbering around 270, and nearly obliterated in a savage and merciless attack.

Dozens of wounded men were treated in the nearby Waxhaws Presbyterian Church, where Andrew Jackson and his brother Robert helped their Co Antrim-born widowed mother Elizabeth stench the soldiers' blood on an improvised straw floor.

The attack caused bitter resentment amongst the frontier settler families, with Tarleton, a Liverpool-born English aristocrat who later became a Tory MP, being despised as "a butcher." It resulted in many farmers and their sons queuing up to enroll in militia units that were soon to go into action at the battles of Kings Mountain and Cowpens.

An uncle of the Jacksons, Robert Crawford, was a major in the militia, and the teenage boys' eagerness to get involved as patriots in the war was given impetus after witnessing the retreat of General Horatio Gates and his men up the road towards Charlotte after General Lord Cornwallis's victory at the battle of Camden.

The Jackson boys were among 40 local militiamen gathered at Waxhaws Presbyterian Church on April 9, 1781 when a company of British dragoons attacked them with sabres drawn. Eleven of the 40 were captured, and the church burned down.

Andrew, then only 14, tried to escape on horseback with his cousin Lieutenant Thomas Crawford, but they were pursued by the dragoons and captured. In detention, Andrew was ordered to clean the boots of a British officer, but he refused, stating he expected the treatment normally accorded a prisoner of war.

Insensed by what he saw as a defiant act of insubordination, the officer then used his sword to strike Andrew's left hand and forehead, leaving a scalp on both which he carried for the rest of his life.

The British then ordered Andrew to lead them to the house of a patriot sympathiser called Thompson, but by taking a roundabout route Thompson was able to escape. As punishment, Andrew, brother Robert and 20 other militiamen were forced to march 40 miles without food and water to Camden, where they were confined to prison on a strict diet of bread and water.

Smallpox was detected in the prison stockade and Elizabeth Jackson persuaded the British commander to include her sons in an exchange of prisoners. Robert Jackson, however, never recovered from injuries received in the fighting at Waxhaws and died.

Elizabeth and young Andrew were distraught, but she felt the need to travel the 160 miles to Charleston to nurse American soldiers imprisoned by the British there. A few months later she died with others from a cholera fever that engulfed the prison ship and was buried in an unrecorded grave at a spot known as Charles Town Neck. Her small bundle of possessions were sent to son Andrew at the Waxhaws.

Andrew, whose Ulster emigrant father Andrew died just before he was born in 1767, was alone. His eldest brother Hugh died while fighting for the American patriot cause, and now the war had claimed the lives of his mother and other brother.

American losses in the Buford massacre were 113 killed and 203 captured, but Colonel Buford and several dozen mounted men escaped. It was a well-planned operation by Tarleton, who recorded his casualties as 19 men and 31 horses killed or wounded.

For all the professional militarism of his victory and being labelled a hero by his own side, Banastre Tarleton lost the propaganda battle in America minds when details emerged that he had allowed "no quarter" even in death for the defeated patriots.

"The demand for quarters was at once found to be in vain; not a man was spared and it was the concurrent testimony of all the survivors that for fifteen minutes after every man was postrate they went over the ground plunging their bayonets into each one that exhibited any signs of life," was one American account of the massacre.

In American revolutionary folklore Lieutenant Colonel Banastre Tarleton became known as "Bloody Tarleton," and "Tarleton's Quarter"—a cynical term for "no quarter"—was coined after that ill-fated battle at the strongly Scots-Irish influenced Waxhaws and Charlotte area which strengthened the resolve of the patriots to resist.

One Ulsterman who was at Charlotte with his family at the time was Patrick Jack, who emigrated in 1762 from a farm at Ardstraw in the Sperrin mountain region of Co Tyrone. Jack first settled at Chambersburg, Pennsylvania before moving along the Great Wagon Road to North Carolina, and he and his five sons were active participants as militiamen in the Revolutionary War.

The Jacks were continually on a wanted list by the British forces and the family home at Charlotte was burned by forces led by Banastre Tarleton in the hunt for Patrick Jack, who hid in a surrounding forest.

James Jack, a nephew of Patrick, was killed in the Revolutionary War, and his 17-year-old son James took his place in the battle lines. James and

Jeremiah Jack are listed as revolutionary patriots at the Battle of Kings Mountain in October, 1780.

SCOTS-IRISH EVOKE THE SPIRIT OF GIDEON AT KINGS MOUNTAIN

The Battle of Kings Mountain in South Carolina on October 7, 1780 is recognised as a very significant turning point in the course of the American War of Independence and this encounter on the patriot side was fought and won overwhelmingly by a group of Scots-Irish militiamen known as the Overmountain Men.

British colonial forces suffered a major set-back in this battle, and after a second reversal in a battle three months later at nearby Cowpens, Crown rule in the American colonies effectively came to an end and independence was ratified.

The Overmountain men who had settled on the western Watuaga region across the Blue Ridge Mountains had become a thorn in the flesh for Crown interests in the inner colonies during the 1770s and the British commander General Patrick Ferguson threw down the gauntlet to them and threatened to squash their defiance.

Ferguson sent a message to them "to desist from their opposition to the British arms, and take protection under his standard." If they did not, Ferguson intended to march his loyalist army over the Blue Ridge, hang the Overmountain leaders and lay waste their country "with fire and sword."

Ferguson's message had the opposite effect: it inspired the Overmountain men to start preparations for anything which Ferguson saw fit to throw at them and they resolved, with heart and hand, to maintain their cultural identity and their independence. The Overmountain men (Wataugans) were led by French Huguenot John Sevier, Welshman Isaac Shelby and two Scots-Irish Presbyterians William Campbell and Charles McDowell, whose families had settled in the Shenandoah Valley of Virginia and North Carolina.

Patrick Ferguson, a career army officer from Aberdeen in Scotland, was considered the top British soldier of his day and was the inventor of the first breech-loading rifle. He served under Lord Charles Cornwallis at

Charleston, and as loyalist militia inspector of the Southern Province, he raised a force of some 4,000, mostly from the Carolinas and New York, many of highland Scots stock like himself.

The Overmountain men, by comparison, were poorly equipped in arms, ammunition and resources and, according to accepted army manuals, were not considered a match for Ferguson's force. Colonel John Sevier tried personally to raise funds, but he found that the Wataugan settlers had mortgaged themselves heavily and their lands along the banks of the Holston River, and there simply was no money to spare.

Sevier, however, had not given up, and with Isaac Shelby, he approached John Adair, the land entry-taker in North Carolina, who had just received $12,735 in payments from the Scots-Irish settlers. Co Antrim-born Adair was a patriot sympathiser and a staunch Presbyterian and he did not need much persuasion to hand the money over as a loan to be used in recruiting the militia for the cause of independence.

With conviction, the intrepid Adair declared: "Colonel Sevier, I have no authority by law to make this disposition of the money. It belongs to the impoverished treasury of North Carolina and I dare not appropriate a cent of it to any purpose. But if the country is over-run by the British their liberty is gone. Take it, if the enemy, by its use, is driven from this country, I can trust that country to justify and vindicate my conduct. So take it."

Both Sevier and Shelby personally pledged to repay the money received from Adair after the war. It enabled the Overmountain men to be fully armed and prepared to face Colonel Patrick Ferguson and his loyalists at Kings Mountain.

The call to arms spread like wildfire through the North Carolina region mountain and the Tennessee territory, and on September 25, 1780 more than 1,000 would-be combatants gathered for enrolment on the low ground at Sycamore Shoals, which today is part of Elizabethton, near to Johnson City in northeast Tennessee.

Few of the men and boys musketing at Sycamore Shoals had the appearance of soldiers going into battle; they were small dirt farmers, who had just left their lands garbed in rough mountain-style clothes and carrying the barest of untensils. The most effective weapon each shouldered was the Kentucky long rifle, the traditional firepower of the 18th century American frontier.

Colonel John Sevier commanded 240 men from Washington County (then North Carolina now Tennessee); Colonel Isaac Shelby led a similar force from nearby Sullivan County; Colonel William Campbell headed 400 Virginian riflemen, and Colonel Charles McDowell commanded 160 from South Carolina. More joined from the Carolina piedmont. By the time they reached Kings Mountain they numbered about 1,400, ranged against 1,100 under Patrick Ferguson.

The womenfolk and the children also gathered at Sycamore Shoals to bid their farewells and to ensure that the volunteers had joined had enough food and clothing for the assignment. And present to offer spiritual guidance was the Presbyterian frontier pastor, the Rev. Samuel Doak, whose parents had emigrated from Co Antrim to the Shenandoah Valley of Virginia.

Doak, a cleric in the best traditions of 18th century Calvinism, likened the cause of the patriot Overmountain settlers to that of Gideon and his people in opposing the Midianites in Old Testament Biblical times. The battle cry was "The Sword of the Lord and of Gideon," with the assembled gathering loudly echoing Doak's words before starting off on horseback and foot to face Patrick Ferguson and the loyalists.

Virginian William Campbell, a six-foot six-inch giant of Ulster stock whose family had moved from Argyllshire in the 17th century Plantation years, was chosen as Overmountain men leader by Sevier, Shelby and McDowell, and it took 10 days journeying before the patriot force got to within sight of Ferguson's Redcoat army.

Campbell's men dug into the wooded terrain, while Ferguson decided on an open base for his base. After reviewing the platoons under his command, William Campbell advised anyone who did not wish to fight to head for home immediately. There were no takers and after he ordered them to "shout like hell and fight like devils," his men, screaming at the top of their voices, responded to the first fire mounted from the loyalist ranks.

The battle of Kings Mountain lasted 65 minutes, with the patriot forces using Indian-style tactics to out-manoeuvre the loyalists from the back of every tree, rock and shrub. There was much hand-to-hand fighting and the sharp shooting of the long riflemen took its toll.

The Redcoats were forced to defend their position with bayonets as the Overmountain men closed in. Colonel Ferguson, probably sensing defeat, had to personally head, off attacks from all sides. A rifle shot struck him in the head and slumping in the saddle, he dropped from his horse dead. His command was taken by Captain Abraham De-Peyster, who had engaged the Overmountain men in a previous battle at Musgrove's Mill.

The loyalists were hopelessly encircled, and in panic some Redcoat soldiers waved white flags of surrender. But the shooting continued, with many of the patriots unaware of the significance of the white flags. They were not professional soldiers and the revenge factor surfaced as previous atrocities committed by loyalists came to minds.

Colonel Campbell managed to bring about a ceasefire among his ranks by calling out: "For God's sake, don't shoot. It is murder to kill them now, for they have raised their flags."

British officer De-Peyster protested at the behaviour of the patriots: "It's damned unfair, damned unfair." Campbell calmly ignored the protestations, calling the loyalists to sit down as prisoners. The Overmountain men had only minimal casualties compared to the loyalists: 28 killed and 62 wounded against 225 dead; 163 wounded and about 800 taken prisoner.

Kings Mountain was the watershed in the Revolutionary War, the left flank of Lord Cornwallis had been effectively shattered and the British were never again able to muster a loyalist force of size recruited from American society. Patrick Ferguson was buried close to the ridge he had chosen to defend.

Ferguson was just 36 when he died, a soldier whose bravery and technical military skills were as much admired by those whom he fought as those who had served under him.

Early in his American service, Patrick Ferguson wrote a letter to his mother which underlined his deep faith: "The length of our lives is not at our command, however much the manner of them may be. If our Creator enables us to act the part of honour and to conduct ourselves with spirit, probity and humanity, the change to another world whether now or in 50 years hence, will not be for the worse."

The loyalist prisoners were taken to Hillsborough in North Carolina, where they were exchanged for patriot prisoners. Most of the Overmountain men drifted back to their farms and their families—their involvement in the war had ended.

A week elapsed before Lord Cornwallis learned of the news of the Kings Mountain defeat and it had a devastating effect. Plans for a major offensive in the southwest were abandoned, although British authorities tried to dismiss the Battle result as having no consequences.

General George Washington did not hear of the Kings Mountain battle until October 26, and with elation, he spoke of "that important object gained" as "proof of the spirit and resources of the country."

In later years, United States President Thomas Jefferson was to recall "that memorable victory" at Kings Mountain—"the joyful annunciation of that turn of the tide of success which terminated the Revolutionary War with the seal of independence."

The Overmountain men leaders at Kings Mountain became leading statesmen, politicians and civic leaders. John Sevier was the first Governor of Tennessee, Isaac Shelby the first governor of Kentucky, while William Campbell represented Washington County in the Virginia House of Delegates before an untimely death 10 months after Kings Mountain. Many others were to distinguish themselves in politics, and in subsequent army careers, but most went back to being simple farmers.

Most of the Overmountain men (Wataugans) who fought at Kings Mountain were first, second and third generation Americans of Ulster-born parents or grandparents. A good many were born in Ireland, the overwhelming number of them in the north of Ireland, from the Presbyterian tradition.

Robert Leckie in his book *George Washington's War* said no breed of frontiersmen existed in America hardier than these settlements of mostly Scots-Irish along the Watauga River. "Fiercely independent, hunters, Indian fighters, deadly shots with those rifles, to which they gave names such as "Sweet Lips" or "Hot Lead," they could campaign for days on their horses with no other equipment than a blanket, a hunting knife and a bag of parched corn sweetened with molasses or honey," he wrote.

The Battle of Cowpens in South Carolina on January 17, 1781 involved quite a number of the Overmountain men from Watauga and Scots-Irish settlers and militia soldiers of other ethnic groups from the Carolinas. The battle was another set-back for the British, with 1,000 patriot troops under the command of General Daniel Morgan routing the Redcoats under Colonel Banastre Tarleton.

British losses were more than 100 killed, more than 200 wounded and 600 captured. Militia casualties were 12 dead and 60 wounded and, as from

Kings Mountain, support in the aftermath of Cowpens solidified support in the region for the American patriot cause and forced the British into desperate counter-manoeuvres.

Two months later, on March 15, 1781 at the battle of Guilford Courthouse in North Carolina, the British forces, although acknowledged to be victorious, lost more leeway in their desperate bid to hold on to the Carolinas. American casualties were less than 80 killed and 200 wounded, compared to nearly 100 killed and 400 wounded for the British.

The patriot militia retreated, while Lord Charles Cornwallis moved his exhausted Redcoat forces to Wilmington on the coast of North Carolina, effectively ceding the state to the enemy. The battle result and after-effects provoked radical parliamentarian Charles Fox to declare in the House of Commons in London that "another such victory would destroy the British Army."

Scots-Irish settlers were also heavily involved in the fighting at Guilford Courthouse.

The main thrust of the Rev. Samuel Doak's sermon to the Overmountain militia men at Sycamore Shoals before they headed to Kings Mountain: "My countrymen, you are about to set out on an expedition which is full of hardships and dangers, but one in which the Almighty will attend you. The Mother Country has her hands upon you, these American colonies, and takes that for which our fathers planted their homes in the wilderness-our Liberty.

"Taxation without representation and the quartering of soldiers in the homes of our people without their consent are evidence that the Crown of England would take from its American subjects the last vestige of Freedom.

"Your brethren across the mountains are crying like Macedonia unto your help. God forbid that you shall refuse to hear and answer their call, but the call of your brethren is not all. The enemy is marching hither to destroy your homes.

"Brave men, you are not unacquainted with battle. Your hands have already been taught to war and your fingers to fight. You have wrested these beautiful valleys of the Holston and Watauga from the savage hand.

"Will you tarry now until the other enemy carries fire and sword to your very doors? No, it shall not be. Go forth then in the strength of your manhood to the aid of your brethren, the defence of your liberty and the protection of your homes. And may the God of justice be with you and give you victory. Help us good soldiers to wield the Sword of the Lord and of Gideon.''

ONLY REVOLUTIONARY BATTLE ON TENNESSEE SOIL

The only engagement of the Revolutionary War to be fought within the boundaries of the existing state of Tennessee was the battle of Boyd's Creek in Sevier County in the heart of the Great Smoky Mountains on December 16, 1780. Then, a consignment of East Tennessee militia riflemen, led by Colonel John Sevier, defeated a large force of Chickamauga Cherokee and renegade Indians, who were operating in support of the British.

The Cherokee tribes had earlier attacked the Watauga Scot-Irish settlements along the Holston and French Broad rivers, while Colonel Sevier and his Overmountain men were away fighting at the battle of Kings Mountain, and at Boyd's Creek the Indians suffered heavy casualties.

Early in 1780, the Chickamauga Cherokees, led by their militant chief Dragging Canoe, were persuaded by British agents to begin attacking the frontier settlements in the south east and this squalid agreement became more important to colonial commander Lord Charles Cornwallis after the defeat of Colonel Patrick Ferguson's force at the battle of Kings Mountain.

Sensing weakness of the Watauga settlements while their men were still in South Carolina at Kings Mountain, senior British officer Colonel Thomas Brown sent one of his agents to Dragging Canoe and little encouragement was needed to send the Chickamaugas on the march north.

They passed through the Overhill Cherokee towns, and on the way, Dragging Canoe recruited more warriors to follow him. However, a few Cherokees were unhappy with the plan to attack the frontier settlements, and Nancy Ward, who had connections to both the white and native American races and was known on the frontier as the "beloved woman of the Cherokees," sent two traders—Isaac Thomas and Ellis Harlan—to alert the Watauga people of the danger.

On arrival back from Kings Mountain, John Sevier learned of Dragging Canoe's intentions and almost immediately he marched southwards with several hundred men, intent on halting the Indians before they forded the French Broad River.

Sevier and his men confronted a small band of Indians on December 15, and, after driving them off, they pressed on, crossing the French Broad River and camping at Boyd's Creek.

On the morning of December 16, their scouts discovered the main Indian camp about three miles away, and as Sevier's men approached, they found the Cherokees stalked out in a half-moon formation, planning an ambush.

A small group of Overmountain men attacked the Indian lines, while the main body feigned a retreat to lure the Indians into a trap. As a number of Indian warriors fell, Dragging Canoe and others retreated into a nearby swamp away from the battle field.

The engagement did not last long, the Cherokee threat to the Watauga settlements had ended with Dragging Canoe and his surviving warriors fleeing the region. Minimal casualties were reported on the patriot side, but more than 30 Indians were killed.

Within a few days, Colonel John Sevier was joined by the Kings Mountain patriot commander Colonel William Campbell and his aide Major Joseph Martin, and, as the entire Overmountain force headed south, they burned several Cherokee towns in retaliation.

Boyd's Creek in Sevier County is close to Dumpling Creek, where, on June 10, 1785 a treaty was conducted between the white settlers led by John Sevier, David Kennedy, Ebenezer Alexander and the Cherokee Indians, led by "king" Ancoo of Chota. This authorised that all of Jefferson, Hamblen, Sevier, Knox and Blount counties, in what was to become 11 years later part of the new state of Tennessee, be opened up to settler homesteads.

The treaty outlined that "liberal compensation" be made to the Cherokees for the land that had been ceded and granted by them to the white people on the south side of the Holston and French Broad rivers to the region of the Tennessee river close to Knoxville. Within three years, more than 1,000 families, most of them of Scots-Irish origin, had moved in and established homesteads on these historic Indians lands.

It was very dangerous territory for the early white settlers and, as a means of protection and communal vantage point, they established fort stations or blockhouses. The McGaughey, McTeer, McCroskey, Hunter and Houston forts on the trail between Sevierville and Knoxville acted as safe havens for the various families.

The McFarlands were a typical Scots-Irish Presbyterian family on the North Carolina /Tennessee frontier during the Revolutionary War, and several generations fought with distinction on the patriot side. The McFarlands, who had moved through the Shenandoah Valley of Virginia, settled at Hamblen County in northeast Tennessee, the region known as the "Irish Bottom" due to the preponderance of Scots-Irish settlers there.

Colonel Robert McFarland, a militia leader in the War, followed in the soldiering tradition of his father Robert, who fought at the Battle of Mount Pleasant in 1774. Robert Sr. and his father John and other members of the family had emigrated from Co Antrim about 1746 and settled first at Augusta County in the Shenandoah, where he became a local church elder and a militia lieutenant.

Born in Virginia, Colonel Robert McFarland entered military service in 1776. He served through the Revolutionary War in various battles on the frontier region and took part in the Colonel Arthur Campbell-led campaign against the Cherokee towns of Chota, Chilhowee, Little Tellico and Chestowah in December 1780, after the aborted attack on the Watauga settlements by Dragging Canoe and the tribes.

A son of Colonel McFarland, also named Robert, was commended for his heroism at the War of 1812 in the battle of Lundy Lane in upper Canada, while his son, another Robert, led the 31st/39th Tennessee Mounted Infantry at the Civil War battle of the Piedmont in Staunton, Virginia on June 6, 1864.

HISTORICAL PERCEPTIONS OF THE SCOTS-IRISH REVOLUTIONARY WAR INFLUENCE

Reputable historians over the past two centuries are agreed that Scots-Irish support for American independence was generally ardent. The commitment to the patriot cause by the immigrant families from Ulster manifested itself in the actual fighting in the Revolutionary War, and their courage and devotion to duty was a shining example.

Scots-Irish backing in the 1770s for breaking the colonial link with Britain was practically unanimous in Pennsylvania, Virginia, New Jersey and Massachusetts, and in large settlements in North Carolina, South Carolina and Georgia similar sentiments were expressed and acted upon with fervour.

Many Scots-Irish families, however, in the South Carolina Piedmont area remained loyal to the Crown and fought bitter battles against American patriots from the same ethnic community. But, at least three-quarters of the Scots-Irish backed the struggle for independence.

They played a key role in ushering in the new American nation, at both the level of leadership in politics and in the armed forces, and as foot soldiers of the Revolution. In the making of America, the Scots-Irish were most certainly in the vanguard and their contribution was monumental.

The Scots-Irish in the Shenandoah Valley of Virginia were particularly patriotic. The people of Augusta County, which had a predominance of Scots-Irish settlers, sent 137 barrels of flour to relieve the poor of Boston after the Boston "Tea Party" in 1773.

The main town in Rockbridge County, another Scots-Irish stronghold, was named Lexington after the opening battle of the war in Massachusetts in 1775. And the classical academy in Lexington, founded by Ulster Presbyterian clergy, changed its name to Liberty Hall (later becoming in 1798 the Washington and Lee University!) and resolutions in support of American independence were frequent.

The French-Indian War of 1754-63 proved to be an effective training ground for the revolutionary forces in America, particularly those from the Scots-Irish settlements, and, in this earlier conflict, the armies in the Lake George and Lake Champlain region (Fort Henry, Ticonderoga and other frontier posts) and Montreal were largely made up of men of Scottish and Ulster-Scottish origin who inhabited the highly dangerous territory.

In Pennsylvania, Kittanning and Fort Duquesne, the American forces fighting the French and the Indians were almost exclusively Ulster-Scots, who were largely responsible for the reversal of General Braddock's defeat. They were the people who erected the local forts and organised the local militia, called Rifle Rangers, frontline units which were eventually incorporated into George Washington's army.

The Scots-Irish have always been a patriotic people, with a strong fighting tradition. On the American frontier in the 18th century, one had to possess these sturdy qualities to defend family, home and property and, more than any other race, the Scots-Irish stood out.

They were successful, through their exploits in the French-Indian and Revolutionary Wars, in opening the way for the advancing settlements of western Pennsylvania and the Ohio Valley, down to the Mississippi River and beyond.

William C. Lehmann, in his book *Scottish-Irish Contributions to Early American Life and Culture*, interestingly observes that the brunt of the fighting in Pennsylvania fell to the Scots-Irish by default. "The Quakers were pacifist and the Germans lacked a tradition of political involvement and generally lived in the more settled regions," he said.

T. J. Werterbaker (*author of Early Scotch Contributions to the United States*—published Glasgow, 1945), praising the excellence of the American soldiers who were Scots-Irish, said they were "the backbone" of George Washington's army, with the famous Pennsylvania Line mostly of this vintage. "At Valley Forge when many deserted him, they remained, despite cold and hunger, to keep alive the waning cause."

George Washington, of course, said: "If defeated everywhere else, I will make my stand for liberty among the Scots-Irish in my native Virginia."

The town of New Londonderry in New Hampshire—first settled in the early 1720s by Ulster Presbyterians from the Bann Valley around Coleraine and Ballymoney—sent more soldiers to aid George Washington's armies than any other colonial town.

Ralph Barton Perry (author of *Puritanism and Democracy*—published New York, 1944) said that "when account is taken of the Scotch-Irish Presbyterians, the Germans of the middle and southern colonies and the New England congregationalists, it is safe to say that the bulk of the revolutionary armies came from dissenters of the Reformed or Calvinistic sects. From the clergy of these sects came also the religious leadership."

A citation submitted by a British major-general to a House of Commons committee in London stated that "half the Continental Army were from Ireland"-Scots-Irish.

General Nathaniel Greene, one of George Washington's Continental Army commanders and who gave Lord Cornwallis a "bloody nose" at the battle of Guilford Courthouse in March, 1781, thought highly of the mostly Scots-Irish settlers who had just moved down the Great Wagon Road into the backcountry. "Coastal dwellers are sickly but indifferent militia, but the backcountry people are bold and daring in their make-up," he said.

The British Government of the day, of course, was well aware of the Scots-Irish leanings in the war, thus the remark by Prime Minister Horace Walpole, who said in a jibe to his cabinet: "I hear that our American cousin has run off with a Presbyterian parson."

This view was shared by Captain Johann Heinrchs of the Hessian Jaeger Corps in British service: "Call it not an American rebellion; it is nothing more nor less than an Irish-Scotch Presbyterian rebellion."

A representative of Lord Dartmouth, writing from New York in November, 1776, agreed: "Presbyterianism is really at the bottom of this whole conspiracy, has supplied it with vigour, and will never rest until something is decided upon."

Jonathan D. Sergeant, member of the Continental Congress from New Jersey, said that the Scots-Irish were the main pillar supporting the Revolution in Pennsylvania.

Horace Walpole and others in the court of King George III in London were convinced the whole war was nothing more than an uprising of rabble-rousing Presbyterians, largely Scots-Irish—"a sort of latter-day Cromwellian outburst against the due civil, ecclesiastical and a political order of a sensible and free British Empire."

It was significant that the only churchman in the American Continental Congress of 1776 was Scottish-born Presbyterian cleric, the Rev John Witherspoon, and he was a principal signatory of the Declaration.

Daniel I. Rupp (author of *History and Topography of Pennsylvania Counties*—Lancaster, Pennsylvania, 1846) stated: "When the alarm of the American Revolution echoed along the rocky walls of the Blue Mountains, it awakened a congenial thrill of blood of that race which years before, in Ireland and Scotland, has resisted the arbitrary powers of England."

David Ramsey, son of Ulster emigrants and considered the "most remarkably judicious" of early historians of the American Revolution, noted: "The Irish in America, with a few exceptions, were attached to independence, Presbyterians and therefore mostly Whigs. They are inferior to none in discipline, courage or attachment to the cause."

General William Howe, a British commander in the war, spoke of the excellent markmanship of the Scots-Irish-"learned as hunters and Indian fighters, and to their rifles perfected with knowledge of ballistics." Another British officer referred to patriot forces in Pennsylvania during the War as the "line of Ireland".

Tennessee state historian and author Wilma Dykeman observed that the Scots-Irish character—"prompt to resent an affront, unrelenting to foes"—was to leave an imprint on the history of the Revolutionary War at Kings Mountain.

"The Scotch-Irish were the group that left their image stamped indelibly on the frontier. They were both venturesome and cautious, taciturn to a fault, but spoke their mind freely when aroused. Friend and foe alike were objects of their steadfast attention and their nature rebelled against anything that savoured of injustice or deceit, not did they take kindly to restraint of any kind," she said.

Dr. Thomas Smyth, in his critique, said: "The battles of Cowpens and Kings Mountain are amongst the most celebrated as giving a turning point to the contests of the Revolutionary War. General Daniel Morgan, who commanded the patriots at Cowpens on January 17, 1781, was a Presbyterian elder and lived and died in the communion of that Church.

"General Andrew Pickens, who made all the arrangements for the battle of Cowpens, was also a Presbyterian elder from the South Carolina Piedmont and nearly all under his command were Presbyterians.

"In the earlier battle of Kings Mountain, on October 7, 1780, Colonel William Campbell, Colonel James Williams (who fell in action), Colonel Benjamin Cleveland, Colonel Isaac Shelby and Colonel John Sevier (of Huguenot stock) were all Presbyterian elders and the body of troops were collected from the Presbyterian settlements."

The Scots-Irish, of course, had made a significant contribution in the first years of the war, with their hardy and skilled marksmen taking a leading part in the defeat, surrender and capture of British soldiers under General John Burgoyne at the battles of Saratoga along the Hudson River in September-October, 1777.

American historian George Bancroft said the Scots-Irish brought to America no submissive love for England, and their experience and their religion alike bade them meet opposition with prompt resistance.

"The first voice publicly raised in America to dissolve all connection with Great Britain came not from the Puritans of New England or the Dutch of New York or the planters of Virginia, but the Scots-Irish," Bancroft pointed out. "The Presbyterians of Pennsylvania and throughout the colonies arose as one man for the rights and liberties of America," he added.

Another distinguished 19th century historian J. A. Froude wrote: "Throughout the revolted colonies all evidence shows that the foremost, the most irreconcilable, the most determined in pushing the quarrel to the last extremity were the Scotch-Irish, whom the bishops, Lord Donegall and others of their kind, had driven out of Ulster."

Author W. F. T. Butler commented: "It was the Presbyterians of Ulster, driven from their homes by the mistaken religious and economic legislation of the 18th century, who furnished the backbone of the armies that put an end to the rule of England in what is now the United States."

HAZARDS OF FRONTIER MILITIA LIFE

The patriot militia during the Revolutionary War was an all-embracing institution on the American frontier, particularly in states like Tennessee and Kentucky which were just being explored and settled by Scots-Irish families from Pennsylvania, Virginia, the Carolinas and Georgia.

War pension records from militia personnel in East Tennessee at the time provide an insight into how the backwoods militia was constructed and viewed by those from the frontier settlements who readily volunteered for service.

Every able-bodied man on the heavily influenced Scots-Irish settlements was required to go into militia action, armed with a long rifle, the muzzle-loading, flintlock firearm which was modified from a short, large-bore rifle.

Each considered himself a soldier, ready to join his fellows at short notice in an emergency, to defend both his family and community from Indian attack, or from British colonial forces not friendly disposed to those who refused to accept their diktats.

Until the period of the revolution, the colonial wars in America were fought by British regulars, reinforced by American militia, known as "Provincials," recruited largely from the settlements of European immigrants such as the English, Germans, Dutch, Scottish highlanders, and indeed, a significant number of Scots-Irish.

The patriot militia units that engaged in the battles of Lexington and Concord, were in service during the Boston Siege, and fought at Bunker Hill, formed the nucleus of the American Continental Army.

Militia service had a long tradition in the American colonies from the middle to late 17th century and most townships had a "muster field" where citizen soldiers assembled at designated times for rifle training and general defence duties. Their effectiveness as a force with quick manoeuverability and capability for swift, decisive action worked to the advantage of the American patriots in the Revolutionary War.

However, the part-time nature of the militia units meant that they could not always be relied upon to endure for long periods at a time. In one instance during the Revolutionary War, only a quarter of the 8,000 men in militia regiments serving under George Washington at Long Island in August, 1776 were still present when the battle ended.

Washington fully realised the limitations of the militia, and, reporting to the Continental Congress in a letter on August, 1776, he concluded: "If I were called upon to declare on oath, whether the militia had been most servicable or hurtful, I should subscribe to the latter." Washington, however, was later to record his gratitude to the militia for the outstanding contribution they made in the winning of the war for the patriots.

American historian Claude H. Van Tyne, in an interesting observation on the patriot militia of the Revolutionary War, said: "Fortunately, for America's success, its army was not merely the armed and disciplined force, obedient throughout the years of war to its patriot leaders, but the ill-trained farmers, citizens, shopkeepers, ready to leave their work and fight when the enemy approached, and forming at all times a potential force far beyond the army in being. It was a nebulous, incalculable and very occasionally a mighty force."

The composition of the American patriot militia confounded the full-time British Redcoat soldiers. One British officer wrote of the assault on Quebec: "You can have no conception what kind of man composed the (American) officers. Of those we took, one major was a blacksmith, another a hatter."

The militia was "incalculable" in that it could never be counted upon by its friends, but equally could never be ignored by its enemies. The patriot militia, with the Scots-Irish in the front line of battle, defeated the British at Lexington, Concord, Saratoga, Kings Mountain and Cowpens.

Significantly, in these battles the militia units were led by experienced officers, who managed to inspire them to fight like regular soldiers, with techniques that were ideally suited to the forest and mountain terrains of the frontier backcountry.

Because of their pacifist convictions, settlers from the Quakers, Mennonite and Amish faiths were exempt from military service, while arrangements were made in Virginia for Methodists and Baptists to serve under their own officers in the local militia units.

Some militia groups in the Carolina Piedmont were loyal to the British Crown, but elsewhere they generally ended up on the patriot side.

The frontier militia men were not attached to a regiment in the established military sense and the mountain, river and bush warfare in the Tennessee and Kentucky territories was largely independent of the main battle theatres of the Revolutionary War of the eastern seaboard.

Militia service extended to three to nine months at a time, resulting in the sturdy backwoods farmers and hunters having to leave their families and farms unprotected for long periods. Periodically, they were allowed to return home to put in crops in their fields.

Very often, the consequences for women and children being left virtually unprotected on the frontier were dire and many militia men returned home from service to find loved ones brutally massacred and their homesteads destroyed in Indian attacks.

Tennessee historian Wayne C. Moore observes that frontier warfare was designed to break the Indians' will to fight, or, conversely, to destroy the whites' determination to persist in their frontier settlements.

Frontier militiamen, paradoxically, adapted much of the fighting tactics of the Indian tribes they were confronting, and on their own familiar homeland terrain, they used these to good effect against the British Redcoat regiments in decisive Revolutionary War battles like Kings Mountain. Patriot militia commanders led their men into battle, doggedly urging their men to give the enemy "Indian play."

From behind bushes and in deep undergrowth, through rivers and over mountain tops, they relentlessly tracked the enemy, destroyed their food and armament supplies, and laid ambushes and conducted their campaigns with a determined "eye-for-an-eye" retribution.

As they strove tirelessly to maintain their defences on the frontier, a clannish bond developed among the settlers (Scots-Irish, English, Pennsylvania Dutch, Scottish Highlanders and Welsh!) which brokered no division. Few transgressions by the Indians against the white settlements in the 18th century Appalachian territory went unpunished.

Militia duty took the frontiersmen hundreds of miles from their homes, very often into neighbouring but hitherto unknown states, and they had an exploratory eye to their duties when viewing with awe large stretches of good fertile land that so far had lay uninhabited.

Many readily returned to these lush regions with their families and kinsfolk to settle the lands when their militia duties were ended. Tennessee and Kentucky were settled in this way after the Revolutionary War.

Payment for militia service, depending on rank and length of service, was in most cases conducted by the allocation of sizeable land grants in the new territories being opened up in Tennessee and Kentucky, west to the Mississippi and beyond.

Militia life brought its dangers, for the settler farmers cum soldiers, but there were considerable dividends for those who survived the hostilities in the Indian campaigns and the Revolutionary War battles.

ULSTER PATRIOTS AT GEORGE WASHINGTON'S SIDE

JOHN ARMSTRONG:

This highly distinguished soldier of provincial Pennsylvania from Carlisle township was a militia commander in the expedition against Fort Duquesne during the French-Indian War and in February 1775 he was the first patriot brigadier-general to be appointed by the Continental Congress.

Ulster-born Colonel Armstrong, who served two terms in Congress— 1779-80 and 1787-88—recruited his men almost entirely from the Scots-Irish settlements of Cumberland, Lancaster and Dauphin counties, and his French-Indian War expedition was the first offensive against the Indians in Pennsylvania.

Armstrong assembled 300 men at Fort Shirley on the Juniata River in August, 1756, and he made rapid progress towards the Indian stronghold of Kittanning on the Allegheny River. The Indians were taken by surprise and decisively defeated, with more than 50 of the tribe killed. Casualties among Armstrong's men were minimal.

The region echoed with praises of Armstrong and his men, with the Colonel being honoured by the corporation in Philadelphia. The Indian threat had subsided and a greater sense of security prevailed.

In the expedition against Fort Duquesne in 1758, led by General John Forbes, John Armstrong had 2,700 militia men under his command and his close friend George Washington a similar number. Of this force from Pennsylvania, the Scots-Irish mustered the greater part of the contingent, and their heroism led to the capture of Fort Duquesne (later to be known as Pittsburgh!) and the expulsion of the French from Pennsylvanian soil.

John Armstrong took part in the successful defence of Charleston in June, 1776 in his role as commander of South Carolina forces, and at Brandywine in September, 1777, he was in charge of the Pennsylvania militia, before moving on to Germanstown a month later. He graduated to major-general in 1778 and held this militia rank for the rest of the war. He died in 1795, aged 78.

A son, Major John Armstrong Jr., was also a Revolutionary War soldier, serving at Saratoga in October, 1777. After the Revolution, he entered politics and was a United States Senator in 1800-04, minister to France in 1804-10 and secretary of war under President James Madison in 1813-14.

John Armstrong Jr. was blamed for the failure of the U.S. expedition against Montreal and for the British capture of Washington and was forced to resign. He retired to become an author, completing works on the War of 1812 and biographies on Revolutionary War generals Richard Montgomery and Anthony Wayne.

ANDREW CALDWELL:

This naval man of Ulster stock was commander of the Pennsylvania navy and commanded the fleet which repelled the British war ships *Roebuck* and *Liverpool* in 1776.

The Caldwell clan, some of whom were closely related marriage to American Vice-President and leading South Carolina Statesman John C. Calhoun, made outstanding contributions during the Revolutionary War on several fronts.

The Rev. James Caldwell, son of Donegal-born Major William Caldwell, was known as "the fighting parson" in the Revolutionary War. This Princeton College-educated cleric was minister of the First Presbyterian Church at Elizabethton, New Jersey.

In the Carolina backcountry, Belfast-born John Caldwell, who emigrated with his parents to America in 1760, was a militia soldier and scout and fought at the battles of Kings Mountain and Cowpens. Other Caldwells listed in these battles were Samuel, William and Thomas.

The Caldwells, of Newberry, South Carolina, were active patriots in the War, and Major John Caldwell was killed. His bothers, James and William, both militia captains, fought at Cowpens.

JOHN COCHRAN

This medical director of the Continental Army at the time of the Revolutionary War was the son of Ulster parents from Co Armagh, who settled at Sadsbury in eastern Pennsylvania. John Cochran received his education under the tutorship of Donegal-born Presbyterian cleric, the Rev.

Francis Allison, and he entered the British service as a surgeon's mate during the French and Indian War of 1754-63.

Cochran helped found the New Jersey Medical Society and when the Revolutionary War started, with others, he prepared the plans for reorganising the Continental Army's medical department. George Washington was highly impressed and in 1777 he appointed Cochran as the Army's physician and surgeon general.

After the war, John Cochran settled in New York, and, in 1790, President Washington made him commissioner of loans.

A grandson, John Cochran, was a leading politician and he ran for the American vice-presidency in 1864. He was also a brigadier-general in the Civil War.

GILBERT CHRISTIAN:

This son and grandson of Ulster Presbyterians who left Ireland for Virginia in 1732, earned his spurs as a Revolutionary war soldier in the frontier battles against the Indian tribes.

Grandfather Gilbert Christian (born in 1678) and his wife Elizabeth Margaret Richardson (born in 1702 in Ireland) settled on the Beverley lands in Augusta County in the Shenandoah Valley about 1733. Their son Robert, who was also born in Ireland, was a recruiting officer for the militia in Augusta County during the Revolution.

Gilbert II commanded the Sullivan County (now part of Tennessee) militia and his prowess as an Indian fighter in the frontier region was legendary. He was in the front line in the battle of Kings Mountain in October, 1780, and was promoted to major and, eventually colonel, during expeditions to quell Cherokee Indian unrest.

Christian was a justice of the peace in Sullivan County, commander of the territorial militia, and the senate speaker of the state of Franklin, which dissolved after several years. His son Robert married the daughter of John Adair, the Co Antrim man, who raised the money to arm the patriot forces in the battle of Kings Mountain.

Colonel William Christian, uncle of Gilbert Christian, also commanded militia units in expeditions against the Cherokee and Chickamauga Indians during the Revolutionary War years. Their Holston River settlement of Christiansville is now the present-day north east Tennessee town of Kingsport.

SAMUEL FINLAY:

Samuel Finlay, of a Scots-Irish family, was a Revolutionary War commander of artillery and major of the cavalry in the Virginia Line. After the war he founded the town of Chillicothe, Ohio and was appointed by George Washington as receiver of public monies in the North West territory. During the War of 1812, he raised a regiment and served as general of militia

JOSEPH GRAHAM:

Joseph Graham was a militia leader in North and South Carolina during the Revolutionary War and contributed to the Mecklenburg Declaration of May, 1775, which preceded the Declaration of Independence.

Joseph, whose father James was an Ulsterman who settled in Pennsylvania in 1733, moved to Spartanburg, South Carolina in 1763 with his widowed mother and about five years later transferred to Mecklenburg county in North Carolina.

Graham was commissioned as lieutenant in the North Carolina Rangers and he was later promoted to captain in the 4th North Carolina Continentals. He distinguished himself in battle at Charlotte in September, 1780, receiving nine wounds. When he recovered, he organised a dragoon company with a role as major.

After the War, Graham became a successful businessman, and, in his later years, he published letters and articles giving a personal account of the events which centered on the signing of the Mecklenburg Declaration. He also provided first-hand accounts of the Revolutionary War, fighting in western North Carolina and in South Carolina.

CHARLES MCKNIGHT:

The surgeon Charles McKnight was the grandson of Rev. John McKnight, an Ulster Presbyterian minister, and was recognised by George Washington for his outstanding medical service during the Revolutionary

War. Washington appointed him senior surgeon of the flying hospital of the patriot soldiers, and he served until 1782 before taking up a post at Columbia College, New York.

REV. ALEXANDER MCWHORTER:

This Presbyterian minister, born in Delaware in 1734, was the son of Hugh and Jane McWhorter, from Armagh. His father was a linen merchant and settled in Delaware in 1730 and later moved to North Carolina.

Alexander McWhorter studied theology under Rev. William Tennant, the celebrated long cabin tutor who was also from Armagh, and when the Revolutionary War began he strongly favoured the aims of the patriots.

In 1775, McWhorter was appointed to visit western North Carolina to try and persuade royalist sympathisers to join the American cause. On this mission McWhorter enjoyed some of success, and by 1776, he visited General George Washington at Trenton, New Jersey to devise measures for the protection of the North Carolina state. He was present when American troops crossed the Delaware River and captured the Hessians.

McWhorter was chaplain to the brigade of General Henry Knox in 1778 and was appointed president of Charlotte Academy in North Carolina, but he left after only a short service due to the draconian measures of Lord Charles Cornwallis and his Redcoat army.

A committed churchman and Calvinist, he was active in arranging the Confession of Faith and Constitution of the Presbyterian Church of the United States.

GEORGE MATHEWS:

George Matthews, a post-Revolutionary War governor of Georgia, was the son of an Ulster immigrant who settled in the Shenandoah Valley of Virginia. George was a renowned Indian fighter and served through various battles of the War, taking part in the battle of Point Pleasant under General Andrew Lewis.

He rose from lieutenant-colonel to colonel with the 9th Virginia company and fought at Brandywine in February, 1777 and at Germantown in

October of that year. He was captured and spent several months on a prison ship in New York harbour.

When he moved to Georgia in 1785, Mathews became militia brigadier-general and was elected governor in 1787. He represented the state in Congress in 1789-91.

In 1798, President John Adams nominated him to be the first governor of the Mississippi territory, but his name was withdrawn because of alleged dubious land speculations.

Mathews also got involved, independently of the US federal government, in territorial advances on the then-Spanish held Florida lands, and in March, 1812, with backing from the English-speaking population in the region and volunteer recruits from the adjoining Georgia, he took formal possession of the township of Fernandina.

The action was repudiated by the U.S. government, and Mathews died a short time later. Interestingly, Florida became part of America seven years later through the Florida Purchase Treaty.

JAMES McHENRY:

James McHenry, from Ballymoney in Co Antrim, had a distinguished career as a soldier and surgeon during the Revolutionary War, and he was imprisoned for a time by the British.

His Presbyterian family had moved to Maryland in the mid-17th century and through the south-eastern American states they made extensive settlements

McHenry, who was educated in Dublin, helped run an importing and shipping company in Baltimore, then studied and worked in Philadelphia as a physician.

From his role as a Revolutionary War soldier, McHenry became heavily involved in politics and served as American secretary of state for war during the 1796-1800 period under both President George Washington and President John Adams. Fort McHenry at Baltimore is named in his honour.

A Co Antrim Presbyterian associate of James McHenry was Blair McGlenachan, who was a banker, ship-owner and general merchant in Philadelphia.

ANDREW PICKENS:

Andrew Pickens, son of Ulster-born Presbyterian immigrant parents who settled in eastern Pennsylvania before heading southwest down the Great Wagon Road, was a distinguished commander of the patriot militia in the South Carolina piedmont region during the Revolutionary War.

This tall, lean, austere figure was a born leader, and while not being noted for speech-making, he was a doer, who, when he spoke, everyone listened. As an Indian fighter in the Carolina backcountry during the war, Pickens played a decisive role in thwarting the Cherokee assaults on the largely Scots-Irish frontier settlements there.

William Pickens and his wife Margaret, Andrew's grandparents, arrived in Pennsylvania from Ulster in 1720 with their six sons. Andrew's father Andrew married Nancy Davis, whose family had also moved from the north of Ireland.

Young Andrew was born near Paxtang in Lancaster County in Pennsylvania in 1739 and in 1740 the family headed to Augusta County, Virginia when the Shenandoah Valley lands were being opened up to Scots-Irish and German settlers.

By 1750, the Pickens were in South Carolina and Andrew married Rebecca Calhoun, a close relative of John C. Calhoun, who was American Vice-President over an eight-year period (1828-1836) to John Quincy Adams and Andrew Jackson.

The family lived for 10 years on 800 acres in the Waxhaws region along the Carolina borders and then moved to Long Cane near Abbeville in the southwestern part of South Carolina, where Andrew became a leading citizen.

To the Cherokee tribes, Pickens was known as "Skyaguusta," the wizard owl. They feared and honoured him as a battle leader who defeated them repeatedly on their home ground, but he was a firm believer in fair treatment for the Indian nations.

Pickens was convinced the white settlers and the Indians could live harmoniously, each on their own lands, and he believed the treaties he helped to frame were just to both races. In later years, he expressed disappointment at the way the Indians were treated by the white settlers.

When the war began, Pickens, father of six children, was a farmer, Presbyterian elder and justice of the peace, and as captain of the local militia he defeated local pro-British Tory loyalist and Indian forces at Ninety Six in 1775. There, he negotiated a treaty with the Tories that was later repudiated as the bitterness of the war increased.

Pickens rose to brigadier-general and, in February 1778 at Keetle Creek, Georgia, he demonstrated his tactical ability in charge of 300 men, who circled a 700-strong Tory force and won a significant battle which eroded British influence in the Carolina backcountry and led to the fall of Charleston and Camden in 1780.

Pickens was captured by the British in 1780 and later paroled, but when Redcoat forces burned his house, he angrily broke the parole and rejoined the revolutionaries. At the battle of Cowpens in January, 1781, Pickens rallied the militia to defeat the British, and for this service the Continental Congress presented him with a sword. His son Robert also fought at Cowpens as a lieutenant.

Andrew Pickens was elected to the South Carolina state legislature in 1782, and that year he raised and commanded a company of 500 men, who in six weeks defeated the warring Cherokee tribes. He successfully negotiated an extensive land treaty with the Cherokees in 1785, a deal that was upheld by the U.S. Congress. He was a Congress man in 1793-95, and Pickens township and county in South Carolina was named in his honour.

The doughty militia leader lived until he was 78 and is buried at Clemson in South Carolina, with his tombstone identifying him as "a Christian, Patriot and Soldier."

Francis Wilkinson Pickens, grandson of Andrew Pickens, was a South Carolina attorney and member of the State House of Representatives in the 19th century. He was a U.S. Congressman, state senator for South Carolina and American minister to Russia in 1858-60. At the outbreak of the Civil War, he was governor of South Carolina and demanded the surrender of federal forts in Charleston harbour.

STAMP ACT THAT SOWED THE SEEDS OF DISSENSION

The 1765 Stamp Act which provoked so much hostility from the Scots-Irish Presbyterian settlers in the American colonies was designed to raise £60,000 a year from taxes for the Crown to pay off the estimated £350,000 cost of maintaining British troops in America.

The Act passed the British Parliament without debate and its Tory framers did not anticipate the hostility it would provoke, as they felt it necessary for the American colonists to pay for their own protection.

Americans, with the Scots-Irish in the vanguard, at first based their objections on the inability to pay, but moved to the more reasoned principle of "No Taxation Without Representation" and viewed the vice-admiralty enforcement courts as a breach of their civil liberties.

John Hughes, who was then distributor of stamps for Pennsylvania, in a report of October 12, 1765 stated: "Common justice calls on me to say, the body of people called Quakers, seemed disposed to pay obedience to the Stamp Act and so do that part of the Church of England and Baptists, that are not some way under Proprietary influence. But Presbyterian and Proprietary minions spare no pains to engage the Dutch and lower class of people, and render the royal government odious."

The Stamp Act was the first direct taxation the British had introduced in America and, at a time when the seeds of revolution were being planted, it aroused opposition right across the colonies. Sons of Liberty organisations were set up to take action and the strength of feeling among the increasing patriot population was such that all of the stamp agents were forced to resign.

Georgia was the only colony where the Stamp Act was put into effect, albeit on a limited scale. In the other colonies the taxation courts closed rather than use the stamps, and within a year the Act was repealed, largely due to the support for the American position by influential British statesman William Pitt and lobbying by Benjamin Franklin, who was then a colonial agent in London.

Franklin was sympathetic to the aims of the Stamp Act, largely influenced as he was by Philadelphia law associate and prominent loyalist Joseph Galloway, who was a leading member of the Pennsylvania provincial assembly.

Interestingly, Galloway in a submission held that it was the Scots-Irish Presbyterians who supplied to colonial resistance a lining without which it would have collapsed.

George Bryan—Presbyterian Power in Philadelphia During the War

George Bryan, Pennsylvania's vice-president and acting president at the height of the Revolutionary War, was a Dublin-born Presbyterian. He emigrated to America in 1752 as a 20-year-old and became a highly successful Philadelphia merchant and civic leader able to harness his ethnic-religious inheritance—Irish Presbyterianism.

Samuel Bryan, George's father, was a wealthy Dublin merchant who influenced a Philadelphia business associate James Wallace to enlist his son as a mercantile partner in a city that was literally teeming with Scots-Irish immigrants.

The Bryan and Wallace partnership lasted several years before George Bryan found it more profitable to branch out as an independent merchant, trading between Philadelphia and England and Ireland in cotton and wool products and Irish linen, along with domestic goods such as shears, needles, pins and buttons.

He teamed up with Ulster merchants Redmond Conyngham (from Donegal!) and John Nesbitt to construct a 100-ton ship *Hayfield*, so as to transport their imports across the Atlantic. *The Hayfield's* first trek across the ocean took it to the Ulster port of Newry in Co Down in 1756 to participate in the flax seed trade. The ship returned eleven months later with a full cargo.

The Hayfield was headed back to Newry in December, 1757 to further the flax seed trade link, and on this voyage it also berthed at Dublin and Louisburg, Nova Scotia before returning to Pennsylvania. Over a number of years *The Hayfield* made a number of successful trips across the Atlantic, travelling as far as Amsterdam in Holland, and, buoyed by the business that was flowing in his direction, George Bryan was by 1760 the owner of six vessels.

These were the years of the French and Indian War and the trade off-shoot from the hostilities were a bonus to Philadelphia merchants like Bryan. Gradually, Bryan built up his fortune and diversified his investments by acquiring land property. His most significant purchase was in 1761 when he bought more than 4,000 acres in Sussex and Morris counties in New Jersey from the London-based Pennsylvania land company for the then substantial sum of £2,750.

Like other men of his class, Bryan married money, with his wife Elizabeth Smith, daughter of prominent Philadelphia Presbyterian merchant Samuel Smith. He not only married within his social status, but increased his contacts among the city's highly influential Presbyterian merchants.

Bryan's rise in the Pennsylvania business world was matched by a strengthening interest in Presbyterian church matters in the region, and, from his election to the congregational committee of First Philadelphia church in 1758, he became obligated as his father had advised him to "God and religion."

Presbyterianism in the American colonies at the time of George Bryan's involvement was undergoing dramatic changes, after the out-pourings of the Great Awakening, inspired by English evangelist the Rev. George Whitefield.

There was the New Side faction who argued that those who could testify to having been "saved" by God could be members of the church. Against this, the Old Side Presbyterians questioned the ability of revivalist ministers to pass judgment on an individual's alleged salvation.

The protracted New Side/Old Side debate lasted from 1742 to 1758, when the Articles of Union passed by the Synod of Philadelphia provided the basis for compromise. George Bryan's First Philadelphia Church was Old Side, while Second congregation in the city was New Side. Their rivalries extended beyond Calvinist theology, and was evident even in the business transactions of the main protagonists!

In church life in Pennsylvania, George Bryan had made his mark and, increasingly, he was looked upon by his peers as a man who could speak with authority for Presbyterian political interests. Described by one church elder in 1766 as "our own hero," Bryan and his Presbyterian party had just reached a zenith in political influence in the state by removing the Quakers from the seat of power in Philadelphia.

George Bryan had been involved in dissenting politics since the mid-1750s, alongside Ulster-born Philadelphia teacher Charles Thomson. Initially, Bryan and his Scots-Irish Presbyterian co-religionists supported Benjamin Franklin and the Quaker establishment in the war against the Indians and in 1756, of the 24 elected officers in the city regiment, at least eight were Presbyterians.

However, as the hostilities continued with Indian attacks on isolated Scots-Irish settlements in the south-eastern and western parts of the province, tensions emerged and the relationship changed. There was resentment at an alleged comment by Nathaniel Grubb, a Quaker party assemblymen, who, when informed in 1756 that several back-country frontiersmen had been murdered by Indians, remarked: "There are only some Scotch-Irish killed, who could well enough be spared.

Grubb denied the remark, but it added to the general feeling of mistrust between the Quakers and the Presbyterians, with the pacifism of the former at a time of great danger to life and limb, an irritant to the settlers from Ulster, who had one aim in view—of defeating the Indians.

The Quaker government in Philadelphia did not feel the need to build forts, establish militia or train scouts and Indian fighters. Their religious convictions and moral conscience demanded that they co-exist peacefully with the native Americans. German settlers in Pennsylvania, particularly members of the Mennonites, Moravians and the Amish sects, were also inclined, like the English Quakers, to retire rather than fight the Indians. Not so the Scots-Irish!

Some Presbyterian leaders, like Charles Thomson and Francis Allison, tried to keep relations cordial with Benjamin Franklin and the Quakers, but George Bryan by 1758 felt alienated from the Philadelphia assembly and decided that the best course was to campaign for its removal. He felt there had to be direct military confrontation with the Indians, stating: "We can expect no lasting peace, unless we bring the Indian enemy to reason."

Bryan's position, however, was not helped by violent vigilante activity by a group of about 50 Scots-Irish settlers from Paxton township at Conestoga and Lancaster in Lancaster county who, in December 1763, avenged Indian killings of their people by putting to death 20 innocent Indians (men, women and children), some of them Christian converts.

The action of the "Paxton boys" in so irresponsibly taking the law into their own hands stunned and revulsed the Pennsylvania establishment, and with the approval of the Philadelphia assembly, Governor John Penn placed a substantial reward on the heads of the Paxton leaders and called for their capture and removal for trial.

The Scots-Irish settlers, however were in no mood to be rebuked or threatened with the law over the killings. They remained defiant, arguing that their frontier settlements had been left largely unprotected in the pervading climate of war by their political masters among the pacifist Quaker fraternity in Philadelphia.

The settlers perceived that the government was supporting the Indians with funds that could have been used by them for adequate frontier defence against attack.

The Paxton group organised a march from Lancaster to Philadelphia to air their grievances before the province's legislature, but before reaching the capital they were intercepted by four assemblymen led by Benjamin Franklin, who promised government relief if they returned home.

The Scots-Irish outlined the frontier grievances at length, with, the chief complaint being the inequality of backcountry settler representation in the Philadelphia assembly.

Governor Penn was still anxious to proceed with lawful proceedings against those responsible for the Conestoga and Lancaster murders, but the white settlers maintained it was improper to "deprieve British subjects of their known privileges" if the trials were to take place outside the counties of residents of the defendants.

The matter dragged on, but the issues of properly administering justice to those guilty of the killings and ensuring proper defence for the white settlements were not effectively dealt with in the assembly debates which followed.

As a result, Governor Penn found it politically expedient to ignore the assembly demands for the immediate prosecution of the Paxton Boys, and no one was ever charged for the killings.

The Paxton Boys insurrection placed George Bryan and his colleagues in a difficult position. Bryan, while unsympathetic to the Indians, was appalled by the Lancaster county massacre and alarmed by mob law. He reminded the Scots-Irish settlers of the "necessity of supporting order" and described the Paxton group as "mean and lower sort of people."

The Paxton group was also condemned by other leading Presbyterian dissenters in Philadelphia. However, in the cross-exchange that followed with George Bryan and others accused the Quaker assembly members of sowing the seeds of the violence by their pacifism, and pressing charges against those involved in the Paxton incident became less of a priority.

Relations worsened between the Presbyterians and the Quakers when Benjamin Franklin decided early in 1764 to petition the king-in-council to remove proprietor rule and bring the colony under royal government. The Scots-Irish, victims of royal rule in the homelands, completed vehemently opposed Franklin's strategy. In a petition circulated throughout the colony, only 3,500 signatures favoured the transfer and 15,000 were against.

The scene was set for the bitterly fought assembly elections in October, 1764, and the Presbyterians forged alliances with the German Lutheran and Calvinist frontier communities and got surprise backing from some Anglican church leaders in Philadelphia.

George Bryan assumed a prominent role in the organisation of the Presbyterian vote in Pennsylvania, and he and former mayor Thomas Willing were selected for the task of ousting on a New Ticket platform the two most prominent Quaker politicians, Benjamin Franklin and Joseph Galloway, from the city's two seats.

Willing represented Philadelphia's wealthy and genteel society and was a leading importer of German immigrants, while Bryan appealed to the Calvinists, of Scots-Irish and German extraction.

The election was one of the most exciting and hotly contested in the history of Pennsylvania, with 3,900 voters participating in the county elections alone. By the narrowest of margins, Bryan and Willing defeated Franklin and Galloway, with eight of the 10 New Ticket candidates returned for the city and county of Philadelphia.

Overall in Pennsylvania, the Quakers still maintained a commanding majority, but their grip on power was loosening—the voice of the Scots-Irish was at last being listened to in the legislative corridors.

George Bryan and his 10-strong minority group operated for a year in the assembly, but in the 1764 their numbers were reduced to four and Bryan's political career went into decline. His financial affairs suffered a major set-back through a loss of trade, and in 1771 he was declared bankrupt and also faced health problems.

The early 1770s were lean years for George Bryan, but in 1777 his political career shot back into prominence when he became a Philadelphia city assemblyman and was appointed Pennsylvania's vice-president and acting president. He was one of the driving forces in the Pennsylvania government, and under his leadership three aims were achieved: support of the state's war effort against the British, the subjugation of the state's Tories who opposed independence and the establishment of the state's revolutionary constitution.

Bryan was not a member of the 1776 constitutional convention which drew up the Declaration of Independence, but he was a trusted aide of those were involved. Philadelphia in 1777 was in a state of chaos, after the upheaval from the signing of the Declaration and with the city's population fearful of attack from the British. Gradually, however, through the guidance of Bryan and others, order was established by a Supreme Executive Council, which reorganised the courts and government departments.

For help in running the city, Bryan turned to two Presbyterian associates, including Declaration signer Thomas McKean, who took on the chief justice's role. The assistant justice post went to John Evans and attorney-general to John Dickinson, both Presbyterians of Ulster stock.

Later, London-trained lawyer and leading Philadelphia Presbyterian Joseph Reed's assumed the presidency with Bryan as his deputy. Reed's grandfather had emigrated from Carrickfergus in Co Antrim.

Other senior civil and military appointments were made from within the Presbyterian fold in Pennsylvania, men who George Bryan obviously felt he could trust at a time of great uncertainty and instability..

After decades of being subservient to Quaker rule, the Scots-Irish Presbyterians from the city and backcountry were now calling the shots in Philadelphia under the banner of the Constitutional Party. By 1780, George Bryan and his friends were at the pinnacle of their power, keeping Presbyterian interests foremost among their concerns.

Their influence continued right through the war years, certainly right up until 1789 when Londonderry-born Charles Thomson was authorised by the Continental Congress to travel to Mount Vernon in Virginia to tell

George Washington that it was the wish of Congress that he become the first president of the United States.

SCOTS-IRISH SIGNERS OF THE AMERICAN DECLARATION OF INDEPENDENCE

The 56 men from the 13 colonies who signed the American Declaration of Independence in July, 1776 were almost entirely of British family origin. Thirty eight are firmly established of being of English extraction, eight Irish (including six Ulster-Scots), five Welsh, four pure Scottish and one Swedish.

Those with Ulster links were John Hancock, Thomas McKean, George Tayor, James Smith, Matthew Thornton and Edward Rutledge, with Thomas Lynch Jr. and George Read from family ties to the south of Ireland. William Whipple, Robert Paine and Thomas Nelson are also believed to have links with the north of Ireland.

Of the 56 signatories of the Declaration, 24 were lawyers and jurists, 11 were merchants, nine farmers and the rest large plantation owners, men of means and well-educated.

PENNSYLVANIA (9)—Benjamin Franklin, Robert Morris, Benjamin Rush, John Morton, George Clymer, James Smith, George Taylor, James Wilson, George Ross.

VIRGINIA (7)—Thomas Jefferson, Richard Henry Lee, Benjamin Harrison, Francis Lightfoot Lee, Thomas Nelson, George Wythe, Carter Braxton.

MASSACHUSETTS (5)—Samuel Adams, John Hancock, John Adams, Elbridge Gerry, Robert Treat Paine.

NEW JERSEY (5)—John Witherspoon, Richard Stockton, Francis Hopkinson, John Hart, Abraham Clark.

CONNECTICUT (4)—Robert Sherman, Samuel Huntington, William Williams, Oliver Wolcott.

MARYLAND (4)—Charles Carroll, Thomas Stone, William Paca, Samuel Chase.

NEW YORK (4)—Philip Livingston, Lewis Morris, William Floyd, Francis Lewis.

SOUTH CAROLINA (4)—Thomas Heyward Jr., Arthur Middleton, Edward Rutledge, Thomas Lynch Jr.

DELAWARE (3)—Caesar Rodney, Thomas McKean, George Read.

GEORGIA (3)—Lyman Hall, Button Guinnett, George Walton.

NEW HAMPSHIRE (3)—Josiah Bartlett, William Whipple, Matthew Thornton.

NORTH CAROLINA (3)—William Hooper, Joseph Hewes, John Penn.

RHODE ISLAND (2)—Stephen Hopkins, William Ellery.

"All America lies at the end of the wilderness road, and our past is no dead past, but still lives on within us. Our forefathers had civilisation inside themselves, the wild outside. We live in the civilisation they created, but within us the wilderness still lingers. What they dreamed we live, and, what they lived, we dream"—T. K. Whipple, *Study Out The Land*

Ulster-born Charles Thomson, secretary to the American Continental Congress, also signed the Declaration, but strictly on account of the office that he held.

ULSTERMEN WHO LED THE PENNSYLVANIA LINE

Colonel William Thompson's battalion of riflemen was one of the foremost regiments in General George Washington's Pennsylvania Line, composed mainly of Scots-Irishmen. This regiment, the first to be enlisted under the authority of the Continental Congress, formed the nucleus of the

American army, with soldiers absolutely loyal to the patriot cause, purporting to "know no fatherland but the wilderness."

Thompson's men were recruited in pursuance of two resolutions of Congress, adopted June 14 and 22, 1775, which authorised the enlistment of nine companies of expert riflemen. Congress had originally stipulated only six companies, but so many volunteers presented themselves from the Scots-Irish settlements that another three had to be formed.

Seven companies of this regiment—the first, second, third, fourth, fifth, eighth and ninth—were composed almost exclusively of Scots-Irishmen; one, the seventh was made up almost entirely of Germans from Berks County, and another, the sixth recruited from German settlements in Northampton County.

The commanders, chaplains and officers of the regiment were overwhelmingly Scots-Irish Presbyterians, with the original command taken by the Ulster-born Colonel William Thompson, a surveyor and justice of the peace from Carlisle, Pennsylvania.

Thompson had served as a captain in the French-Indian War of 1756-63 under another Ulstermen John Armstrong and was involved in locating lands granted to officers on the western frontier of Pennsylvania province.

Other notable officers in Thompson's battalion were Lieutenant-Colonel Edward Hand, Colonel James Chambers and Major Robert Megaw. The regiment became the Second Regiment of the Continental Line, and after January 1, 1776, the First Regiment.

SCOTS-IRISH INFLUENCES IN THE DECLARATION OF INDEPENDENCE

The influence of Ulster-Scots Presbyterians was heavily stamped on the American Declaration of Independence of July 4, 1776 and in the unfolding events which led to the establishment of the United States as a nation.

The historic Declaration contained sentiments closely identified with the aspirations of the Presbyterian immigrant stock from the north of Ireland who settled in the American colonies during the 18th century.

A significant assertion was: "We hold these truths to be self-evident, that all men are created equal, that they are endowed by their Creator, with certain unalienable rights, that among these are Life, Liberty and the pursuit of Happiness."

Historical folklore records the far-seeing contribution of the Scots-Irish (Ulster-Scots) in the struggle for American independence, with General George Washington reportedly stating: "If defeated everywhere else I will make my last stand for liberty among the Scotch-Irish of my native Virginia."

THOMAS MCKEAN, leading Delaware signer of the Declaration , was the son of William McKean, an Ulster emigrant from North Antrim who came to Pennsylvania via Londonderry as a child and later married Letitia Finney, whose family had also emigrated from the north of Ireland.

The lawyer Thomas McKean led the movement in Delaware for American independence and served as commander of a patriot militia group known as the Pennsylvania "Associators."

McKean was appointed chief justice of Pennsylvania in 1777, a position he held for 20 years. He was also president of the Continental Congress for a short period in 1781 and was later Governor of Pennsylvania.

GEORGE TAYLOR, a signer for Pennsylvania, emigrated from Co Antrim as a 20-year-old in the 1720s, and he settled in the Scots-Irish dominated Chester County.

Taylor, involved in the iron producing business, would have been classified as a moderate radical who represented the small farmer Scots-Irish settlers of south east Pennsylvania. He was a delegate to the second American Continental Congress and served on the Supreme Council of Pennsylvania.

JAMES SMITH, another Declaration signer from Pennsylvania, emigrated from the north of Ireland as a 10-year-old at about 1719 and, like George Taylor, he also settled with his Presbyterian family in Chester County.

Smith emerged as a leading lawyer, and in 1774 he submitted a paper on the constitutional power of Great Britain over the colonies in America, in which he urged an end to the import of British goods and promoted the idea of a congress of the 13 colonies, to promote colonial grievances and ambitions.

He raised a militia group in York, Pennsylvania and joined the American Continental Congress in July 1775, a year before the Declaration was ratified.

MATTHEW THORNTON, signer from New Hampshire, landed on American soil as a four-year-old in the passage of five ships carrying 120 Presbyterian families from the Bann Valley (Coleraine-Ballymoney-Aghadowey-Macosquin).

Thornton graduated as a doctor and practiced at Londonderry, New Hampshire, a Scots-Irish township which became heavily involved in the struggle for American independence. His patriot sympathies won him political recognition, and it was from his position in the Continental Congress that he readily lined up to sign the Declaration.

Londonderry in New Hampshire is reputed to have sent more soldiers to aid George Washington's armies in the Revolutionary War than any other backcountry colonial town.

EDWARD RUTLEDGE, whose father Dr. John Rutledge left Co Tyrone in the north of Ireland in 1735, was a signatory of the Declaration from South Carolina.

With his brother John, Edward Rutledge was elected to the Continental Congress in July, 1774, and their commitment to the American patriot cause won the respect of Pennsylvania statesmen Benjamin Franklin and President to be from Massachusetts John Adams.

Edward Rutledge was captain of the Charleston battalion of artillery and he defended the city against the British. He later became a United States Senator and was South Carolina governor for two years from 1798.

Other Declaration signers - JOHN HANCOCK, WILLIAM WHIPPLE, ROBERT PAINE and THOMAS NELSON - are also believed to have some Ulster links, while THOMAS LYNCH Jr. and GEORGE READ had family ties to the south of Ireland.

Patriot merchant and militiaman COLONEL JOHN NIXON gave the first public reading of the Declaration in Philadelphia Square on July 8. Nixon was the grandson of Ulster immigrants.

John Nixon was not just a leading Revolutionary soldier, but a merchant and a financier of high repute in the American colonies. He was one of the signers of Pennsylvania paper money in the 1760s, and in 1779 he was an auditor of public accounts and was involved in setting up and adjusting the American Continental currency.

Nixon helped organise the bank of Pennsylvania to supply the needs of the Army, and in 1784 he became a director of the Bank of North America.

The Scots-Irish people who settled in America in the 18th century were a progressive community, and it is interesting to acknowledge their main interests of achievement alongside the German Palatinate Lutherans who were on the frontier at the same time. Scots-Irish excelled in education, government, law, the stage, invention and the military, while Germans were best at art, music, science, philanthropy and music.

CHARLES THOMSON:

Distinguished Ulster-born 18th century American statesman Charles Thomson was a devout Presbyterian church elder who completed translations of the Old and New Testaments of the Bible from the Greek Septuagint version.

Thomson, who designed the first Great Seal of the United States, was born near Maghera in Co Londonderry, and he emigrated from Ulster as a 10-year-old.

He was, outside of George Washington, the most influential man in the government of the United States after the Revolutionary War and was an original signatory of the Declaration of Independence of July 4, 1776.

Charles Thomson, who remained a staunch Presbyterian throughout his life, was for 15 years from 1774, secretary to the Continental Congress, the legislature which then was the effective government of the United States.

When the new federal constitution was adopted in 1789, Thomson was delegated to convey to George Washington at his home in Mount Vernon, Virginia the request of the Continental Congress that Washington become the nation's first president.

The original Declaration of Independence bore only two signatures, that of John Hancock, president of Congress, and Charles Thomson, secretary. The text was written in Thomson's handwriting. In the political upheaval of the time, there was plenty of support for the concept of independence, but no great rush to sign the Declaration, largely because of the dire consequences of failure.

However, Hancock, also of Scots-Irish roots, and Thomson, were obviously of stern qualities, with Thomson earning the reputation of being "the Venerable Patriot."

Charles Thomson came from a farming family background in the Sperrin Mountain region of Co Londonderry and was born at Gorteade, Upperlands near Maghera in 1729.

The family, of lowland Scots roots, worshipped at Maghera Presbyterian Church for several generations, and today a plaque is inserted at the Church in his memory.

John and Mary Houston Thomson had six children, five sons and one daughter—William, Alexander, Charles, Matthew, John and Mary—and when his wife died at the birth of their last child, John decided on emigration to America, selling up the family farm and bidding farewell to the kinsfolk in the Maghera Church.

In 1739, John Thomson and the children set sail from Londonderry and, after a rough journey across the Atlantic which took a heavy toll on many passengers, John died of fatigue as the ship was entering Delaware Bay. The Thomson children arrived on American soil as orphans, anguished over the tragic death of their father so soon after the loss of their mother.

Years later, Charles Thomson recalled: "I stood by the bedside of my expiring and much loved father, closed his eyes and performed the last filial duties to him."

The body was buried at sea to save the cost of a land burial, and unscrupulously, the ship's captain held on to John Thomson's monies deposited in the ship safe at the beginning of the journey in Londonderry.

The Thomson children found placements in Pennsylvania with family and kinsfolk, and Charles started out as an apprentice blacksmith. However, through the generosity of a kindly and wealthy women, he was sent to the new classical school at Thunder Hill, New London, Pennsylvania.

His tutor was Rev. Francis Allison, an Ulster Presbyterian minister from Leck outside Letterkenny in Co Donegal, and he graduated as a teacher of classical subjects in 1750, teaching Latin and Greek at Philadelphia University.

Thomson was also heavily influenced by Scottish-born Rev. John Witherspoon, a signator of the Declaration of Independence and by Rev. Joseph Clark and James Armstrong, two Scots-Irish clerics who were to become American Presbyterian church moderators and militia leaders during the Revolutionary War.

In 1760, Charles Thomson gave up teaching to develop a mercantile career and, it was through his contacts in the business world of Philadelphia that he moved into politics. He became associated with the Whig movement and espoused the radical politics of Benjamin Franklin, Thomas Jefferson and John Adams, which increasingly pushed for American disengagement from Britain.

After independence was declared in 1776, the four were authorised to design a seal for the new state, but six years on and the work not fulfilled, Thomson, assisted by young Pennsylvanian lawyer William Barton, set about the task.

Within a week, he had the mould of a new seal before the Continental Congress and the inscription was written into law on June 20, 1782. From Thomson's original design emerged the Great Seal of the United States of America, which since has had artistic variations and six new dies cut—in 1825, 1841, 1854, 1877, 1885 and 1904.

Charles Thomson was involved in treaty negotiations with the Delaware Indians, and for his honesty and absolute Christian integrity in dealings he was given the name "Wegh-Wu-Haw-Mo-Land," which translated means "the man who speaks the truth."

In retirement, Charles Thomson spent much of his time on translations of the Old and New Testaments of the Bible from the Greek Septuagint version. This was quite an outstanding work for the period, but few in American theological circles recognised its worth at the time and, regrettably, after Thomson's death, copies were sold as wastepaper.

Charles Thomson, whose first wife died in childbirth, died on August 16, 1824, aged 95. He was buried as per his wish alongside his second wife Hannah in the family plot at Harriton, Pennsylvania. The couple was later re-buried at Laurel Hill, four miles from Philadelphia. His memory is cherished in Pennsylvania, and in Maghera!

WILLIAM IRVINE—DISTINGUISHED DOCTOR AND SOLDIER

Brigadier General William Irvine, born in Enniskillen, Co Fermanagh, was another Ulsterman with a distinguished Revolutionary War service in George Washington's patriot army as a soldier and surgeon.

Irvine, a graduate in medicine from Trinity College, Dublin was a surgeon on a British war ship sailing in American colonial waters during the Seven Years (French-Indian) War of 1756-63, and at the end of hostilities, he doctored in a strong Scots-Irish settlement at Carlisle in eastern Pennsylvania.

There he married Anne Callender, daughter of Captain Robert Callender, another Scots-Irish Presbyterian settler, and they had eleven children, five sons and six daughters.

Irvine was a member of the provincial convention in Philadelphia of July 15, 1774 which denounced British "tyranny" in Boston, and he actively campaigned for American rights of independence. In close liaison with George Washington, Irvine raised and commanded the 6th Pennsylvania Regiment (the Pennsylvania Line) at Monmouth, New Jersey. He was involved in expeditions to Canada and was captured and spent almost three years in British custody.

In March, 1782, he took command of the isolated frontier outpost at Fort Pitt (Pittsburgh), where, despite having depleted forces, courageously fended off numerous Indian attacks. He resigned from the Continental Army in 1783 and was appointed to purchase lands for the distribution to the Pennsylvanian militia veterans.

When the War ended, Irvine wrote to George Washington, complementing him on his success. Washington replied: "With great sincerity, I return you my congratulations."

Irvine was a Congressman over two terms (1786-88 and 1793-95). In 1790, he served on the Pennsylvanian constitutional convention and, in 1794, he acted as arbitrator and commanding officer of the state troops in quelling the whiskey rebellion in Pennsylvania, involving the Scots-Irish settlers. He died in Pennsylvania in 1804, not before the Pennsylvania legislature rewarded his many valued services to the commonwealth by voting him a large tract of land on Lake Erie, known as Irvine's Reserve.

William Irvine's brother Andrew joined him on the Canadian campaigns as a lieutenant, and later as captain. Another brother Matthew was a surgeon's mate in Thompson's Pennsylvanian rifle battalion until 1775 and a surgeon of General Henry Lee Dragoons from 1778 to the end of the war. Three of William Irvine's sons were army officers.

A grandson, William Irvine Lewis, was one of the 189 men who died with Davy Crockett at The Alamo in Texas in March, 1836. Lewis was a great grandson of Donegal-born John Lewis, the first Scots-Irish settler in the Shenandoah Valley of Virginia in 1732.

RICHARD MONTGOMERY—SOLDIER ON TWO SIDES OF THE AMERICAN REVOLUTION

Richard Montgomery, the son of an Irish MP from Donegal, had distinguished military service in both the British and American Continental armies and he lost his life in the patriot assault on Quebec on January 1, 1776.

As an 18-year-old just graduated from Trinity College in Dublin, Montgomery became an ensign in the 17th Foot regiment in 1756, and within a year he was in the thick of the action of the Seven Years War, taking part in the siege of Louisburg in Canada.

As a lieutenant he took part in the successful British operations at Toconderoga, Crown Point and Montreal and in the West Indies he was at the capture of Martinique and Havana. On his return to Britain after the war, he associated with leading Opposition Whig politicians Edmond Burke and Charles Fox and was greatly influenced by their radicalism.

However, Montgomery felt he had no future in England, and in 1772, after selling his army commission, he headed back to America, then deeply embroiled in the early stages of the Revolutionary War. He settled on a 67-acre farm at King's Bridge, New York and married Janet Livingstone, of a prominent Scots-Irish family.

He accepted a commission in the Continental Army in June, 1775 and was appointed a delegate to the first provincial congress in New York. It was a big step for a man who for 16 years had gallantly worn the uniform of the British Army, and, leaving his young wife, he headed north to become second in command to General Philip Schuyler in the Canadian invasion.

Montgomery assumed full command on Schulyer's illness, and he showed outstanding military prowess in leading an offensive into Canada, despite having to cope with the inadequacies of inexperienced troops and serious logistical problems.

After taking St John's and Montreal in September-November of that eventful year, he pushed on to launch the unsuccessful attack on Quebec in late December and was killed in action on New Year's Day, 1776.

The British forces instantly recognised his body and ordered it to be "decently buried." In 1818, the body was transferred for re-burial at St Paul's Church in New York County.

Highest praise for this outstanding soldier came from London, from both his former friends and from his political enemies. Edmund Burke, speaking in the British Parliament, contrasted the "disgrace" of the large colonial army shut up in Boston with the movements of the hero who in one campaign had conquered two-thirds of Canada.

Prime Minister Lord North replied: "He was brave, he was able, he was humane, he was generous, but still he was a brave, able, humane and generous rebel."

Charles Fox retorted: "The term of rebel is no certain mark of disgrace. The great asserters of liberty, the saviours of our country, the benefactors of mankind in all ages have been called rebels."

The city of New York erected a monument to the memory of Richard Montgomery and a tablet was raised on the spot where he fell at Quebec.

Richard Montgomery was described as being "tall, of fine military presence, of graceful address, with a bright magnetic face and winning manners." He was one of the outstanding soldiers of the Revolutionary War, on either side.

ANDREW LEWIS—PATRIOT GENERAL FROM THE SHENANDOAH VALLEY

This Continental Army general was the son of Co Donegal-born Presbyterian

John Lewis, reputed to be the first Ulsterman to settle in the Shenandoah Valley of Virgina in the early 1730s. Andrew Lewis, also Donegal-born and six feet tall with a very strong physique, was one of George Washington's key officers during the Revolutionary War.

The Lewis family settlement was at Staunton, Virginia and, on his way to becoming the first military leader in the region, Andrew became militia lieutenant in Augusta County and a justice of the peace, and as a landowner, he amassed a considerable wealth.

During the French-Indian War of 1754-63, Lewis served alongside George Washington and took part in various expeditions against the Indians—at Sandy Creek (1758) and Fort Dequense (1758). He spent a time in captivity, but, on release, took part in important land negotiations with the Indians.

Lewis commanded 1,000 men in Dunmore's War against Shawnee, Miami, Wyandot and Ottawa Indian tribes in southwest Virginia in 1774, winning a crucial victory at Point Pleasant. His brother Charles was killed in this battle, and Andrew was appointed brigadier-general in the Continental Army in March, 1776, taking command of the units at Williamsburg, Virginia.

At Gwynn Island in July of that year, Lewis commanded action that forced the royalist Dunmore out of the Old Dominion of Virginia. A higher command to major-general looked certain, but, when this did not come, an aggrieved Lewis resigned his commission, allegedly for ill-heath. He continued, however, to serve in the Virginia militia and on the state's executive council, chaired by Thomas Jefferson.

Andrew's older brother Charles served in the Virginia House of Burgesses and in the state conventions that ratified the Federal Constitution. Another brother, William, rose from lieutenant in the 1st Virginia company to major in the 10th and was captured at Charleston in 1780, with his release only coming when the war ended.

William's grandson, William Irvine Lewis, died with David Crockett at The Alamo in Texas in March, 1836. Other members of the Lewis clan distinguished themselves in political and military careers through the 19th and into the 20th centuries.

John McKinly—Militia Chief in Delaware

Ulster-born John McKinly was governor and militia commander in chief in Delaware at the height of the Revolutionary War. Such was his standing within the American patriot movement, that he was captured by the British and evacuated to Philadelphia, away from his popular base.

This was in September, 1777, just after the battle of Brandywine, when the British were occupying McKinly's town of Wilmington. When the British left Philadelphia, they took him to New York County, where he was paroled a year later.

McKinly, born in the north of Ireland in 1721, had settled at Wilmington, Delaware after emigrating in the mid-18th century, and in addition to his practice as a doctor, he rose rapidly in local civil and militia affairs. He was Wilmington sheriff for two years and chief burgess for 17 years, posts which left him in charge of the militia.

In 1771, he was elected to the Colonial Assembly and, as brigadier-general, was instrumental in calling up the Delaware state militia and sending delegates to the Continental Congress. After his release in 1778, McKinly was elected to the Continental Congress, but he did not serve and spent the last 18 years of his life as a medical practitioner in Wilmington.

Courage was the Mettle of "Scotch Willie" Maxwell

General William Maxwell, "Scotch Willie" to his compatriots in the Revolutionary War, had a humble upbringing as a farm boy in New Jersey after he moved to America with his parents in 1747 from their Co Down homeland in the north of Ireland.

Maxwell, a tall, ruddy-faced bachelor who spoke with a burr, had a chequered career as an officer in George Washington's army, and while his judgment and tactical ability in the field of battle was often the target of much criticism, his courage and commitment to the patriot cause could never called into question.

His shortcomings as a general could probably be attributed to a liking for alcohol, and after the battles of Brandywine and Germantown in the autumn of 1777, Maxwell was charged with misconduct and was not exonerated, but at the November hearing the charges were unproved.

Maxwell joined a British regiment at the age of 21 and was on General Braddock's expedition in 1755 during the French-Indian War. He rose from being an ensign to lieutenant in the New Jersey regiment and, during the final years of the war, took part in the attack on Ticonderoga and is believed to have been with General Wolfe at Quebec.

As a colonel he was subsequently on duty with the British commissionary department at Mackinac, and in 1774, he returned home as a veteran of 20 years military service to take an active role in the Revolutionary War movement in New Jersey.

"Scotch Willie" was a member of the New Jersey provincial congress in 1775, and in November he was commissioned colonel and raised the second battalion of the New Jersey militia. In February, 1776, he marched north at the head of five full companies in support of the ill-fated Canada invasion and suffered defeat at Trois Rivieres in June.

On return to New Jersey, Maxwell, as a brigadier-general, joined George Washington in attempting to resist the British troops at the Delaware River and was put in charge of four new regiments of Continental troops.

However, things started to go wrong during the preliminary assignments of the Philadelphia campaign, and Maxwell failed to arrive for the action at Brunswick, New Jersey in June 1777 because the order was not delivered to him. It was September before his troops went into action, at the battle of Gooch's Bridge.

Maxwell's main critic was Major William Heth, a veteran of Morgan's Rifles, and it was a complaint from Heth which led to his trial. But Maxwell's army career continued and his men from the four New Jersey regiments took up arms at Valley Forge.

In May, 1778, Maxwell was involved protecting Washington's flank and he had a measure of success against the British at the battle of Monmouth a month later. He moved to protect the New Jersey coastline and then got caught up in an expedition against the Iroquois Indians.

Disillusioned with his role, Maxwell resigned his army commission in July 1780 and moved into less dangerous territory as a member of the New Jersey Assembly. He died in 1796, aged 63.

EDWARD AND JOHN RUTLEDGE—DECLARING FOR INDEPENDENCE IN SOUTH CAROLINA

The Rutledges of Co Tyrone are one of the best-known families who emigrated from Ulster in the 18th century. This is largely due to the contribution of Edward Rutledge, South Carolina governor and a signatory of the American Declaration of Independence, and his brother John, who was also a South Carolina governor.

Dr. John Rutledge, Edward's father, left the north of Ireland in 1735, and shortly after arrival in Charleston, he married 15-year-old Sarah Hext. The couple had seven children, with Edward, the youngest, just a year old when his father died.

The Rutledges were a well-connected affluent family, and after Edward Rutledge got his early education in Charleston, he was sent to London to study law at the Temple Bar, where his eldest brother John had also been called. Five years later he returned to South Carolina, and his public life began in July, 1774 when he was elected to the First Continental Congress in Philadelphia along with brother John.

The Rutledges talked and argued a lot in the Congress debates, much to the irritation of some in the chamber, but more senior colleagues like U.S. president-to-be John Adams and Benjamin Franklin put this down to their youthful vigour and obvious commitment to the American patriot cause.

Edward Rutledge had made himself popular in Charleston by instituting legal proceedings on behalf of Thomas Robinson, publisher of the *South Carolina Gazette*, who had been imprisoned for printing his newspaper on unstamped paper, thereby violating the disputed Stamp Act, initiated from London.

The Rutledges were re-elected for a second Congressional term in February 1776, and as John returned to South Carolina to canvas opinion on support for independence, his brother maintained a presence in the Philadelphia legislature.

When word came through from Charleston on July 2 that South Carolina was weighing in behind independence, Edward Rutledge and three other South Carolina delegates—Thomas Heyward Jr., Arthur Middleton and Thomas Lynch Jr.—signed the Declaration. Rutledge was the second youngest signer.

In November of that year, Edward returned to take command of the Charleston battalion of artillery, and as captain of that unit he was involved in a number of battles, including the defence of Charleston. When the city fell to the British in May, 1780, Rutledge was captured and sent to St. Augustine, Florida, but in July, 1781, along with Thomas Heyward and Arthur Middleton, he was involved in prisoner exchange and set free.

Rutledge was soon back in his state legislature, and he drew up the bill proposing the confiscation of the properties of all Crown loyalists, feeling this measure was necessary to negate the pro-British sympathies which were still deeply embedded, particularly in parts of the South Carolina piedmont area among elements of the Scots-Irish.

When the war ended, Rutledge, a rapid conservative, continued to represent South Carolina in Congress until 1796. He was also a U.S. Senator and in 1798 became governor of South Carolina, but his health at this time was poor, and he died in January 1800, aged only 51. Edward Rutledge was married twice—to Henrietta Middleton, a sister of his fellow signer Arthur Middleton, and on her death 18 years later to widow Mary Shubrick Eveleigh.

John Rutledge was the first patriot governor of South Carolina, elected in 1779, and he managed to escape Charleston just before it was captured by the British in May, 1780. He turned up in North Carolina and joined the army of General Horatio Gates and visited Philadelphia to lobby George Washington and the Continental Congress to send American regulars to liberate the South.

After the war, John Rutledge was elected chief justice of South Carolina and senior associate justice of the U.S. Supreme Court. He died in 1800, aged 61.

American historian R. L. Meriwether said of John Rutledge: "He was the most gifted and devoted leader of the ruling group of 18th century South Carolina. He embodied, perhaps, more perfectly than any other man, the ideas of his class."

Another of the Rutledge clan from Co Tyrone to distinguish himself in the Revolutionary War was George Rutledge, who was a militia officer at the Battle of Kings Mountain in October, 1780.

Edward (born in Co Tyrone in 1755) was brigadier general and state militia commander when John Sevier was appointed as first Tennessee governor in 1796, and he represented Sullivan County in the Tennessee legislature. His wife was Annie Armstrong, of a Co Fermanagh family who had moved from the Shenandoah Valley of Virginia.

George Rutledge's family can be traced back to George and Nelly Gamble Rutledge, from Co Tyrone, whose five children William, Thomas, John, Jane and Catherine emigrated with their off-spring to America in 1763, and they too moved through the Shenandoah Valley, settling at Tinkling Spring at Staunton, and worshipping at the Presbyterian Church there. George's father William married Eleanor Caldwell, from Co Cavan.

The grandfather of Thomas Lynch Jr., one of the four South Carolina representatives and the youngest at 26 to sign Declaration of Independence, was also born in Ireland and settled as a wealthy estate-owner in the colonial territory around Charleston.

Thomas Lynch Jr., although born in Winyaw, South Carolina, was educated at Eton and Cambridge in England, and graduated in law at the Middle Temple in London. He was elected to the South Carolina Provincial Congress and in 1775 was appointed captain of the First South Carolina Regiment, before he and his father Thomas moved to the Continental Congress in Philadelphia.

Thomas Lynch Sr. took seriously ill early in 1776, and he died before the Declaration could be signed later that year. Thomas Jr., however, was on hand to vote for independence on behalf of his state and to sign the document in his father's absence, but his health was also poor, largely as a result of a "swamp fever," or malaria, he picked while in war service in North Carolina. He died in 1779, aged only 30.

JOHN DUNLAP—THE PATRIOT PRINTER

American pioneer printer John Dunlap who printed the first copies of the Declaration of Independence was born in Strabane, Co Tyrone and lived with his uncle William, also a printer, in Philadelphia after his emigration as a young man.

Dunlap was printer to the American Continental Congress throughout the Revolutionary War, and in 1777, he founded the Philadelphia Packet newspaper, which he published daily after 1783. He was a close associate of Charles Thomson, the Ulster-born secretary of the Continental Congress.

As a soldier, John Dunlap served in the first troop of the Philadelphia cavalry, which acted as a bodyguard to General George Washington at the battles of Trenton and Princeton. He was a very generous man and personally contributed $20,000 to supply the U.S. Army with provisions and clothing in 1782 during a crucial period in the War. He died in 1812.

A letter written by John Dunlap on May 12, 1785 to Robert Rutherford, a friend back in Ulster, urged others to follow him to America. He wrote: "The young men of Ireland who wish to be free and happy should leave it and come here as quickly as possible. There is no place in the world where a man meets so rich a reward for good conduct and industry as in America."

Strabane, where John Dunlap was born, is the part of Ulster described as "the emigration hinterland" of Londonderry, and in 1780 his father was registered as a saddler in the town.

Soon after the Declaration of Independence was signed, John Dunlap's printed copies were circulated throughout various states, and the first newspaper outside America to publish the first text was the *Belfast News Letter*, today Northern Ireland's leading morning paper.

Details of the Declaration had arrived in Londonderry by way of a ship from Pennsylvania in late-August, about six weeks after it was signed, and they were taken the 100 miles to the offices of the *Belfast News Letter*, then published by brothers Henry and Robert Joy.

For the *News Letter*, founded in 1737 and claimed today to be the longest existing English-language newspaper, it was a European scoop. King George III in London had not even been acquainted of the news of the Declaration—*News Letter* readers in Belfast were among the first to know on their side of the Atlantic, with the report carried in the edition of August 23-27.

Later in its edition of September 6-10, 1776, the *News Letter* reported on the unfolding events in Philadelphia: "The 4th of July, 1776, the Americans appointed as a day of fasting and prayer, preparatory to their dedication of their country to God, which was done in the following manner: 'The Congress being assembled after having declared America independent, they had a crown placed on a Bible, which by prayer and solemn devotion they offered to God. The religious ceremony being ended, they divided the crown into thirteen parts, each of the United Provinces taking a part.'"

The *News Letter* was an influential vehicle for relating news of the migration of the Scots-Irish Presbyterians to America during the 18th century. The paper carried many advertisements for the ship's passage from the Ulster ports of Belfast, Londonderry, Larne, Portrush and Newry to America, most of them carrying details of special provision for contracted labour in the new lands.

Conscious of the strong links between the Ulster and the American colonies, the *News Letter* kept its readers fully informed about developments affecting their kinsfolk across the Atlantic. Reports on various battles of the Revolutionary War, obviously dispatched on the various ships that kept moving regularly across the Atlantic, were carried.

"I love Highlanders, but when I come to the branch that has been grafted on to the Ulster stem, I take off my hat in veneration and awe!" - Lord Roseberry.

TREKKING INTO THE UNKNOWN—ACROSS THE
CUMBERLAND GAP.

·⌒ 9 ⌒·

THE HAZARDOUS JOURNEY
INTO KENTUCKY

The Scots-Irish (or Ulster-Scots) were prominent in the first flow of pioneer settlers who headed for Kentucky from the years immediately after the American Revolutionary War. They came along the Wilderness Road, via the Ohio River and over the Cumberland Mountains to a region many considered too dangerous to encounter.

By the late 1780s the population flow towards Kentucky moved at a rate of 10,000 a year, made up of English, Scottish Highlanders, Welsh, German Lutherans and French Huguenots. The 1790 United States census revealed that close on 70,000 people had climbed on foot or on horseback over the steep path.

The stream of immigrants increased to a flood, with some arriving by boat down the Ohio River from Pittsburgh. However, most took the safe overland route. The early settlers of the Kentucky mountains were principally an overflow from the great stream of immigration heading west from Pennsylvania, New York, New Jersey, Maryland, Carolinas and Virginia. Main Kentucky settlements were at New River Valley and Big Sandy Valley, while some families spilled into central Tennessee at Cumberland Plateau via the Clinch and Holston Rivers.

Kentucky officially became the 15th state of the Union in 1792, but before that the Commonwealth of Virginia laid disputed sights on the territory.

In 1763, a proclamation by King George III restricted English and Scots-Irish settlements to the eastern slopes of the Appalachian Mountains, but the desire of the pioneers to move westwards was overwhelming, and by 1768, land negotiations were started with the north-western Indians. However, while Kentucky had been surveyed for most of a century, it remained a land of mystery to the mid-18th century settlers in neighbouring Virginia and North Carolina.

The mystique was summed up by a John Marshall, who wrote at the time: "The country beyond the Cumberland Gap still appeared to the dusky view of the generality of the people of Virginia, almost as obscure and doubtful as America itself to the people of Europe before the voyage of Christopher Columbus.

"A country there was, but whether land or water, mountain or plain, fertility or barrenness preponderated; whether inhabited by men or beasts or both or neither, they knew not. If inhabited by men, they were supposed to be Indians, for such has always infested the frontiers."

For several centuries, Kentucky was a battleground for territorial conflict between the Cherokee, Iroquois and Shawnee Indians, and because of the stand-offs between the tribes, the early white explorers experienced little resistance. The Cumberland Gap was a popular crossing in the Appalachian mountains for the pioneering families heading into Kentucky.

In 1750, Dr. Thomas Walker, a Virginian of Scottish descent, discovered the Gap, naming it and the Cumberland mountain range after the Duke of Cumberland, son of King George II. Daniel Boone, the explorer, first sighted the Gap in 1769 after leaving his North Carolina farm with five Scots-Irish hunting and scouting companions.

After descending the west side of the Appalachian mountain range, Boone and his long hunter companions marvelled "from the top of the eminence, the beautiful level of Kentucke," a fertile land of cane and clover. They talked about an abundance of game—"hundreds of acres principally covered by Buffelowes." After several trips through the Gap, Boone returned in 1773, and with about 30 woodsmen, of Scots-Irish descent, and their axes, felled a road through the forest.

The frontier was opened up to Kentucky, Tennessee and Ohio by virtue of Boone's Wilderness Road. By 1800, it is estimated three-quarters of the settlers moving into Kentucky, a big percentage Scots-Irish, made it via the Cumberland Gap. It was a high-risk route, with constant danger of attack from the Cherokee and Shawnee Indian tribes and from white renegades and marauders.

Harrodsburg, on the banks of the Kentucky River, was the first permanent white settlement, coming after a surveying mission by James Harrod and Thomas Bullit, who left Fort Pitt (Pittsburgh) in Pennsylvania in 1773 and descended the Ohio River.

There, they met Scots-Irish McAfee brothers—Robert, William, James and George—who left Virginia on a similar mission. The two parties, numbering about 35, joined forces, and proceeded via the Ohio River to Salt River Valley, locating two settlements, one at Harrodsburg, and the other at McAfee's Fort, a few miles north.

These early settlements had to withstand persistent Indian attacks. Harrodsburg was the capital of Kentucky County, with a population in 1776 of 198 persons, of which 81 were eligible for military duty. Hugh McGary, son of an Ulsterman, was the fort commandeer and a justice in Kentucky's first court.

Harrodsburg residents, most of them Scots-Irish, were said to be industrious and thrifty and in 1775 John Harman raised the first corn. The first woolen mill and gristmill on the western frontier were operated here, and pottery, flour and textiles were also manufactured. Like his Scots-Irish frontier compatriots, Daniel Boone was a farmer, blacksmith, and a weaver, as well as being a long hunter.

To survive on the frontier one had to adapt, and among the settlers were carpenters, coopers, tailors, wheelwrights, wagon-makers, rope-makers, wine-makers, surveyors and teachers. The first school in the state was conducted within the fort in 1778. The teacher had no textbooks and the children used smooth boards for paper and juice of ox galls for ink. However, they managed to read and write with remarkable proficiency, and patiently studied the Bible and Presbyterian hymnals. By 1800, Harrodsburg was a prosperous community with rich farm lands surrounding the town growing flax, hemp and tobacco.

John Adair, eighth governor of Kentucky and son of Ulster-born parents, lived there. During the Revolutionary War, some Kentucky settlements faced grave danger from British-backed Cherokee Indian attacks and in 1778 a 25-year-old Ulster-Scot General George Rogers Clark led a force of 175 men from Virginia to relieve the situation. They covered 180 miles of swamp and forest to capture three forts.

The Protestant non-conformist character of the population was evident, and one pastor among the first to cross into Kentucky was Londonderry man the Rev. John Brown, who founded in 1755 the first classical school at Timber Ridge Presbyterian Church—Lexington in the Shenandoah Valley of Virginia.

Among those who moved in the early trek to Kentucky was Thomas Lincoln, who left Virginia, married Nancy Hanks and fathered President Abraham Lincoln. Kentucky historian William Haney revealed that while English blood is predominant in the Kentucky mountain people, their amalgamation with the Scots-Irish "gave them greater courage, endurance and sturdiness to battle with the difficulties with which pioneers of any country may contend."

In the minds of the frontier settlers, all men were free and equal, and should have due regard to the freedom and equality of others. They believed that the purpose of government was to ensure universal freedom and equality. The Kentucky mountain people are in the main descended from soldiers of the American revolution, a great many of them Scots-Irish.

SAM HOUSTON, GOVERNOR OF
TENNESSEE AND TEXAS.

·◦❀10❀◦·

FRONTIERSMEN WHO WERE ALSO SOLDIERS AND POLITICIANS

SAM HOUSTON:

Sam Houston, who boldly wrested Texas from Mexican control and was the Lone Star State's first president, and later governor when it was admitted to the Union in 1845, was the grandson of an east Co Antrim Presbyterian who emigrated to America about 1740.

This teacher-lawyer-soldier-statesmen was a forceful and courageous personality on the American frontier in the early part of the 19th century, and showing a strong streak of independence and all the traditional Scots-Irish characteristics, he blazed a trail from Tennessee to the Tex-Mex border.

The Houston (Huston) family connection can be traced back to the Ballyboley/Ballynure/Brackbracken area that lies halfway between Belfast and Larne. The Houstons were an enterprising plantation farming family from lowland Scotland who moved into Ulster in the early 17th century.

John Houston left the port of Larne for Philadelphia with Presbyterian kinsfolk, and within a few years he had reached the Shenandoah Valley of

Virginia, where he was instrumental in setting up the Timber Ridge and Providence Presbyterian churches at Lexington in Rockbridge County.

Sam Houston was born at Timber Ridge on March 2, 1793, son of Sam and Elizabeth Paxton Houston. His father Sam, a major and later colonel in the militia, was a veteran of the Revolutionary War who soldiered on the frontier until his death in 1807.

The widowed Elizabeth Paxton Houston moved with her nine children—six sons and three daughters—to Maryville, Blount County in the Great Smoky Mountain region of East Tennessee. It was a long and dangerous trek in a covered wagon through territory that skirted Cherokee Indian settlements, but Elizabeth was a determined woman, seeking a secure future for herself and young family.

The Houston home in Blount County was at Baker's Creek, a point close to the Little Tennessee River, which divided the pioneering settlements from the Cherokee Indian lands. The family enrolled at New Providence Presbyterian Church, and twice and often three times a week Elizabeth and the children walked the considerable distance over the hills to worship.

At New Providence, Sam Houston was tutored by highly respected Scots-Irish pastor, the Rev Isaac Anderson, who described him as "a young man of remarkably keen and close observation." Sam was a quick learner, and he soon had a firm grasp of the classics. By 18, he had graduated as a teacher and found a position at a small country school which he occupied until he was 20.

In his earlier youth, Sam Houston was attracted to the ways of the Indian tribes, and he alienated his family when he took up residence at a Cherokee encampment, adopting the Indian dress and costumes and learning the language.

Soldiering was an ambition for Sam, and in 1813, he enlisted in the 7th United States Infantry for the war with the Creek Indians and in 1814 he distinguished himself at the Battle of the Horseshoe Bend. Here he received three wounds—pierced in the thigh with a barbed arrow and shot twice in the right shoulder. His bravery under fire and his persistence in vigorously attacking the Creeks, even while he was severely wounded, earned respect from General Andrew Jackson, who was directing the war. The two men became firm friends, and within a year, Houston was promoted from sergeant to second lieutenant, becoming first lieutenant in 1818.

Jackson used Houston to cultivate relations with the Cherokees and his knowledge of the Indian language and culture helped him to avert a threatened uprising by tribesmen after the chiefs had surrendered a vast amount of land to the United States government. Sam later led a Cherokee delegation to Washington to receive payment for their lands and to legally settle on the bounds of their allotted reservation.

Houston resigned his army commission after becoming disillusioned over allegations of complicity in the smuggling of black slaves into the United States. His position was later vindicated in a Washington inquiry, and he moved to Nashville, Tennessee, where he studied law and was admitted to the bar. He, in turn, was appointed a district attorney, an adjutant general for the state of Tennessee and major-general in what were to be significant stepping stones to a political career

Sam was elected as a Jacksonian Democrat to the United States Congress in 1823, and re-elected in two years later. He became governor of Tennessee in 1827, and was re-elected in 1829. However, when his Presbyterian marriage to 18-year-old Flora Allen faltered after only three months, he resigned the governorship and sought refuge with his Cherokee Indian friends, who, by this time, had been moved to Oklahoma in the Andrew Jackson-directed Trail of Tears campaign.

Once again, Houston took on the dress, customs and manners of the Cherokees and hunted, fished, attended war councils and lived up to the tribes' habit for intemperance. He was even given a certificate of adoption into the Cherokee tribe and cohabited with a half-breed Indian woman, Tyania Rodgers Gentry. Their association ended when she refused to desert her people on Sam's request. His own wife, a young woman of position and character in middle Tennessee, later obtained a divorce for abandonment and she re-married. Houston was a man of varied moods, and when taken to bouts of heavy drinking, he could be a difficult individual.

In 1833, Sam Houston headed to Texas, then in the middle of a revolution seeking to end Mexican rule. He was warmly welcomed by the American colonists at Nacogdoches, and adopting a hardline stance on independence for the region, he participated in the convention at San Felipe de Austin (later to become the city of Austin!), which led to the breaking of the American link.

Sam, always promoting the welfare of the native American Indians, took part in talks with Comanche Indian chiefs on disputed boundary questions in the San Antonio region.

In the spring of 1836, Sam Houston was appointed commander-in-chief of the Texas revolutionary troops and he made the call: "Volunteers from the United States... come with a good rifle and come soon. Liberty or death!"

Houston was called into almost immediate action by the events that unfolded from The Alamo in San Antonio. There, Mexican President Antonio Lopez de Santa Anna and a 5,000-strong army had laid siege on 189 Texas Rangers and volunteer soldiers from Tennessee, along with a collection of women, children and black slaves. Tennessee frontiersman Davy Crockett and another Tennessean Colonel Jim Bowie, two former associates of Houston, were among those besieged at The Alamo, but reinforcements did not arrive, in time and a terrible massacre occurred which stirred the American settlers in the territory.

With 700 auxiliary soldiers hastily recruited, Sam Houston confronted Santa Anna and 1,800 Mexican troops at the Battle of San Jacinto on April 21, 1836. The odds were against them, but in 20 minutes Houston's "Texians," charging to the cry "Remember the Alamo," were victorious. The Mexicans lost 630 killed and had 730 taken prisoner, among them the hated Santa Anna, who was first to concede independence for Texas.

Sam Houston, injured in the right ankle at San Jacinto, became President of independent Texas, serving two terms—1836-38 and 1841-44. In March, 1846 Sam was elected as a U.S. Senator for Texas, which had admitted to the Union four months earlier, and in this role he served 14 years.

In a speech on November 25, 1841, Sam Houston declared: "Texas has achieved her entire independence and successfully asserted her right. How has this been accomplished? By the spirit and energy of her citizens—by the valour of her sons—by the inspired language breathed by her daughters."

During his senatorship, Sam opposed the South's state doctrine that Congress had no right to legislate on slavery in the territories. He also advocated California as a state of the Union and the development of the Pacific railroad through Texas.

In 1859, Sam was elected governor of Texas as an Independent and he served until 1861, when on the enrolment of the state as a member of the

Confederacy, he refused to take the necessary official oath and recognise the authority of the new convention.

Houston was forced out of office by Confederate politicians, but he was now an old man and war-weary, and did not resist. He wanted no more blood spilt among his own people. He retired to his farm at Huntsville, Alabama and, after an illness of five weeks, died on July 26, 1863, aged 70, as the Civil War raged.

Sam married again, in May, 1840, to Margaret Lea of Marion, Alabama. They enjoyed a happy stable relationship which produced eight children. Margaret was the daughter of a Baptist pastor, and it was her influence which led to Sam's Christian conversion at Independence, Texas in 1854. From being brought up in a solid Presbyterian family background where some of his close relatives were men of the cloth, Houston later experienced the heathen faiths of the Cherokees and for a brief time in Mexico Roman Catholicism. His addiction to drink did not endear him to church people during a considerable period of his career.

After his conversion to the Baptist faith, Sam regularly corresponded with his wife when away from home, providing resumes of sermons he had heard preached. He joined the Sons of Temperance organisation, leaving behind his excessive drinking habits from earlier years, but spurned a request from a delegation of Texas ministers who asked him to use his influence in getting a Sunday alcohol prohibition law passed.

After outlining his reasons, Sam added "I am a sincere Christian. I believe in the precepts and examples as taught and practised by Christ and His Apostles to be the bedrock of democracy."

He often referred to his wife Margaret as "one of the best Christians on earth" and significantly his dying words—"Margaret, Margaret, Texas, Texas."

A newspaper report of Sam's death concluded: "To his numerous friends it will be doubtless a matter of great satisfaction to learn that in his last hours he was sustained by the Christian's hope and that he died the death of the righteous."

Sam made his will a few days before his death, and in the fifth clause he said: "To my eldest son, Sam Houston, I bequeath my sword, worn in the battle of San Jacinto, to be drawn only in defence of the constitution and laws, and liberties of his country. If any attempt be made to assail one of these, I wish it to be used in its vindication."

Houston, whatever his accomplishments as a politician, statesmen and soldier, never acquired real wealth, to that attained by some of his contemporaries. He was not good at finance management and, although his estate at the time of his death listed 89,288 dollars in assets, very little of this was liquid cash, and his wife Margaret experienced great difficulty in making ends meet.

This fulsome tribute was paid to Sam Houston by President John F. Kennedy: "He was one of the most independent, unique, popular forceful and dramatic individuals ever to enter the Senate chamber. He was in turn magnanimous, vindictive, affectionate, yet cruel, eccentric yet self-conscious, faithful yet opportunistic. But Sam Houston's contradictions actually confirm his one basic consistent quality, indomitable individualism, sometimes spectacular, sometimes crude, sometimes mysterious, but always courageous."

Sam Houston was a man of many parts, and American historian Ernest C. Shearer accurately described his moods: "He was as inconstant as a weather vane, solid as a rock, mercurial as a chameleon; intense as the heart of the sun, enthusiastic as a child, vain and proud as a peacock, humble as a servant, direct as an arrow, polished as a marquis, rough as a blizzard and gentle as a dove. In short, it was difficult to fit him to any set pattern."

In 1850, 18,000 native Tennesseans lived in Texas, the largest contribution to the region from any other state in the Union and obviously largely due to the influence of Sam Houston and associates like Davy Crockett and Jim Bowie.

DAVID CROCKETT:

Brave frontiersman Davy Crockett died at The Alamo five months before his 50th birthday, but in his 49 years this rugged Tennessean lived life to the full and created a legend and myth that lies at the heart of American folklore.

This highly colourful and courageous character was born in a humble log cabin in a valley alongside the Big Limestone River and the Nolichuckey River in Greene County, North Carolina (a region later to become Tennessee!)

on August 17, 1786. Forget the story that Davy was born on a mountain top in Tennessee—he was born in a holler.

Davy, who preferred to be called David, may have been a rural back-woodsman, but he had enough intelligence, commonsense and cunning to survive and outwit even his most devious adversaries and highly educated political opponents. He was in every respect a man of the people—humble, straight-talking and honest, the fifth child of a family of nine (six sons and three daughters) born to John and Rebecca Crockett. He was a romantic adventurer, explorer and hunter who left an indelible mark on the rugged landscape of his Tennessee homeland, and the stories of his exploits and achievements will always be a cornerstone of American life.

Crockett was also a soldier and politician of standing, as well as being a celebrated storyteller, folklorist and wit. He was a man with the common touch, someone who was fully aware of precisely where he had come from and where he was going.

Before spending the last few months of his life in Texas, where he stood at The Alamo in 1836 stoutly defending liberty and democracy for his country, Davy lived at seven different locations in Tennessee. He spent the first twenty five years in East Tennessee, the next ten in Middle Tennessee around Nashville and the last fourteen in the wild and sparsely-inhabited West Tennessee towards Memphis.

The Crocketts had arrived in America from the north of Ireland in the early 18th century, having lived in the Tyrone-Donegal counties in the province of Ulster after moving there from Scotland during the 17th century plantation.

Historical records claim the family derived from French Protestant Huguenot stock (Crocketagne), and it is recorded that several Crocketts defended the Ulster city of Londonderry in the famous siege of 1688-89.

One of the first Crocketts to reach America was Joseph Louis, with his wife Sarah Stewart, from Co Donegal. These Crocketts landed in Pennsylvania, settling for a time in Maryland and then moving down the Shenandoah Valley of Virginia and further on to North Carolina, Tennessee and Missouri. Other branches of the Crockett family emigrated from Co Antrim in the 1730s.

Davy Crockett is the great grandson of Joseph Louis Crockett, and his grandfather David passed through the Shenandoah Valley, verified by the fact that his son Robert was born at Barryville in the region in 1755. By 1771, the Crocketts were in North Carolina with deed records of Tyron County confirming David Sr. had bought a 250-acre farm on the south side of the Catawbe River.

In November, 1777, Davy Crockett's grandparents were massacred in a Cherokee Indian attack on their homestead at Carter's Creek beside the Holston River in Hawkins County, near the present-day town of Rogersville in East Tennessee. There, within a radius of three miles David Crockett Sr. and his three sons John, William and Joseph lived on separate farmlands. Davy's father John was away at the time of the killings, but his uncle James was taken captive and did not return home for 20 years.

The massacre, marked on a gravestone in a cemetery in the centre of Rogersville, left the small clutch of Scots-Irish families in the region fearful and vulnerable, but they re-grouped to form a cohesive defensive strategy to combat the daily threat posed by Indian attack.

John Crockett took part in Revolutionary War battles in the region, including Kings Mountain in 1780, along with six other members of the wider family circle.

His wife Rebecca Hawkins, who was born in Maryland, also reached North Carolina via the Shenandoah Valley with her Scots-Irish family, and she and John eventually settled at Limestone Creek in Greene county.

Davy Crockett spent the first five years of his life at Limestone Creek. The family moved to Cove Creek where his father had a partnership in a mill, but it was a short stay as the mill and the Crockett home was destroyed in a flood. The next stop was Morristown in Jefferson County, Tennessee, where John Crockett opened a tavern on the main road from Abingdon in Virginia to Knoxville.

When he was twelve, Davy was hired out as a cattle hand to a Dutch settler Jacob Silver in Rockville, Virginia. He found the work rewarding, but was homesick and trekked the 400 miles home, only to be sent back to school by his father. But the classes only lasted four days, and fearing punishment at home for his truancy, he finally decided to make his way in the wider world.

Davy tried a succession of jobs over a three-year period, and after passing through Virginia, worked for a time at Baltimore docks. He was employed by a Quaker John Kennedy, who allowed him to attend educational classes. But Davy preferred the freedom to roam the forests and mountains of his rugged and wild Tennessee homeland, as a hunter living and working off the land.

In 1806, Davy married pretty Polly Finley (Finlay), who was Scots-Irish on her father's side, and, while Polly's mother was looking for better than the intrepid Crockett, the marriage blended with three children to their name, sons John Wesley and William and daughter Margaret Polly. The couple lived for a few years on a rented farm near the home of Polly's father in Jefferson County, but the going was hard and they moved west into Middle Tennessee, beyond the Cumberland mountains. By 1811 they had settled at Mulberry Creek, on the Duck and Elk Rivers in what is now Moore County. The surrounding forests were rich in deer and smaller game, the ideal spot for a man of Davy Crockett's tastes.

Within two years Davy moved the family to Bean Creek in Franklin County, to a home called "Kentuck" and stayed there until after his involvement in Andrew Jackson's war with the Creek Indians in 1812-14. Crockett originally volunteered for 90-day service in the Second Regiment of Volunteer Mounted Riflemen, but the military duties were extended and he was selected as a scout to spy on the Indian territories, along with a close friend George Russell. It was during this expedition that Davy gained the reputation of being a bear hunter, with his trusty Kentucky long rifle.

Davy joined the regular army and fought the Indians at Fort Strother and Fort Taladega and encountered British forces in Andrew Jackson's Florida campaign. Around this time Polly Crockett took ill at her Mulberry Creek home and Davy had to return home. Polly had always been a delicate, frail person and the many moves and natural hardship she faced on the frontier wilderness sapped her energy and strength. She died in 1815, leaving a distraught Davy to care for three young children, and for a time a younger brother and his wife helped out.

Within a year, Davy married again, to a widow Elizabeth Patton, the mother of two children whose husband had been killed in the Creek War. Elizabeth was also of Scots-Irish origin, of a good family background from North Carolina and her sizeable farm helped Davy to increase his social status. Elizabeth came to Texas in 1854 and died there in 1860, aged 72.

Davy, despite having taken on another wife and two more children continued to hunt and explore, and with neighbouring settlers he looked over the Alabama territory, which had just been acquired from the Creek Indians. On that mission, he contacted malaria and was fortunate to get home alive. He later took advantage of the treaty of 1816 with the Chickasaw Indians and found another settlement at Shoal Creek near Lawrenceburg in Middle Tennessee. Within two months he was a justice of the peace and later became lieutenant colonel of the local militia. His new found civic duties, on his own admission, were seriously taxing his educational abilities, but he claimed that he got by on his "natural born sense," rather than any knowledge of the law.

Davy was elevated to colonel in the militia, and in 1821 was elected to the Tennessee state legislature for Lawrence and Hickman counties. While electioneering, he admitted he never read a newspaper and knew nothing about government, but he had talents as a soap box orator and a humour which endeared him to ordinary grassroots voters.

Crockett was also a gifted storyteller, but for all his natural instincts and talents, he was looked down on by representatives of the moneyed classes and slightingly referred to as "the gentleman from the cane." But Davy knew his constituency and the poor backwoods families rallied to his cause.

While attending the Tennessee legislature at Murfreesboro, Davy's large grist powder mill and distillery on Shoal Creek were swept away in a flood—a repeat of the misfortune which struck his father at Cove Creek—and he was forced to move the family to Rutherford Fork, 150 miles distance. He was re-elected to the legislature in 1823, defeating Dr. William E. Butler, a nephew of the wife of Andrew Jackson and one of the region's most wealthy men.

Butler had education, money and influence, but Crockett had the uncanny knack of persuading voters over to his side. In his accounts, Davy tells of a special hunting short which he wore when campaigning. It was of buckskin, outsize and had two pockets. In one pocket, he carried whiskey and in the other tobacco. Davy reckoned that when he met a prospective voter he would treat him first with whiskey and before leaving him he would hand him a twist of tobacco to replace the "chaw" he had disposed off when he took the drink. The reason was that if a man was in good humour, in as good a shape as when he found him, the vote was secure on polling day. Butler was routed at the polls and Crockett returned to represent five counties.

Davy Crockett was, in many respects, a socialist, although he espoused the capitalist free market ideals of the American dream. The major issue for the 1823 legislature was the disposition of lands belonging to the state and the mopping up of the territory formerly under the control of North Carolina in the late 18th century. Crockett, who was joined by President to be James Knox Polk in the debate, deeply mistrusted the federal government over its legislation on the territorial state remits of Tennessee and North Carolina.

Davy, who had two terms as a Tennessee state legislator, also opposed legislative handling of divorce cases and had numerous run-ins with Andrew Jackson, shortly to become president. Later as a Congress man, he irked the Washington establishment when he put forward a resolution to abolish the nation's military academy at West Point.

His main argument was that only the sons of the rich and influential could get into West Point and that the bounty of the government should go to the poor rather than to the rich. He contended that the War of 1812 had shown that a man could fight the battles of his country and lead his country's armies, without being educated at West Point; as shown by the success of Andrew Jackson who had since progressed to the highest office in the land.

In 1827 Davy was elected to Congress for West Tennessee, defeating General William Arnold and Colonel Adam Alexander, who both dismissed the Crockett bandwagon, convinced it was a straight fight between them. Davy won by 2,748 votes, and he held the seat at the next election.

However, Crockett's opposition to Andrew Jackson's Indian Bill prevented him getting a third term. Davy's attitude was: "I am at liberty to vote as my conscience and judgment dictate to be right, without the yoke of any party on me, or the driver at my heels, with the whip in his hands, commanding me 'gee-whoa-haw' just at his pleasure."

Davy was his own man, even in the presence of more powerful company, and when an usher at President Jackson's home one evening cried: "Make way for Colonel Crockett," there came the reply: "Colonel Crockett makes room for himself."

Although he fought alongside Andrew Jackson in various battles, he parted company with the President over land and river issues that greatly affected the livelihoods of his people. Crockett said in March, 1830: "To

General Jackson I am a firm and undeviating friend. I have fought under his command… I have loved him… and still love him; but to be compelled to love everyone who… for self-aggrandizement pretend to rally around the 'Jackson Standard' is what I can never submit to. The people… ought to look for breakers! The fox is about; let the roost be guarded."

Crockett and other Tennessean representatives were disappointed at Jackson's stand against financial aid for the improvement in the transportation facilities of the state. Davy strongly believed in human rights, including those of the native American people, and he led opposition to Andrew Jackson's Indian policy of forcing the tribes living east of the Mississippi River to move to the western part of the Louisiana territory.

When the bill approving the measure at a cost of 500,000 dollars was put before Congress in 1830, Davy was the only Tennessean to vote against it. His main objective was that he did not want to see the poor remnants of "a once powerful people" forced to move "against their will." Davy represented four counties in West Tennessee on the border of the Chickasaw Indian country, and he was appalled at the decision to drive these tribes west of the Mississippi. He also knew that many by now-peaceful Cherokees would prefer "death in their homes" to moving away from their natural environment in Tennessee.

During his last term in Congress, Davy toured major eastern cities and New England states and, wherever he went, he was met by huge crowds and great ovations. He was in big demand as a speaker at banquets and dinner parties, and when he visited Philadelphia he was presented with his famous rifle "Betsy." This bore the gold and silver inscription: "To the honorable Davy Crockett of Tennessee by the young men of Philadelphia."

"Betsy" was to accompany Davy on his last fateful journey to Texas for the battles with the Mexicans—and, nostalgically, the trusted weapon was recovered by his family after the fall at The Alamo.

THE CROCKETT TRAIL TO TEXAS, AND THE ALAMO

Davy Crockett left his West Tennessee home for Texas on November 1, 1835, three months after his election defeat for Congress. His political career was over and the tremendous urge to explore new territory had again seized him. His aim was to improve his economic well-being on the Texas frontier. He told contemporaries: "You can go to hell, I'm going to Texas."

Davy moved to Texas down the Mississippi River through Arkansas and into the Red River Valley. This verged on Comanche Indian country where the tribes were on the warpath, as menacing to the American settlers as the Mexicans under their President, General Antonio Lopez de Santa Anna.

Soon after his arrival in Nacogdoches, Davy took the oath of allegiance to the provisional government of the independent republic of Texas. He was joined by his nephew William Patton, who had accompanied him to Texas in an initial 17-strong party which was to be become known as the "Tennessee Mounted Volunteers."

Texas was in revolt against the ruling junta in Mexico and the stakes were high as both sides prepared for a fight to the death. Crockett and his men reported for duty at Bexar on January 13, 1836 and they were warmly welcomed by Colonel William Travis, who, because Crockett also bore the title of colonel, offered him command of the fort. Crockett refused, stating he had come to defend Texas as a private.

When word came through on February 11 that Santa Anna and a large army had crossed the Rio Grande into Texas, it was decided that all the men of the Texas garrison should go as soon as possible into the enclosure of The Alamo, an old walled Franciscan mission station, in what today is the centre of the city of San Antonio.

The movement into The Alamo was not completed until February 23, and it was there over the next few weeks that 189 men, together with some women, children and black servants, were to take refuge from the advancing 5,000-strong Mexican army led by Santa Anna.

Most of the volunteers including Crockett, were Tennesseans; the rest were Kentuckians and Virginians. Among them was a Tennessean of Scottish roots, Colonel Jim Bowie, the man credited with inventing the Bowie knife. Illness from tuberculosis prevented Jim from taking an active role in the battle. Colonel William Travis, aged only 25, was in command, and he kept repeating even at the height of battle: "Victory or death! I shall never surrender or retreat!"

Sam Houston, like Crockett of Ulster-Scots extraction, was major-general of the regular army in the new independent republic of Texas, but it was an army which had still to be recruited. The siege lasted 13 days and, while guns were fired daily at sunrise to alert army reinforcements, it was to no avail.

The siege began on February 23, 1836, and Crockett's pledge to Colonel Travis was "Colonel, here I am. Assign me a position and I and my boys will try to defend it." The "boys" were the Tennesseans and they were assigned to the most vulnerable point at the station.

In a memorandum dated February 23, Crockett wrote: "Early this morning the enemy came in sight, marching in regular order. They'll find that they have to do with men who will never lay down their arms as long as they can stand on their legs." Ominously, in another recorded message on March 3, Crockett declared: "We have given over all hope of receiving assistance from Goliad or Refugio."

Eighteen cannon, were mounted as the siege began and Travis in his report said: "The Hon. David Crockett was seen at all points animating the men to do their duty." The accurate rifle fire of the Tennesseans kept the Mexicans at bay, but time and supplies were running out. And there was no sign of the army reinforcements that had been promised.

A detachment of 32 men arrived on March 1, but two days later there came the news from a courier that 400 men had turned back because of difficulties on the way and, because the officers felt another Texas station was more in need of defending than The Alamo.

Santa Anna decided the fort should be taken by assault and the first two charges were beaten back with huge losses on the part of the Mexicans. In a third assault, concentrating on the north wall of the fort, the Mexicans managed to breach the defences and gain access to the plaza of the mission.

The Texans were outnumbered and had to retreat to the buildings around the plaza and the mission church. Their cannons were seized and used to batter down the doors. The defenders took their last stand in hand-to-hand combat, and many died at the receiving end of a Mexican bayonet.

An estimated 189 Texans were killed, with their bodies placed on a funeral pyre and burned. The only survivors were non-combatants, mostly Mexican women and children, several black slaves of Colonel Bowie and Colonel Travis, and a Mrs. Dickinson, wife of an officer of the garrison.

Various accounts of how Davy Crockett died at The Alamo have been rendered. It is claimed he was one of six survivors who surrendered to Santa Anna and was shot dead on the Mexican leader's orders. But is generally accepted that he fell behind the south wall, which he and the Tennesseans were charged to defend. Mrs Dickinson, who was led from the church, said in her testimony: "As we passed through the enclosed ground in front of the church I saw heaps of dead and dying. I recognised Colonel Crockett lying dead and mutilated between the church and the barrack building and even remember seeing his peculiar cap lying by his side."

Two slave witnesses, Santa Anna's cook Ben and Colonel Travis's servant Joe, claimed Crockett's body was surrounded by Mexican corpses. Ben reported seeing Davy's knife buried "up the hilt in the bosom of a Mexican found lying across his body." It was said that Crockett fought to the end, killing many Mexicans. His last act of helpfulness was loading Jim Bowie's rifle and pistol.

General Sam Houston found the fall of The Alamo an agonising nightmare. Ironically, Sam was presiding at a convention in Washington dealing with the independence of Texas, and when word reached him of the last message ever dispatched by Colonel Travis, he walked out, mounted his battle horse and, with three companions, headed for The Alamo.

The party rode hard all day, only stopping when their wearied horses could go no further. He knew that the signal gun would be fired as long as The Alamo held out. The last one was fired on the day that he had read Travis's message (Sunday March 6)—the day the Mexicans butchered 189 men. Sam Houston was too late to render assistance at The Alamo, but through his leadership, and, against all the odds, he managed to retrieve the position for the Texan cause in the days that followed.

The Alamo, by restricting Santa Anna's army for two weeks, had allowed the Texan army to get organised. The battle cry had now become "Remember the Alamo," and under Houston, the Texans, heavily outnumbered but determined to "save Texas," won a famous victory at the Battle of San Jacinto. It was 700 brave, but largely untrained, Texas against 1,800

Mexicans, and, buoyed by the frenzied cries of "The Alamo," Houston's men won the day in 20 minutes.

The Mexicans had 630 killed and 730 prisoners taken, including their commander Santa Anna. The Texan losses were eight killed and 23 injured.

Houston, who suffered an ankle injury, secured from Santa Anna a treaty recognising Texas independence, and by September of that year, he was president of the new republic. Texas later became a state of the Union—the 28th—on December 29, 1845.

The *Telegraph and Texas Register* in Austin reported in its issue of March 24, 1836: "The end of Davy Crockett of Tennessee, the great hunter of the west, was as glorious as his career through life had been useful. He and his companions were found surrounded by piles of assailants, whom they immolated on the altar of Texas liberties. The countenance of Crockett was unchanged: he had in death that freshness of hue, which his exercise of pursuing the beasts of the forest and the prairie had imparted to him. Texas places him, exultingly, amongst the martyrs of her cause."

John Wesley Crockett, Davy's son, who later represented his father's old constituency of West Tennessee in the American Congress, wrote to his uncle George Patton, of North Carolina: "You have doubtless seen the account of my father's fall at The Alamo in Texas. He is gone from us and is no more to be seen in the walks of men, but in his death like Sampson (Samson), he slew more of his enemies than in all of his life. Even his most bitter enemies here, I believe, have buried all animosity and joined the great lamentation over his untimely death."

Davy's last reported memorandum, written on March 5 carried the words: "Go ahead, liberty and independence forever!"

Some military strategists may look back on The Alamo as a disaster—that a significant body of soldiers were allowed to be surrounded by a force vastly superior in numbers—but it is widely accepted that the supreme sacrifice made by Davy Crockett and the others in the little mission station largely contributed to securing independence for Texas.

Shortly after the Alamo, John Wesley Crockett went to Texas to retrieve his father's rifle "Betsy" and, with other personal belongings, the weapon became a treasured possession in the family, being handed down from generation to generation. Davy Crockett once wrote: "I'll leave the truth for others when I'm dead. First be sure you are right and go ahead."

James Wakefield Burke, in his book David Crockett—The Man Behind the Myth, wrote of the legendary Tennessean: "David Crockett possessed the essential attributes for the American frontier. He was an adventurer, with a talent for falling in with strangers, a memory for names and faces, a gift of storytelling, inexaustable invention, indomitable valiance, a remarkable ability for sharp-shooting and that freedom from conscience that springs from a contempt for pettiness and bureaucracy.

"He was a free soul who sought the company only of those of like temperament. There seems to have been graven into this liberated man from the dirt farms of Tennessee a reluctance to be tied down, to be obligated for long to any engagement, to own anything save his long rifle."

Obviously this was a man in the highest traditions of his Scots-Irish family heritage. The legend and myth of Davy Crockett was indeed real.

DAVY CROCKETT'S LAST LETTER HOME

Seven weeks before Davy Crockett's death at The Alamo he wrote his last letter. The letter, written from Nacogdoches, Texas on January 15, 1836, was to his daughter Mary (Polly) and her husband Wiley Flowers: "My dear son and daughter, I am now blessed with excellent health and am in high spirits. I have got through safe and have been received by everybody with the ceremony of friendship. I am hailed with a hearty welcome to this country. A dinner and party of ladies have honored me with an invitation.

"The cannon was fired here on my arrival and I must say as to what I have seen of Texas it is the garden spot of the world, the best land and the best prospects for good health I ever saw and I do believe it is a fortune to any man to come here. There is a world of country to settle, the richest country in the world. Good land, plenty of timber and the best springs and good mill streams, good range of clear water… game aplenty.

"I have taken the oath of government and have enrolled my name as volunteer for six months and will set out for the Rio Grande in a few days with the volunteers. I am rejoiced at my fate. I had rather be in my present situation than to be elected to a seat in Congress for life.

"I am in hopes of making a fortune yet for myself and family. I hope you will all do the best you can and I will do the same. Do not be uneasy about me. I am among friends,

Your affectionate father. Farewell David Crockett!"

FRONTIER WOMEN HELD TOGETHER THE
HOME, COMMUNITY AND SOUND VALUES.

·⟿ 11 ⟿·

Hardy Women of the Frontier

Human endurance on the American frontier in the 18th and early 19th century is perhaps beyond the comprehension and the imagination of those of us in live in the comfortable modern society of the early 21st century.

The settlement of a vast wilderness and the creation of a civilisation in what today has become the most powerful, most democratic and free nation in the world is undoubtedly one of the epic stories in global history. At every opportunity, there should be fulsome recognition of a courageous people who were not deterred by the personal hardships and tragedies that they faced.

Settling the American frontier may have a romantic ring to it, perpetuated by the images created in the Hollywood western movies, but there was a starkness about life in the vast territories which the European immigrant settlers encountered in their long overland treks that was far from cosy and glamorous.

Indeed, at a time when travel and accessibility was very difficult, and at times hazardous and extremely dangerous, it is incredible just how much territory was settled, and in such a short span of years.

Many trekked long journeys on foot, while the others managed to move on horseback, either alone or as part of a train of Conestoga wagons.

There have been some incredible stories of men and women who lived through wars, famine, disease and drought and survived to secure a firm foothold on lands that was to be theirs and their families for generations and centuries to come.

The men were in the vanguard of the great march West, over a century and a half from the eastern seaboard states of New England through the Appalachian territories, and beyond the Mississippi River over the Rockies to the Pacific Ocean in the West and to Texas in the South.

Women too were an integral part of the onward journey by the hardy settlers through dense forests and over mountains in the Appalachians to the great plains of the south and west. Their contribution to the frontier settlements as the backbone of the home, the community and the church was far-reaching.

The wonderful womenfolk of the American frontier showed extraordinary tenacity and true grit in facing the awesome and grinding challenges of largely hitherto uninhabited lands, variable climates and a dangerously hostile environment that resulted in many lost lives.

They encountered a life of constant toil, home-making, child-minding and subservience that could not have been easy or even tolerable by the standards that we all come to expect today in our modern society. But with love and care they ensured that the family life became paramount and the values that uphold society prospered.

Men invariably get the credit for extending the American nation and civilising the bleak wilderness that extended from the 18th century North Carolina, Tennessee and Kentucky frontier regions beyond the Mississippi River to the territories in the direction of the Pacific Ocean which, in the 19th century, became known as The West.

The men were the ones who cleared the land, built the homes, grew the food in the fields, chased off the marauding Indian tribes with their long Kentucky rifles and set up townships where ordered, close-knit communities were established.

The men folk were not, of course, the whole story on the frontier. When America was offering free land for those prepared to take it up in the 18th and 19th centuries, it was not just men who arduously trekked across the Atlantic from Europe to seize the opportunity.

Women too wanted to be in on the great American dream, and many staked claims for 100 acres of land and more and got it.

Some of the women were unmarried and had to continually struggle for their rights in a male-dominated society, but they were characters with nerves of steel and a determination beyond belief as they ventured into the great unknown of the vast North American continent.

They came of Scots-Irish, German, English, Dutch, Scandinavian and Scottish Highland descent—strong, self-reliant, resourceful, loyal and, in most cases, God-fearing.

• Some married out on the frontier.

• Most accompanied husbands and parents in the hazardous journey in wooden ships across the Atlantic.

• Some were sisters whose parents or brothers persuaded them to make a claim for land too.

• Some were daughters landed as children on American soil with their parents.

• Some became widows when their husbands were killed in the conflicts with the Indians or in the battles of the Revolutionary War.

When many of these hardy women folk went to the "New World" in the early to mid-18th century, they had very few worldly possessions and with their families had to live on a very basic diet of pumpkins and potatoes until they and their husbands or fathers could grow grain and other foodstuffs.

Indeed, the very early 18th century settlers had little more than wild fruits, berries, game and fish to live on. And they made a primitive porridge out of Indian corn.

Life for women on the American frontier was continuously one of toil and danger, facing drudgery, and, in many cases, illness brought on early in middle age by years of physical and mental fatigue.

But their experiences did create very strong, independent and resourceful personalities, and the tough characteristics and survival inheritances that they brought with them from the "Old World" did equip them for the perils which they faced, and allowed them to turn adversity into situations that were ultimately beneficial to their calling in life.

Women of the 18th century period on the American frontier were conditioned to lives of constant labour, and they certainly lived up to the designation of "Janes-of-all trades," as they coped with the perennial chores of the home, and on the farm lands that they cultivated.

The earliest of the European immigrant settlers in colonial American of the 16th and early 17th century were male. Very few women ventured across the Atlantic on the exploratory trips into Virginia and the other eastern seaboard regions. It was considered much too dangerous a place for women.

Even by 1625, men in Virginia outnumbered women seven to one, which made it very difficult for the males to find partners for marriage. However, by the 18th century, the large influx of European settlers in the eastern seaboard and Appalachian regions happily resulted in a more even spread of the sexes.

The 18th century settlers, particularly of a Scots-Irish hue, brought their own flax seeds to plant and grow for linen-making in the one-room log cabin homes. There was the complex, laborious process of preparation, bleaching, spinning and weaving and the women were in the forefront of this work.

During harvest time and threshing day—normally a popular neighbourhood event in frontier communities—women and the older girls in the family helped out in the fields when they could, but they also had to prepare in the household for both the noon-day and the evening meals.

In many of the early American frontier settlements, clothes worn by all of the family were home-made, with deerskin and leather breaches generally the garb of the men and the boys, and when woolen and linsey yarn was not available, the women and girls had to use the same materials as the males.

The linsey gown was spun and dyed and fashioned together by the women themselves, and for head gear they worn sunbonnets.

Descriptions, however, of how the settlers dressed varied from region to region, and depended on the prosperity or otherwise of a region.

For "Sunday-go-to-Meeting" garb, the clothes had a distinctive look, accurate historical recollection of dress from the 1770s-1780s Scots-Irish settlements of the Carolina backcountry reveals.

On the American frontier, the more adult women were lumbered with the task of carrying, over a considerable distance from the river creek to the log cabin home, heavy pails of water. The family laundry had to be done by hand at the stream, in all weathers on an almost daily basis, and fresh water in wooden buckets from the wells had to be borne to the log cabins.

Women scoured the land for anything burnable on the home fire and, if firewood was not available, they were forced to rely on dried twigs, tufts of grass and old corn cobs. Garden crops which added to a staple diet were attended to by the women and they also produced a variety of food, clothing and household utensils to sell locally in the market places for very necessary income.

Teenage girls and the older children had to assist with the work in the fields, dropping seed corn and gathering flax, which they later hatchelled, spun and wove. They were adept at the loom and with the needle in the cottage industries that abounded in the backcountry settlements.

Care of the vegetable garden and the dairying was also a women's chore, as well as looking after poultry, and they also engaged in the making of sugar from maple sap.

On a more business footing, there were women on the frontier who enterprisingly and with considerable courage ran village shops and wayside taverns. And, of course, midwifery and nursing had to be an inevitable calling for some of the women in the various localities.

Child-birthing, with only the most basic facilities and medical help in the wilds of the frontier, was a risky operation for both the mother and the child. But the women of the settlements could always be relied upon to help each other and before and during a birth the necessary precautions, within the very limited means available to protect life, were taken.

Infant mortality was significantly higher on the 18th century American frontier than on the more settled eastern seaboard communities, with no hospitals and few if any doctors, but remarkably the majority of children born in the white settlements survived.

Very often, the mothers were "doctors" to their own children and the women took care, if they were not stricken down themselves, of other members of the family when they were infected by smallpox, malaria, pneumonia, cholera, pleurisy and ague (the frontier fever).

It was generally accepted in the early American settlement years that the proper place for a woman of good family and respectability was at home, but to survive in frontier communities everyone had to be adaptable, even the female members of the family. They all had to work and work hard, and it was accepted that a high degree of managerial skills marked out the women of the frontier!

The work extended, in many instances to tending the livestock and slaughtering of even the largest of animals. British travellers in the 18th century American backcountry were shocked to see females fell animals with an axe and engage in the hard labour of forest and land clearing.

It was noted that backcountry women were not only "up to their elbows in housewifery, but were busy with what other white ethnic cultures took to be man's work."

Women had few if any legal rights in 18th century American frontier society, and marriage was considered a practical social and economic necessity in the harsh and far from accommodating environment for female rights.

Indeed, the conservative view, prevalent mainly in the Southern states, was that the woman's place was in the home, under-written by the Old Testament Biblical philosophy which scrupulously upheld the traditional concept of male supremacy in the family and in the wider community.

However, the legal and social conditions of women in some states did improve considerably by the mid-19th century, permitting them to sue in courts, make contracts, exercise full control over their personal affairs and retain custody of their children in a matrimonial dispute.

When a husband was missing from home for a long period while engaged in militia battles and presumed dead, the wives were permitted to re-marry. If the husband did re-appear and there was existential bigamy, the wife was permitted to choose between spouses.

Conditions were no different for women in the north, particularly in the North-West Territory where the new lands of Illinois were being open up in the late 18th century.

It was said, however, that the support system provided to the men there by the resolute and fiercely loyal women was a crucial factor in ensuring the survival of the new life in the raw settlements of Illinois.

Women may not have enjoyed equal rights to men in holding civic office, but their share of the work load in sustaining a home was at least on a par.

In 1896, eminent Scotch-Irish historian Rev. Dr. Henry C. McCook, of Philadelphia, describing those early frontier women's efforts, said they had to be physician and surgeon, as well as attending to all their own work.

The onerous duties and burdens of home-making and child-caring, he said, largely fell on their shoulders.

McCook, in Scotch-Irish Women Pioneers, wrote: "There was neither bedstead, not stool, nor chair, nor bucket, nor domestic comfort. But such as could be carried on pack horses and the Conestoga wagon through the wilderness. Two rough boxes, one attached to the other served as the table, two kegs for seats and so on.

"Having committed themselves to God in family worship they spread their bed on the floor and slept soundly until morning. Some times they had no bread for weeks together, but they had plenty of pumpkins and potatoes and all the necessities of life.

"The earliest settlers, of course, did not have the luxuries of pumpkins and potatoes, to begin their culinary duties therewith. They had in sooth to invent a cuisine. Everything must be found anew.

"The wild fruits, wild berries and wild game and the fish of the New World were utilised. Indian corn was a new cereal to these Ulster house-wives, but it had to be wrought into the primitive menu, mush and milk!

"It was a novel sort of porridge for our grand-dames but they learned to make it. Cooking was not the only sphere that solicited her faculty. The pioneer woman had to invent a pharmacopoeia.

"Wounds and sickness came, and must be cared for. The forest was full of healing herbs—and, perhaps, our octogenarian members still have recollection of ginseng and snakeroot teas and slippery elm poultices, and the like.

"The frontier woman had to be physician and surgeon, trained in nursing and apothecary, all in one, and often supplied the patient, too in her own person. In times of personal sickness and during the illness of children, the strain upon women thus situated must have been intense.

"Such a life, indeed, developed self-reliance; fertility of resources, strong and independent characters, but many fell under the grievous strain and thus became veritable martyrs.

"In these humble log huts began the work of home building, constructing that prime factor of all strong and good social order, the family. The family is the unity of society, the true basis of the best civilisation and the family pioneer family building woman was the chief architect.

"The husband indeed must fend and fight for wife and weans, for steading and glebe; he must shoot game, and chop down trees and clear up fields and plant grain, but the duty and burden of home-making must fall upon the wife and mother. And well our Scotch-Irish pioneers did their work."

Often, the frontier women had to work in the fields barefoot when moccasins were not available, and when it came to building the log cabins and churches, they helped their men-folk make a clearing in the forest by cutting down the trees.

An example of this challenge was the immigrant women from Co Antrim in the north of Ireland who helped their men-folk build Timber Ridge Presbyterian Church at Lexington in the Shenandoah Valley of Virginia in the early 1750s.

These women of Ulster extraction did 10-mile trips on horseback, through hostile Indian country to carry sand used for "lyme" in the church's construction.

During the 18th century years of American settlement, women were traditionally kept in the background of church life, with the preaching, teaching and decision-making essentially a male preserve.

Female clerics were unheard of and frowned upon by the church establishments in every denomination. Increasingly, however, by the 19th century, women in the American backcountry territories were given an active role in church-support agencies, providing financial backing for mission work, at home and abroad. But the pulpit remained out of bounds for females in most American churches until the mid-20th century, and even today this view holds sway with some congregations in Appalachian backcountry regions.

Many frontier women had to survive stark loneliness and for months and even years they bore the burden of looking after the household chores and the constant care of the children.

The loneliness and mental anguish for the women was most acute when the men were away for long periods, either working the land from dawn to dusk, hunting in the forests, on business and trading commitments or soldiering far from their homes in the locally-recruited militia units in the battles of the Revolutionary War and in the expeditions conducted against hostile Indian tribes.

Stout means of defence was a very necessary requirement on the frontier forts and townships, and very often the women fought alongside the men when they were in a tight spot.

Brandishing a long Kentucky rifle with accuracy and determination at a stockade under siege from Indians was not solely confined to males, and the tales of legendary heroines gallantly defending their home or fort and children are an integral part of frontier folklore.

On the frontier, the white European settlers faced cold and bitter winters and hot, dust bowl summers, swarms of crickets, insects of all descriptions, the wildest of animals, and tornadoes which often ripped through their wooden homes apart, and left them vulnerable.

The Rev Henry C. McCook, vividly describing the character and work ethic of the frontier women, said: "Stalwart of frame, no doubt they were, with muscles hardened under the strain of toil, hale and hearty, vigorous and strong, able to wield the axe against the trunk of a forest monarch or the head of an intruding savage; to aid their husbands and fathers to plow and plant, to reap and mow, to rake and bind and gather.

"They could wield the scutching knife or hackling comb upon flaxen stocks and fibres, as well as the rod of rebuke upon the back of a refractory child. They could work the treadle of a little spinning wheel, or swing the circumference of the great one. They could brew and bake, make and mend, sweep and scrub, rock the cradle and rule the household."

Many frontier women were married in their early teens and had families running into double figures by the time they were 30. Some never reached middle age, worn out with the incessant struggle to keep the family intact and make ends meet as their husbands worked for long hours and little financial return on the bleak and highly dangerous frontier lands.

Very often, it was difficult to distinguish between a young mother and her teenage daughters in physical attributes and looks, such was the short age span between them.

There were always fewer women than men, of course, on the American frontier and this resulted in very short courtships and hurried marriages, nearly always conducted by a church ceremony.

Arranged marriages for the benefit of land and property acquirements were not an uncommon feature of the frontier, such was the need, and perhaps greed to add to one's estate.

No women, regardless of their looks or society ranking, were single for too long, and spinsters were a very rare species in most communities. The husbands were nearly always older than their wives, very often 20 and 30 years separating them. Bachelors were much more common than spinsters in frontier communities.

Widows, just bereaved, had never too long to wait before again being "spoken for," thus the large number of frontiersmen who are recorded as having several wives due to the deaths of spouses.

Having the companionship and care of a dedicated and loving wife was a very necessary requirement for men aspiring to prosperity on the American frontier, but some males had to fend for themselves as bachelors and widowers, and for them it was a very lonely existence.

The Rev Charles Woodmason, an outspoken itinerant Anglican preacher who held a patronising High Church view of the non-conformist immigrants, made an interesting observation of Scots-Irish frontier settlements in the Carolinas during a tour of the Appalachian backcountry in the 1760s.

Woodmason said: "There is not a cabin but has ten or twelve children in it. When the boys are 18 and the girls 14 they marry—so that in many cabins you will see children—and the mother looking as young as the daughter."

Living in the bleak frontier environment, the Scots-Irish women in particular, were strong characters—self-reliant, resourceful and loyal. Devout, patient and cheerful in the midst of difficulties, they pursued with vigour the even tenor of their ways, performing with efficient diligence the duties that lay nearest them.

The elders in the church, politics and in civic society were the men, and they were the ones who took the ultimate decisions that directly affected their communities. However, the women did have considerable influence in many aspects of American frontier life, essentially in the home, in the rearing of children and in maintaining decent upright standards of life.

The contribution of the frontier women in the making of the United States of America in the 18th and early 19th century was immense, and only now is it being fully recognised in this more equitable modern society where male and female rights in most instances are equal, and more readily taken for granted.

Nancy (Anderson) Green—Steely Widow of the Frontier

This formidable Scots-Irish woman of the Carolina backcountry was born in Ballymoney, Co Antrim in the north of Ireland about 1750, of devout Presbyterian Covenanting stock, and the fascinating story of her life on the American frontier is one of tragedy, deprivation and ultimate happiness.

Nancy and her Stinson (Stephenson) family (who included brothers James and William) moved to America in 1772 under the pastoral care of feisty Presbyterian minister the Rev William Martin and they settled at Rocky Creek, a branch of the Catawba River in Chester County, South Carolina.

Just before she left her homeland, Nancy married a Co Antrim kinsman William Anderson and on arrival in South Carolina they were allocated a track of land given as bounty by the colonial authorities as inducement to emigration from Europe.

By 1773, William Anderson had built a log cabin and set about planting some Indian corn to complement the foods that he would readily find by fishing in the rivers and hunting in the forests.

Gradually, the Anderson homestead advanced in size and with three young children (Mary, Robert and William) to feed and clothe William and Nancy had to work long hours to ensure they had a reasonable level of return from what then was effectively an outer frontier region.

The Revolutionary War which had started had heightened tensions in the area and even at church worship on a Sunday the settlers were confronted with the stark choice on which they should react—either succumbing to the rule of the Crown forces or throwing in their lot with the American patriot cause.

For the Rev William Martin, an old-style Presbyterian pastor with strong views on independence for his people and a deep distrust of the British, there was only one option. "My hearers," William Martin said in his broad Ulster accent to faithful worshippers like William and Nancy Anderson, "Talk and angry words will not do. We must fight."

After hearing Rev. William Martin, William Anderson felt he had a patriotic duty to fulfill—to join the local militia and take up the fight.

His wife Nancy fully understood the predicament, but as he bade her and the children farewell at the cabin door before heading off on horseback to join the local unit, she might not have imagined that it would be the last time they would see each other.

A bout of smallpox was visited on Nancy and the family, and with William away, British dragoons stopped off to maliciously plunder on the homestead and drive off the stock in the fields.

Other cabins belonging to Scots-Irish settlers were raided in similar fashion, and the nearby Presbyterian meeting house where Rev. William Martin was pastor was burnt as a reprisal against the patriot militiamen and their supporters.

Nancy was in a hopeless position and for food she had to roast the ears of green corn, or dry the corn in milk and grate it on a rough stone into coarse meal, from which she made mush for herself and her sick children.

William Anderson, meanwhile, joined the forces of General Sumter under Captain John Steel at Clem's Branch on the east side of the Catawba River, and he fought at the battles of Williamsons, Rocky Mount, Hanging Rock and Carey's Fort.

Two months after he left, William was shot dead in a Redcoat attack on his unit. Nancy was now a widow, left alone to look after three young children. Indeed, in the small Rocky Creek neighbourhood four other women were widowed by the deaths of their husbands in battle.

Eventually, the smallpox epidemic cleared and the children recovered, but the onerous tasks of harvesting and attending to the daily painstaking chores of the home kept Nancy and the other widows fully occupied.

The stock had gone, but Nancy Anderson pulled her flax, watered and put it through the break before scuttling it with the hand-scuttle and hackling it on the coarse and fine hackle. She then carefully spun the flax in a manner she had been taught back in her north of Ireland homeland.

Nancy did receive some help from her brother William Stinson, who was engaged at the Battle of Kings Mountain and paid regular visits to Rocky Creek. He had to be very careful as British and loyalist forces were constantly passing through the area, and did regularly harass Nancy Anderson and the other women.

The food which Nancy Anderson and her children lived on over that winter was mainly bread, although occasionally a little meat was given to her by patrolling patriots, after hunting in the forests.

Nancy had to be adaptable and she learned to fish in the adjoining river and steams, using traps, and the catches she got did provide a staple and a very welcome change of diet.

Throughout her ordeal, Nancy Anderson never wavered from her strong Covenanting faith and she constantly prayed for a betterment of the situation.

This was to come in a rather unusual way in the form of the stranger Daniel Green, thought to be a soldier, who accidentally came upon on the Anderson homestead at Rocky Creek.

The tall, quite apprehensive stranger Green introduced himself to Mrs Anderson and her children and, after giving her some firm assurances about his reasons for being in the area, he was invited to partake of a meal.

Nancy and the stranger talked for hours about the extremely difficult personal plight both found themselves in, and while he said he needed to borrow a horse, there was a marked reluctance to take the lone sorrel mare which the poor widow Anderson had.

Several days elapsed and the friendship between Nancy Anderson and the stranger developed into a mutual relationship which grew stronger as time passed. Even a week on the bleak landscape of the American frontier was a lengthy period for a vulnerable widow and a soldier uncertain about his future. Nancy and Daniel had only known each other five days.

Obviously there was no time to hang around and, after borrowing a horse, the stranger rode with Nancy Anderson to the home of the local Justice John Gaston, where, after a short legal ceremony, the pair were pronounced man and wife. A dollar payment was passed over—all the money Daniel Green possessed in the world.

Mrs. Anderson became Mrs. Green in a lightning marriage which led to raised eyebrows among the strict, very conservative Presbyterian Covenanting community of Rocky Creek. Acquaintances were scandalised that Nancy had dispensed with the marital formalities laid down by the church.

In Presbyterian Covenanting tradition an intended marriage had to be published by the minister on three successive Sundays. This Nancy and Daniel Green did not do.

Nancy, however, was undeterred by the criticism. It was her judgment and personal choice that Daniel Green was a loving partner, and a suitable, caring step-father for her three young children.

Daniel was a man of commanding stature, said to be frank and honourable in his dealings, aptly disposed to trust and possessing a sound intellect. Nancy had learned that Daniel was born of a poor family background in New Jersey about 1752, which made them around the same age.

During the early part of the Revolutionary War, he had served in Canada, and moving to Philadelphia, about 30 miles from his home, he had a spell in the marines.

He returned to military service as a patriot soldier and was captured by the British and held on a prison ship at Charleston, before escaping along with a number of Scots-Irish lads from Chester, York and Lancaster counties of South Carolina.

Daniel and Nancy Green eventually overcame their adversities caused by the war, and the murmurings within the Rocky Creek community about the standing of their hurried marriage within church confines. Their prosperity increased, but they had no children and Daniel lovingly treated Nancy's daughter and two sons as his own.

Daniel joined Nancy as a committed churchgoer and he repaired the Presbyterian church at Beckhamville, which was damaged in the war, and built an ornate granite wall around the burial ground. Daniel did not belong to any particular denomination, unlike his wife, but he was highly esteemed by members of different faiths as an excellent man, a sincere Christian.

Nancy lived until she was 77, passing away in June 1827 after a lengthy illness. Daniel, on the day of her funeral, remarked that they had been together for 50 years and had tasted real happiness.

"We have been blessed in our basket and our store, flourishing like a green bay tree beside the waters, but this is not our abiding place. How soon I too may go the way of all living; I know not," he said.

Daniel survived Nancy by only a few weeks. He was a man in his late seventies and had grown very tired nursing and watching his ailing wife in her final days. A severe attack of fever led to his death.

Funeral arrangements for Daniel were made by his step-son William Anderson, a highly respected colonel in the American militia. Just before Nancy's death, William had gone to the spot where his father William had been buried and removed the remains to where he expected soon to open a grave for his mother.

Heavy rains had resulted in the original burying ground being flooded with the bones of people buried there being brought to the surface. It was a harrowing experience and extremely distressful to Nancy Anderson Green when she was told. But due to her very poor state of health, she was unable to be present at the transfer with other family members.

In a quiet reserved spot near the banks of the Catawba River which flows through the beautiful countryside straddling South Carolina and North Carolina, Nancy Anderson is buried between her two soldier husbands, alongside her children, grandchildren and great-grandchildren.

Nancy was most certainly a woman of extraordinary character and courage, typical of those who settled in the 18th century American frontier, and against great odds made a settled home and reared a family.

The *James and Mary* was one of five vessels which that year carried 467 families (more than 1,000 people) of Covenanting (Reformed Presbyterian) stock from Co Antrim to America on an historic passage arranged and led by Rev. William Martin.

James Stinson was a militia captain under Colonel John Sevier at the Battle of Kings Mountain in October 7, 1780, and his brother William also fought there.

William Stinson is listed on a memorial to 65 Revolutionary War soldiers from Rev. William Martin's Catholic Presbyterian Church at Chester County, South Carolina. Most of the soldiers were either north of Ireland born or first or second generation Ulster-Scots.

Maritime records show that James Stinson, Nancy's brother, emigrated from Larne in Co Antrim to Charleston in South Carolina on August 25, 1782 on the *James and Mary* sailing ship.

MARY NEELY—EXTRAORDINARY WOMAN WHO DEFIED HER INDIAN CAPTIVES

The survival of young Mary Neely after being captured by Indians on the death of her father is an extraordinary story which aptly epitomises the determination and courage of settlers on the 18th century American frontier.

Mary was the fourth of a family of ten children, born to William and Margaret (Patterson) Neely near the French Broad River in North Carolina in 1761. The family was of Ulster and Welsh extraction, having emigrated a few years earlier.

William Neely was a restless adventurous man who set his sights on acquiring new land in the Tennessee territory, then belonging to North Carolina. With six other pioneers he headed in the direction of the Cumberland River in mid-Tennessee by means of a large canoe, which he had built from a large poplar tree.

After selling his possessions in North Carolina, William moved in 1779 with 96 cattle and 40 horses from the French Broad River to a point on the Cumberland River, about twelve miles east of present-day Nashville, which he settled and called Neely's Bend. William's teenage daughter Mary travelled with him in the canoe on the perilous river journey through hostile Indian country, while the rest of the family arrived by land.

William Neely was obviously a leader in this frontier settlement, for his counsel was sought in every enterprise, especially when danger protruded from an Indian attack.

In the first year of the settlement William Neely and his people had to live on meat, vegetables and fruit, as their little stock of flour and meal had run out. It was while engaged in corn producing that an incident occurred which led to William's death and changed the whole course of Mary's life.

About 30 of the men from the settlement were at a spring, two and a half miles from the fort, making salt and clearing off ground for cultivation the next year. They appeared relaxed, as no sign of Indians had been noticed for quite some time.

Two hours before sunset, William told the men to return to the fort and he and Mary would stay there alone. Some of the men protested, fearful it was too dangerous to leave him and 19-year-old Mary so exposed, but William was a person without fear and he stayed behind with his daughter.

Indians, however, were lurking in the trees watching the operations, and they pounced shortly after the men had gone, fatally wounding William with a tomahawk blow to the head. Mary stood helpless, shouting frantically to her father to reach for his gun.

She fainted with the shock of the attack and the mortal blow on her father, and when she regained consciousness a few minutes later she realised two Indians were dragging her into towards their canoe.

That fateful memory of those few minutes remained with Mary for the rest of her life, and later when she returned to the white settlements she would describe it as the saddest day of her life.

Mary was taken north of the Cumberland River to an Indian reservation in Kentucky, and she was to spend the next few years in the custody of her captors.

Initially, Mary thought she would suffer the same fate as her father, but death did not materialise, and after deliberations at an Indian council it was decided to offer her the choice of either becoming the wife of a young tribesman or a servant to the chief.

She chose the latter—the idea of becoming wife of the one who may have murdered her father appalled Mary, and to her surprise, the decision she made was honoured.

For a month after her father died, Mary could not shed a tear, and continually watched by the Indians, she longed for her freedom. Even when she was being taken away from the Cumberland region to the reservation, she managed to carve marks on trees to guide those who might pursue, or set a guide to her if she managed to escape.

A favourite past-time of the Indians in the evening was to get out the scalps they had taken and dry them in front of the fire. Mary, as she watched their barbarous actions, must have been horrified that perhaps her father's scalp was one of those being paraded in front of her.

As time passed, the watch on Mary became more relaxed, and one night, while encamped under a beech tree she took the opportunity to escape. She climbed on to the branches of the tree and hid, but the Indians were alerted to her presence, and she was promptly returned to her post.

In the first winter of her capture smallpox afflicted a large number in the reservation, and Mary too was smitten, with sores appearing all over her body. During the epidemic the Indian meat supplies ran out, and they were all forced to drink bear oil, of which the tribes always seemed to carry a supply.

Revolted by its taste, Mary, however, did not partake of the oil and for days she starved, getting by only on pieces of white oak bark which she peeled with the knife that she had carried since her capture.

The Indians, by character, divide whatever they have with their prisoners, and when a bear was killed Mary was given her share. On one occasion, Mary shot a deer with her gun, and the meat from the animal was gratefully devoured by the hungry tribe members.

Over the winter, Mary Neely made several unsuccessful attempts to escape, and by the spring the journeying had resumed for the tribes, heading for most of that year in a north easterly direction towards Indiana, Detroit and Michigan. Reluctantly, Mary was dragged with them, and she endured great hardships, as the weather deteriorated on the advent of a second winter.

At Michigan, the Indians camped close to a French stockade after passing through British lines, and friendships were developed which led to a bartering of goods between the two groups.

It was there that Mary seized the opportunity to prepare a getaway, with the help of a Frenchman, who had befriended her and was on familiar terms with the Indian chief.

The Frenchman decided on a plan which would involve giving the Indians a gallon of whiskey ("fire water" to the tribes!) to drink in a container which he knew servant Mary would be tasked by the chief to return to its owner at the fort.

The Indians drank merrily, and as expected, Mary was ordered to return the vessel to its owner. It was her big chance to escape, and on arrival at the stockade she was hurriedly directed to the home of the Frenchman's mother, who at first concealed her in the cellar.

When they realised that Mary had gone, the Indians arrived at the stockade demanding to know where she was, but her French collaborators were not for giving her up. After spending a few days in the cellar, she was concealed in another part of the house.

Following a long search the Indians eventually gave up, and to ensure her safety Mary, was sent to an offshore island near the Canadian borders, where 90 other people of similar plight to her were detained by the British as prisoners of war.

Mary's plight was just as desperate as it had been in the custody of the Indians, and the urge for complete freedom burned up in her.

After some time being spent at sea in a prison ship on Lake Ontario and Lake Chaplain, Mary saw another escape route and with two girls and an old man began heading south.

The journey was long and trying, but her incessant struggle to be free remained and after completing hundreds of miles, she eventually made it to Philadelphia in Pennsylvania.

There, Mary met a family called Hiddle, who were heading for the Shenandoah Valley of Virginia via the Susquehanna River, and they agreed to let her join them on the trek, on the condition that she should help drive the stock.

The Hiddles and Mary reached their Shenandoah destination in mid-winter—Mary's third since she was taken captive—and she got lodging with a family called Spears, where she was employed as a servant. There, Mary at last felt safe from molestation by the Indians, and for the first time in three years she enjoyed the luxury of sleeping in a bed.

Throughout the period of her detention Mary's brother never ceased in his search for her, although she was given up for dead by other family members. During her three-year absence, Mary's mother and several brothers were killed by the Indians, but one faithful brother kept searching in Tennessee, Kentucky, Virginia and Pennsylvania.

It was an almost impossible mission, but, luckily, while in the Susquehanna River region Mary's brother learned of a young woman who had been held captive by Indians and was now staying at the home of "the old man Spears." Mary was left-handed and her brother was able to use this as a lead to her whereabouts.

On arrival at the Spears' home, the brother was told Mary was at church. It was the Sabbath and she had gone to the morning service with Mrs. Spears and her daughter. On their return, the brother immediately recognised his sister and for Mary too it was a moment of great joy, as they warmly embraced.

Within a few days Mary and her brother set out, on one horse, for Carpenters' Station in Lincoln County, Kentucky, where an older sister was waiting, and other relatives. It was too dangerous to head back to Neely's Bend in Middle Tennessee, with Indian tribes circling the region.

Mary's sister later married a son of the Spears gentleman whom Mary had stayed with in Virginia, and Mary's husband ituation allowed one of the Neely brothers to re-settle his father's farmlands.

Mary (Neely) Spears during her stay with the Indians gained a considerable knowledge of how to treat diseases in the frontier's changing climates and, seeing a great human need, this allowed her to develop a meaningful role as a physician. She had particular expertise in dealing with white swelling (a hip disease) and chronic sores.

The reputation of Mary Neely in caring for the sick, handling the medications of the day and in service generally soon extended far and wide, and her work was acknowledged by eminent doctors in Kentucky.

It was said that Mary never despaired of finding a cure for the worst cases that presented themselves, and, remarkably, she enjoyed a large measure of success. She was very methodical in her habits and prescribed only a minimum of medicines, contending that nature was the best remedy.

Mary had been a member of the Baptist church for most of her life, and it was said her deportment was always that of a genuine Christian, showing charity to others and holding firm to the faith that had been passed on to her by God-fearing parents.

There was no church organisation in central Illinois when Mary and George settled there in the early 1820s, and they and other pioneers established the Clary Grove Baptist church at their log cabin home.

It is believed to have been the first settled church in central Illinois. George Spears, meanwhile, raised a militia unit to protect the region from Indian attack, and he and his men served with Andrew Jackson in the War of 1812-14 against the British.

The couple continued to live in Green County, Kentucky until 1824, when they sold up and moved to Sangamon, Illinois, then a wild and sparsely populated region. Indians still remained in the area, but they were much more peaceful and spent most of their time hunting and fishing.

Mary still practiced her "doctoring", as professional medical help was almost non-existent on this part of the American frontier in the early 19th century. She cared for patients who even travelled from Missouri and Iowa.

Some dismissed Mary as a "quack," but out of a social consciousness she felt she was doing a duty that was incumbent upon her in an isolated community she was so much a part of—to help make well those stricken with infirmity and disease. George Spears died in 1838, after a marriage lasting more than 50 years and Mary was left with her oldest daughter and youngest son.

In 1843, Mary, by now 82, returned to Neely's Creek homestead to visit her 78-year-old brother whom she had not seen for more than 30 years, and so emotional was the reunion that she stayed there for a month.

Mary (Neely) Spears was on personal speaking terms with Abraham Lincoln, later to become President. The friendship developed in the 1830s when Abraham Lincoln was resident and postmaster of Salem, Illinois. Mr. Lincoln never tired of hearing Mary relate the experiences and deprivations of being held captive by the Indians.

Mary died in January 1852, reaching the age of 90 years, five months and 26 days.

Her tragic and eventful life was indeed remarkable and, considering the terrible ordeals she came through as a young woman, it is incredible that she lived to such an age. Mary (Neely) Spears was in the finest traditions of the American frontier woman!

Hardy Frontierswomen who Became Real Heroines of the War

Scots-Irish womenfolk of the Appalachian backcountry performed significant heroics during the Revolutionary War, and many went beyond their normal call of domestic duty in the home to ensure that their husbands, sons and brothers in the American patriot militia units received all the back-up they needed in resources.

Margaret Catherine (Kate) Barry, from Walnut Grove, Spartanburg in South Carolina, is considered one of the outstanding heroines of the

Revolutionary War, for the part she played in saving lives during the Battle of Cowpens in January 1781.

Kate Barry was the daughter of Co Antrim couple Charles and Mary Barry Moore, who emigrated to America in about 1750. She was a woman of hardy resolve, married at 15 to Captain Andrew Barry, who was also from a Scots-Irish family that had settled in the Tyger River region of South Carolina.

Andrew Barry was a captain of the South Carolina Rangers during the War and he commanded militia companies at the battles of Fishing Creek, Musgrove's Mill (where he was wounded!) and at Cowpens.

The couple had eleven children, five sons and six daughters, and Kate performed duties as a volunteer scout and guide for the South Carolina Piedmont patriots, always acting in support of her husband. Her scouting operations centered mainly in Spartanburg County, and being an excellent horsewoman, she was able to cover the thick wooded terrain and Indian trails with speed of movement.

Kate frequently rode to where the patriots were camped to warn of impending danger, and with the help of a black slave Uncle Cato, she completed many successful scouting operations. Hollow trees would be filled with corn to provide against food shortages. Very often, after raids by British forces, settler homes were left destitute and the corn caches in the trees were used to feed the people and the animals.

This highly motivated frontierswoman even engaged in rounding up militia troops when reinforcements were required. At the battle of Cowpens she took responsibility for gathering up patriot groups and moving them to strategic points in the frontline of battle.

Her husband was holding the line with General Andrew Pickens against the British Redcoat troops under the command of Banastre Tarleton, a Merseysider from the north of England, whose butchery made him a much reviled figure in the Scots-Irish communities of Charlotte and the Waxhaws.

As the battle ensured at Cowpens, the women of Nazareth Presbyterian Church, 13 miles away, were assembled in a house near the church, and a vigilant Kate Barry was at the shoals on the Tyger River, waiting for reports from the battlefield.

When news of the crushing victory for the patriots was passed along, she rushed to the Church to inform the women. At Cowpens, 926 of Tarleton's troops were killed, captured or wounded and many armaments were taken. On the American side, 132 were killed and 60 wounded.

On another occasion when the British, led by "Bloody Bill" Cunningham, made an infamous raid into the area, Kate heard them across the river near her father's home at Walnut Grove. She tied her two-year-old daughter Catherine (Little Katie) to a bed post for safety and rode to her husband's company for help. Her action forced the British to retreat.

Once, when the Redcoats came to Kate's home demanding to know the whereabouts of Andrew Barry's company, she refused to co-operate and was tied up and struck three times with a leash. This attack angered the men of her husband's company, for it was said any one of them would have given his own life to save hers.

Again, on a separate front, with the British in hot pursuit, Kate swam her horse across the Pacolet River near Hurricane Shoals. Fortunately, the water rose to a high level just as Kate and the horse reached dry ground on the other side, thus preventing the British from capturing her and the important message that she carried.

The heroic deeds of Kate Barry have been part of South Carolina folklore for more than 200 years, and today her memory is revered by many people of the Spartanburg and Greenville areas.

Kate's nephew was Senator William Taylor Barry, who was President Andrew Jackson's postmaster general in the White House, after soldiering with Jackson in the War of 1812-13. He was also United States minister to Spain.

MARY POLLY FINLAY CROCKETT

The mother of pretty Mary Polly Finlay, a Scots-Irish lass from East Tennessee, had ambitions that her daughter would marry a husband more settled and of greater substance than the intrepid David (Davy) Crockett, who was keeping her company.

Polly's love, however, for this highly colourful and courageous frontiersman overcame her mother's doubts, and in a short but reasonably happy marriage which lasted almost ten years (1806-15), the couple flitted from various homes, through East and into Middle and West Tennessee.

Polly's parents were both of Scots-Irish immigrant families and her father William had been on expeditions with Daniel Boone in the Carolinas and Kentucky.

From first sight, Davy, who had earlier courted another young woman Margaret Elder, was in love with Polly, and he admitted that he was "plaguy well pleased with her from the word go."

David was 20 and Polly a few years younger when they married on a license issued in Dandridge courthouse in East Tennessee on August 12, 1806. The marriage was solemnised a few days later by a preacher after a few traditional frontier customs were observed.

Davy's brothers and a few friends approached the Finlay home on his behalf with an empty jug. If Polly's father filled it up, this was the sign that he approved of the marriage, and to Davy's delight the match was made when his friends came back with a pitcher overflowing. A wedding gift was two cows with calves.

The Crockett marriage produced three children, sons John Wesley and William and daughter Margaret Polly, but life was exceedingly difficult in the wooded wilderness of the Tennessee frontier for delicate and frail Polly.

Davy was for ever roaming the Tennessee forests and the mountains, leaving Polly alone for long periods with the children. It was a lonely, and at times a bleak existence in the rural hills of Tennessee in the early 19th century.

For the first few years of the marriage, they lived on a small rented farm at Bay's Mountain in Jefferson County, East Tennessee near Polly's father's spring settlement, but they struggled to make ends meet, and Davy was convinced their best hope was to move west to more fertile land.

Polly, it was said, kept a comfortable home within the meagre means, and David could at least feed her and the children from his hunting in the forests and rivers, but there was little or no money to pay the rent, much less for the bare necessities of a home.

In 1811, they made the long 150-mile trek over the Cumberland Mountain plateau and took up residence at an attractive spot near the head-quarters of Mulberry Creek, a branch of the Elk River at Maury County in Middle Tennessee.

Davy and Polly then moved to territory straddling Franklin County and Lincoln County, Tennessee, near the Alabama line, to eventually set up a home at Bean's Creek, near the present-day town of Winchester, which they called "Kentuck."

There, on the Mulberry fork of the Elk River tributary of the mighty Tennessee River, Davy marked his initials on a beach tree and laid out a five-acre claim on state land, and built a cabin home. This was great hunting country, and Davy was able to indulge his passion as never before.

Unfortunately, the many home moves and the natural hardship Polly faced during cold and wet winters on the frontier sapped her energy and strength, and several months after giving birth to daughter Margaret, she died a very young woman in her late twenties, leaving David to care for three very small children.

Before Polly's death, Davy had been soldiering as a "mounted gunman" in the American army, battling with the Creek Indians at Fort Strother and Fort Taladega and encountering British troops in the Florida campaign, and it was on leave for the birth of the third child that he found her in sickly condition.

No definite cause of death was established and historians say it may have been either typhoid or cholera. The illness, in the summer of 1815, lasted several weeks and when she died, a distraught Davy buried her on a hill near the cabin at Bean's Creek in Franklin County, Tennessee.

The gravestone, erected by the Tennessee Historical Commission, remembers Polly thus: "Polly Finlay Crockett. Born 1788 in Hamblen County. Married to David Crockett August 12, 1806. Mother of John Wesley Crockett—1807. William Crockett—1809. Margaret Finlay Crockett—1812. Died 1815."

Polly Finlay was very close to Davy Crockett's heart and it was said by associates that he "ever after" held the memory of his "tender and loving wife."

Within a year, however, David Crockett married again, to a widow Elizabeth Patton, mother of two children whose husband had been killed in the Creek War of 1812. Elizabeth, like Davy and Polly Finley, was also of a Scots-Irish background.

Elizabeth was of a good family background from North Carolina and owned a sizeable farm which helped Davy increase his social status in the frontier community.

But although he had taken on another wife and two more children, Davy's wandering lust and love of the wild frontier persisted, coupled with a blossoming political career which made him not just a Tennessee celebrity, but a great national hero in Washington.

In 1854, 18 years after Davy's violent death at The Alamo in Texas in March, 1836, Elizabeth Patton Crockett moved to the Lone Star state—on land allocated to the family in lieu of heroic services at The Alamo, and she died there in 1860, aged 72.

Davy Crockett is remembered at his Limestone cabin birthplace at Greene County in East Tennessee alongside the Big Limestone and Nolichuckey Rivers thus: "Pioneer, Patriot, Soldier, Explorer, State Legislator, Congressman. Martyred at The Alamo. 1786-1836."

Rachel (Donelson) Jackson—Frontierswoman and President's Wife

The extreme harshness of the American frontier during the late 18th century made life very difficult for women young and old as they struggled to keep pace with the enormous challenges encountered by their men-folk in what was a wooded and mountainous wilderness.

Rachel Donelson, who later became the wife of the seventh United States President Andrew Jackson, was only twelve when she and members of her family and Scots-Irish associates embarked on one of the most daunting and perilous journeys in America's early history.

For a girl as young, intelligent and lively as the dark-haired Rachel, the arduous and highly dangerous Holston River voyage to the Cumberland River in Middle Tennessee region in 1780 obviously left a lasting impression, and the harrowing experience was indeed character-building for the numerous personal trials she was to face later in her life.

Rachel (Donelson) Jackson was born in 1767 in Pittsylvania County, Virginia after her parents had moved there from the eastern side of the state where they were married.

John Donelson, Rachel's father was a land-owner and huntsman/surveyor in Virginia and North Carolina who became a leader of the Watauga community which settled during the 1770s on the Holston River of what today is North East Tennessee.

The Wataugans, led by another Scots-Irishman James Robertson, were a hardy, tough breed of people who had the insatiable urge to keep pushing the frontier westwards to new settlements, across the Allegheny Mountains—even against the advice of British land agents who feared the inevitable conflict with the native American tribes. In that region, the Indian tribes were the Cherokees and the Chickasaws.

John Donelson and James Robertson combined with a North Carolina lawyer and agent Richard Henderson to make an assault on new lands on the Cumberland River several hundred miles west. The plans were first prepared in 1777, and Robertson led an exploratory team there over a two-year period, before the decision was taken to move.

A 3,000-acre land grant was negotiated with Richard Henderson, and arrangements were made for the movement of these families who were prepared to risk all to start a new life in a far-distant rugged wilderness.

The journey was split with James Robertson assigned to lead 200 men and boys with their animals (horses, cows, pigs and sheep) and other belongings on the Kentucky route, along the Wilderness Road and through the Cumberland Gap.

John Donelson, with the welfare of his wife Rachel and young daughter Rachel and his nine other children uppermost in his thoughts, led, with male comrades, the 400 women and children on a flotilla of flat boats from Fort Patrick Henry along the Holston River to the Cumberland River and the new settlement of Fort Nashborough, later to be named Nashville.

River travel, because of the obvious dangers of attack from Indians, was not a favoured mode of communication in that part of the Appalachian frontier, but the Wataugan people felt it was there no other option.

It was an extremely cold winter—said to be coldest in living memory in North Carolina, and the Tennessee territory with the deep snow and frozen rivers making the journey for both parties extremely hazardous. But, with dogged determination they persevered, and by Christmas week of 1779, Robertson and his men had arrived at their destination.

They were worn out by the rigours of the journey, but began almost immediately to erect log cabins and cleared stretches of land for the arrival of John Donelson and the families in the spring. The Cumberland River was frozen over, and the animal stock had to be drive across rock solid ice.

The Donelson-piloted party moved in an armada of 40 small flat boats and canoes, moving slowly along the Holston River. The largest boat, *Adventure*, had 30 families on board, including James Robertson's wife Charlotte and five children and John Donelson's own family, his wife Rachel and the children including young Rachel.

It was a journey into the unknown for the families; along unchartered waters; over dangerous shoals, rapids and falls; through territory occupied by hostile Indian tribes and in weather conditions well below zero temperatures.

After only three miles the voyage was halted; ice and snow and cold had set in and the frozen river made progress impossible. There was no movement until mid-February, and when the boats were eventually cut loose, they were hampered again by the swell of the river due to incessant heavy rain.

Several boats sank and some of the voyagers took ill from smallpox and died. As they passed the Chickamauga Indian settlements the boats came under attack from tribesmen massed on the shore. There were casualties on both sides, with settlers countering the Indian assaults with sniper fire from their long Kentucky rifles.

Most of the boats got through, beyond the danger points, and by the beginning of spring they were at the mouth of the Tennessee River and the high water of the Ohio River. They faced difficult upstream currents, and progress was further hampered, when they had to stop and make camp to replenish dwindling food supplies by hunting buffalo and bear in the adjoining woods.

The last lap of the journey came via the Cumberland River, and on Monday, April 24, when the party reached French Salt Lick, site of present-day down-town Nashville, there was a hearty welcome from James Robertson and his men who had prepared well for the arrival.

When they reached Fort Nashborough in 1780, John Donelson settled his family on fertile bottom land, a few miles from the fort, but this was dangerous territory, and with a scarcity of grain and food for the winter, they moved to a more settled area at Harrodsburg, Kentucky in the fall (autumn) of that year.

In 1785, Rachel, in her 18th year, married Lewis Robards, who was from a good family in Mercer County, Kentucky. But it was a relationship which lasted only a few years, and Rachel returned to be with her mother, who had moved back to live near Nashville after the murder of her husband in 1786 by persons unknown on the road between Nashville and Kentucky.

The death of John Donelson was a severe blow to his family, and it was at her mother's home that Rachel met a young lawyer from North Carolina, Andrew Jackson, who was staying as a boarding guest.

The friendship developed and in August, 1791 the pair were married at Natchez, but the marriage to Lewis Robards was never officially wound up, which meant Rachel unwittingly committed bigamy when she wed Andrew Jackson.

Robards had filed divorce proceedings to the Virginia legislature, but dropped these without telling Rachel and it was an inconclusive arrangement that was to haunt Mrs Jackson in later years.

By September 1793, Robards did manage to get his divorce, after charging that it was his wife who had deserted him and she was living an "adulterous relationship" with another man. The charge was not contested, and Rachel and Andrew went through another marriage ceremony, quietly in Nashville in January, 1794.

Rachel came with a settlement of her late father's estate, which included household articles valued $433.33 and two black slaves. The couple had no children, but they had a very happy 27-year marriage, even though the latter few years were marred by allegations made by political opponents of Andrew over the legality of their marriage, after Rachel's break-up with Lewis Robards.

During the early years of the marriage, Andrew Jackson was a lawyer, circuit judge, land speculator, farmer and businessman. He later moved into politics, was a soldier of national renown especially for his victory over the British at the Battle of New Orleans in 1815, and eventually, he became president, to serve two terms in Washington from 1828 to 1836.

From a life as a child and teenager in the harsh Tennessee and Kentucky frontier wilderness, Rachel's personal circumstances improved immeasurably, and in the several large plantation homes where they lived, her role was more supervisory of the housekeeping and manual duties which were carried out by the black slaves.

She hosted regularly gatherings for members of the large family circle and Jackson's political and business friends, but she fretted much over her husband's long absences from home, due to his exploits as a soldier and politician.

In 1808, they adopted one of twin sons born to her sister-in-law Elizabeth Donelson and, eventually, Andrew Jackson Jr. was made President Jackson's heir.

Tragically, Rachel Jackson died a few weeks after Andrew was elected for his first four-year term as President. It came soon after the death of another adopted child, 16-year-old Indian son Lyncoya, and the devastated Rachel's condition rapidly deteriorated on learning of the vicious accusations of "bigamy and adultery," made against her during the Presidential campaign of 1828.

Rachel was heartbroken that she should be targeted in this way and, within a few weeks, her physical and mental condition had considerably worsened. Although Andrew tried frantically to revive her, she died on December 22, 1828.

She was buried in the garden of their Hermitage home outside Nashville on Christmas Eve. Among the pall-bearers at the funeral was Sam Houston, then governor of Tennessee and a close associate of Jackson.

For several days, the incoming president was inconsolable and he told his aides that "a loss so great can be compensated by no earthly gift". He had to prepare for the trip to Washington, to begin his Presidency, but until the day he died in 1845, Andrew grieved for a wife who was so close and dear to him.

Andrew's love for his wife, over thirty three years of marriage, was evident by the inscription he placed on Rachel's tomb.

It was said he kept his pistols polished and in condition for instant use against anyone who cast a shadow of discredit or doubt on the honour of the woman he loved with "such single-minded, fierce and gentle devotion."

The inscription on Rachel's tombstone read: "Here lies the remains of Mrs. Rachel Jackson, wife of President Jackson, who died 22nd December, 1928, aged 61. Her face was fair; her person pleasing, her temper amiable and her heart kind.

"She delighted in relieving the wants of her fellow creatures and cultivated that divine pleasure by the most liberal and unpretending methods; to the poor she was a benefactor; to the rich an example; to the wretched a comforter; to the prosperous an ornament; her piety want hand in hand with her benevolence, and she thanked her creator for being permitted to do good.

"A being so gentle and yet so virtuous, slander might wound, but not dishonour. Even death when he bore her from the arms of her husband, could but transport her to the bosom of her God."

Eliza (McCardle) Johnson—Devoted Wife who Taught her President Husband

Eliza McCardle Johnson, wife of President Andrew Johnson, was a teenager in the small East Tennessee mountain town of Greeneville when she first met her husband.

Andrew, like Eliza of Scots-Irish immigrant stock, could not read or write and had hardly been a day at school before he met Eliza. But she taught him, romance blossomed and Andrew rose to become mayor of Greeneville, governor of Tennessee, a U.S. Senator and 17th president of the United States on the assassination of President Abraham Lincoln.

Eliza McCardle, only daughter of John and Sarah Phillips McCardle, was born at Leesburg, Tennessee in 1810, and her shoemaker father died when she was a small child, leaving her to be raised on a meagre income by her mother, who was skilled at making quilts.

Local folklore in Greeneville relates that one day in September, 1826, Eliza was chatting with classmates from the Rhea Academy when she saw young Andrew, his mother Mary "Polly" (Johnson) Dougherty, her second husband Turner Dougherty and an older brother trek into the town with sparse belongings on board a little one-horse wagon.

They had just crossed the Great Smoky Mountains from the Carolinas in search of a new home, and they found Greeneville on the Nolichuckey River in East Tennessee an enterprising, welcoming town, then with a population of 500.

It was love at first sight, and they were married the following May—Andrew at 19 and Eliza, tall with hazel eyes, brown hair and a good figure, at 16. Eliza was modest and retiring, highly esteemed and "regarded as a model woman by all who knew her."

With Eliza's basic education at Rhea Academy, she began tutoring Andrew in reading, spelling and mathematics and, even when he acquired work as a tailor, she continued to read aloud to him in his shop. She worked hard to smooth his manners and his speech qualities.

Eliza realised that Andrew was rough around the edges, but possessed a keen and engaging mind, a strong will and an unyielding Scots-Irish trait of self-determination.

The lessons eventually paid off and Andrew's stature rose as a citizen and local politician in a frontier town, largely inhabited by Scots-Irish Presbyterian residents.

He became a tailor at the A. Johnson Tailor Shop on Main Street in Greeneville Andrew made coats for $3.50, pants for $1.50, vests for $3.50 and suits for $10. The business flourished, with Eliza a real driving force behind her husband.

Encouraged by his wife, who helped him increase his public speaking abilities, Andrew Johnson was elevated first as a town alderman in Greeneville, and then he became mayor in 1834.

By 1853 he was governor of Tennessee, and on taking office, he immediately gave his enthusiastic backing to public education in the state. Indeed, public schools in Tennessee received funding for the first time in his first term as governor.

Johnson was reported to have said in his later life: "If I had been educated in early life, I would have been a schoolmaster. But I feel proud that I was proprietor of my own shop."

Through Eliza's influence, Andrew Johnson had good reason to say "God bless women."

The marriage between Andrew and Eliza lasted for almost 50 years, and they had five children (three sons Charles, Robert and Andrew Jr. and two daughters Martha and Mary—all born in Greeneville). Ill-health plagued Eliza for a large part of her life, and although he frequently was away from home for long periods, Andrew remained a faithful husband.

Associates were convinced the relationship was an extremely happy one, the firm foundations obviously made by Eliza during the early years when Andrew required educational tutoring.

Eliza's health had deteriorated by the time Andrew had reached the White House in Washington in 1865, and she was so weakened by tuberculosis that she made only two public appearances, as a semi-invalid, during his four years of Presidential service.

Her elder daughter Martha Johnson Patterson carried out the First Lady duties, and Eliza rarely emerged for public engagements from her second-floor room in the White House.

Andrew Johnson's pro-Union stance during the American Civil War alienated him from Confederate supporters in the Southern states, and in the summer of 1862 his home in Greeneville was seized for use as a military hospital. Eliza had to move to the home of her daughter Mary in Carter County, Tennessee, and later to Murfreesboro in Middle Tennessee.

Despite her ailments, Eliza was very proud of her husband's rise to national recognition, as American vice-president and president. She had good reason to be, as her tutorship in the early years of their marriage stood Andrew in good stead.

When Andrew faced impeachment by the House of Representatives in 1868 for alleged crimes and misdemeanors in his handling of the defeated Confederacy, Eliza remained convinced of his innocence.

She predicted that the Senate trial would completely vindicate her husband, as it did—failing to get the necessary two-thirds approval.

One of their daughters Martha Patterson was hostess at White House functions, and she made it clear to the President's aides: "We are plain folks from Tennessee, called here by national calamity. I trust too much will not be expected of us in a social way."

To underline the family's humble backcountry roots, Martha installed two Jersey cows on the lawn of the White House to supply fresh milk and butter. She even replaced the House carpets with simple muslin.

While Eliza remained in the private quarters of the White House, she still remained the matriarch of the family and, being an avid reader, she collected newspaper and magazine articles which she thought would be of interest and assistance to Andrew in fulfilling his presidential duties.

The Johnsons returned to Tennessee in 1868 when Andrew failed to secure the Democratic Party nomination for another term, but he did resume his political career in 1874 by becoming the first president to be elected to the Senate. His health also was in decline and he did not complete his term of office.

Eliza McCardle Johnson survived her husband by only six months. She died in January 1876, aged 65, and both were buried in Greeneville, Tennessee. Today, in Greeneville the memory of Andrew and Eliza Johnson is perpetuated at their pleasant Main Street home.

Mary Patton—Gunpowder Maker for the Frontier Patriot Militias

Mary Patton became a heroine in the Appalachian backcountry for the daring role she played as gunpowder maker for the American patriots during the Revolutionary War.

Mary McKeehan was English-born of Scottish parentage, and she married Ulster Presbyterian settler John Patton in 1772 when their families were living in eastern Pennsylvania and he was a private in the local militia.

Her father, David, taught Mary the art of powder-making when they lived in England, and she passed the skills on to her husband John in his role as a militia man and general merchant.

At the start of the Revolutionary War, John and Mary moved with their two children from Cumberland County, Pennsylvania to the Overmountain region of Sycamore Shoals-Elizabethtown in North Carolina, which today is part of the state of Tennessee.

There, in partnership with another Scots-Irish settler Andrew Taylor, they established a gunpowder mill along the lines of the operation they ran at Carlisle township in Pennsylvania and found a ready business with the local militia, of which Taylor was connected.

Mary, looked upon as a redoubtable woman of steely character and courage, became a celebrated folk heroine of the hardy Overmountain settlers in the Tennessee/North Carolina territory. She was held in the highest esteem for the role she played in the war.

On one occasion when she was returning home alone on horseback, after delivering a consignment of black powder, a masked man rode out in front of her and demanded her money. She promptly said that her husband was some distance behind, carrying the money, and when the bandit hesitated Mary spurred her horse and reached home safely. On her trips, Mary would shoe the horse herself, and when the journey was complete she would remove the shoes to save them for another day.

After the Revolutionary War, Mary continued to make the gunpowder for militia units, riding as far as South Carolina, Virginia and Georgia to sell the powder for about a dollar a pound. She was a real expert when it came to powder making, simply with the use of a large black kettle and the relevant substances.

The processes in the manufacture of black gunpowder were the production of saltpeter and charcoal, and in the thriving cottage industry operation of the Patton household mill, much hand-labour was needed. The powder was packed in lots of 25, 50 and 100 pound kegs and transported to the battle lines on horse-drawn carts.

Mary supplied 500 pounds of black gunpowder to the 850 Overmountain militia soldiers from Sycamore Shoals, who fought at the Battle of Kings Mountain in South Carolina on October 7, 1780.

Her highly potent mix was an essential ingredient in securing a highly significant victory over the British Redcoats for the Overmountain Men, who consisted mainly of Scots-Irish settler farmers from the Watauga community in the North Carolina/Tennessee territory.

Three Pattons—Robert, Thomas and Matthew, all of them from a Scots-Irish background—are listed as having fought at the Battle of Kings Mountain, a decisive encounter for the American patriots in the War.

Mary Patton taught other members of her family and the wider kin to manufacture gunpowder, and the celebrated Patton mill continued in production for upwards of a century to the latter half of the 19th century. The land on which the powder mill was situated stayed in the family until the early 1960s.

Gunpowder supplies from the Patton mill were used by the Confederate Army units in the Appalachian states during the American Civil War.

A large black kettle, belonging to Mary Patton for use in her powder-making, is a prized artifact of the Massengill Museum of the Overmountain History at Rocky Mount in North East Tennessee.

Mary Patton died on December 15, 1836, aged 85, and she is buried on Tennessee soil in the Patton-Simmons Cemetery at Sycamore Shoals near Johnson City.

ELIZABETH PAXTON HOUSTON—MOTHER OF A GREAT AMERICAN LUMINARY

Elizabeth Paxton Houston, mother of Tennessee and Texas Governor Sam Houston, was made of a steely resolve needed for the arduous frontier life in the Shenandoah Valley of Virginia and East Tennessee during the late 18th century and early 19th century.

This mother of nine children—six sons and three daughters, Sam was the fifth child—was a member of a Scots-Irish family—the Paxtons, who, like the Houstons, moved from the north of Ireland to America during the mid-18th century.

Elizabeth was a very devout Presbyterian, who according to records of the time was "gifted with intellectual and moral qualities" above that of most women on the frontier. It was said her life was characterised by "purity and benevolence."

During the Revolutionary War, Sam Houston's father Sam had served as captain, paymaster and later major in Morgan's Rifle Brigade, a crack unit of the American patriot army, and in 1783 he married Elizabeth Paxton, a daughter of one of the richest men in the Shenandoah Valley.

Sam Sr. inherited his father's farm at Timber Ridge outside Lexington, and they worshipped at Timber Ridge Presbyterian Church along with other Scots-Irish settler families. In 1776, Sam donated land for the establishment of an academy in Lexington run by the Presbyterian church to be known as Liberty Hall, and later to become the Washington and Lee University.

When her husband Sam, a major in the Virginia militia, died in 1807 on a tour of frontier army posts, Elizabeth Houston, then aged 52, moved with her family from Lexington in the Shenandoah Valley in a covered

Conestoga wagon train to Maryville, Blount County in the Great Smoky Mountains of East Tennessee.

There, they settled on land which Sam Sr. had purchased with the intention of moving closer to kinsfolk who had settled in East Tennessee.

They worshipped at Baker's Creek Presbyterian congregation, and twice and often three times a week Elizabeth and the children walked in all weathers the four miles over the hills to services. They were also attached to New Providence Presbyterian Church in Maryville.

Sam and his brothers helped their mother erect the log cabin home on a 419-acre site at Maryville, at a point close to a river which divided the settlements of the white settlers from the lands of the Cherokee Indians.

The land was cleared, the house was built and the crops were planted, in typical late 18th and early 19th century frontier style and, with the children grouped all around her, Elizabeth proved a redoubtable industrious citizen of Maryville and its environs, even taking a keen interest in the business affairs of the town by opening a grocery and hardware store.

Elizabeth Houston had shown remarkable courage and determination in moving the large family household such a distance after the death of her husband. She was a woman of big build and forceful personality, qualities that stood her in good stead in the male-dominated world of the Virginia-Tennessee frontier.

Elizabeth Houston's sound Christian counseling was an obvious influence on young Sam, and in later life he admitted that the early impressions passed on by her far outlived all the wisdom of his adult life.

Sam adored his mother—she had nursed him from a serious injury he had received during a battle with the Indians—and on the little finger of his left hand he wore a ring which she had given as a young man. The ring had the word "Honor" engraved on it.

Sam, in one of his nostalgic moments in 1859 four years before his death and long after his mother had passed on, said: "Sages may reason and philosophers may teach but the voice which we heard in infancy will ever come to our ears, bearing a mother's words and a mother's counsels."

The renowned 19th century soldier, statesman and politician was a complex man who did not always live up to the fine Christian principles set by his mother, but he did, however, end his days as a Baptist convert, largely through the steadying influence of his second wife Margaret Lea.

In August 1831, Sam Houston was involved in important land treaty talks with the Indian tribes when he heard that his mother was very ill and dying. He rushed immediately to Maryville in East Tennessee to be with her and arrived just in time.

Elizabeth Paxton Houston was in her last hours and it was a defining moment in Sam's life as the woman who had most influenced him left the scene of time.

Sarah (Ridley) Buchanan—Frontier Woman of Intuition and Initiative

This brave heroine of the frontier settlement at Fort Nashborough in Middle Tennessee during the 1780s and 1790s was noted for her intuition and initiative in the face of real danger from hostile native Americans of the Creek, Cherokee and Shawnee tribes.

Teenager Sarah Ridley had moved with her family in the momentous, highly perilous trek from the Watauga region on Holston River in East Tennessee in 1779-80, led by Colonel John Donelson and Colonel James Robertson.

The settlers who huddled together in the dozen or so forts which encompassed Fort Nashborough on the Cumberland river (the site of present-day Nashville) faced danger at every turn, and they were compelled to work the small plots around their log cabins with guns at their side.

Even to venture a short distance from the forts was ill-advised, but by necessity to obtain water and food it had to be done, and women like Sarah Buchanan were in the front line.

Once, Sarah Ridley and a relative Susan Everett wandered into a party of heavily armed Indians as they were returning home on horseback to their Mill Creek fort, about 500 yards distance. Thinking quickly Sarah urged Susan to imitate the position of a man of horseback, and yelling furiously they raced towards the Indians, as if to indicate this was the head of a troop of militia seeking to confront the tribes. In a panic, the Indians took to their heels and headed off leaving just as frightened Sarah and Susan enough time to make it back safely to their fort.

This incident gave Sarah the title of "the fast rider of Mill Creek." Soon after, at the age of 18, she married widower Major John Buchanan, a formidable Scots-Irish frontiersman whose family had moved from Lancaster in Pennsylvania and who had served under General Andrew Pickens in the patriot militia of South Carolina.

Indeed, Major John was a kinsman of President James Buchanan, who was also born in Lancaster, Pennsylvania.

The couple lived at Buchanan's Station in Middle Tennessee and it was there that she witnessed the killing of her father-in-law at the gates of the fort by Indians. A short time later, her brother-in-law was scalped to death after being surprised by Indians, several hundred yards from the station.

Death from Indian attack was a common occurrence at this settlement and womenfolk like Sarah Buchanan had to be tough to endure. It was a dangerous situation, but Sarah Buchanan was a woman of sturdy resolve and on another occasion, armed with a large hunting-knife, she warded off two horse thieves intent of taking the Major's two horses.

By the early 1780s, peace treaties were being successfully negotiated with the Indian tribes as more and more white settlers moved into the region requiring land.

However, warlike elements in the Cherokee, Creek and Shawnee tribes led by a militant chieftain John Watt still posed danger and, from a base on the Tennessee River below Chattanooga, they continued their attacks on the settlements in the Cumberland River valley region of Middle Tennessee.

Buchanan Station, four miles east of Fort Nashborough, was vulnerable to Indian attack, especially after 500 militia men in the region were stood down at the end of peace talks which some wrongfully thought would bring permanent peace.

An attack came in September, 1792 and, with only about twenty men to defend the station from an estimated 300 Creek and Cherokee Indians, Major John Buchanan feared the worst. The shortage of manpower meant they had to fire their guns often and in volleys, and very soon the ammunition ran out.

Sarah Buchanan, however, was not for giving in, and with her sister-in-law Nancy, she gathered together all the metal plates and spoons at the station and had them quickly moulded into bullets, more than three hundred in all which helped relieve a pretty desperate situation.

The women ranked as soldiers on this occasion and fired repeatedly. Other women were engaged in making bullets or creating distractions to make the besiegers believe that the fort was strongly manned.

The attack on Buchanan's Station lasted for four hours and, against all the odds, there were many more casualties on the Indian side than in the fort, and the tribesmen were forced to retreat.

During the fierce fighting, it was said that Sarah Buchanan aided the successful defence of the station by words and deeds, "as if life and death depended upon the efforts which she made."

Danger from Indian attack prevailed in the region until 1796, but, with enormous strength of purpose and determination, Sarah Buchanan, the most fearless of women, made sure that her homestead remained intact.

Sarah mothered 13 children and, although she had very little early education, she managed to run the home and show inspiring leadership in the most trying of circumstances. She was of Scots-Irish Presbyterian stock, but, while she did not belong to a particular church, Sarah scrupulously kept the Sabbath and taught her children to have regard for religious duties. Sarah died on November 23, 1831—her husband John a year later, and both are buried on the site of the old Buchanan's Station.

Sarah Buchanan's life on the American frontier is summed up by the inscription:

"Oh Pilgrim Mothers, few the lyres
Your praises to prolong;
Though fame embalms the pilgrim sites
And trumpets them in song.
Yet ye were to those hearts of oak
The secret of their might;
Ye nerved the arm that hurled the stroke
In labor or in fight.
Oh, Pilgrim Mothers! though ye lie,
Perchance in graves unknown;
A memory that cannot die,
Hath claimed you for its own."

CATHERINE MONTGOMERY CALHOUN, REBECCA CALHOUN PICKENS AND CATEECHEE—THREE WOMEN DRAWN TOGETHER IN TRAGEDY

The Long Cane Massacre of February 1, 1760 is a tragic event prominently recorded in the annals of the 18th century white settlements in the South Carolina Piedmont. There, two brave upstanding women—Catherine Montgomery Calhoun and Cherokee Indian squaw Cateeche—were to become victims in different ways in a terrible atrocity that is still recalled by people in this part of the Carolinas.

Seventy-six-year-old family matriarch Catherine Montgomery Calhoun, her son James and seven-year-old grand-daughter Catherine were among 56 white settlers killed and a number were taken captive in a vicious attack by Cherokee warriors during the French-Indian War.

Catherine Montgomery Calhoun, grandmother of leading 19th century South Carolina statesman and American Vice-President John C. Calhoun, was born in Londonderry in 1683, and she emigrated with her Co Donegal-born husband Patrick and four sons James, William, Ezekiel and Patrick (John C's father) in 1733.

The family, who were to acquire considerable tracks of land in the American colonies, first settled in Lancaster County, Pennsylvania, then Albemarl County, Virginia and, eventually, Abbeville County in South Carolina.

The Long Cane Massacre occurred as a Conestoga wagon train of 150 settlers, mostly Scots-Irish Presbyterian, were heading in the direction of Augusta, Georgia to seek fortified security refuge from an impending attack by Cherokee tribes. Others were being moved to the Waxhaws in another part of the Carolinas close to Charlotte.

It was a cold winter's morning when the families at the Calhoun settlement at Long Canes were alerted by the Indian woman Cateechee to the danger of an imminent attack.

Cateechee, risking her life, rode seventy miles on horseback to raise the alarm and the settlers made immediate preparations to travel sixty miles south to Tobler's Fort at Beech Island in New Windsor township, just across the Savannah River from Augusta, Georgia.

The journey was hampered by the weather, with the wagons getting bogged down on wet ground and, after travelling a few miles to Long Cane Creek, it was decided to make camp for the night. This was a fateful decision, for the Cherokees had arrived at the abandoned Long Cane settlement and were alerted to the camp location.

The Cherokees struck when the settlers were at their most defenceless, and confusion reigned as only a few of the sixty fighting men could get hold of their guns to fend off the attack. Terrified women and children ran for cover, and some became separated from the main settlement.

The attack lasted about 30 minutes and the death toll was 56 of the white settlers and 21 from the Cherokee raiding party, including their chief Sunaratehee. Five of those killed were members of the Norris family—mother of Robert Norris, his wife, two sons and a daughter.

Grandmother Catherine Calhoun played a brave matriarchal role, even as she faced death, and attempted to shelter the children from the ravages of the attack. Several days after the massacre, her son Patrick and a militia troupe found the bodies of Catherine and 22 other victims, women and children, huddled around a large tree.

They had gathered there in a vain attempt to escape death and it was felt appropriate that they should all be buried there in a mass grave. The other 33 victims were buried nearby in a second mass grave close to where they fell.

A gravestone was erected by Patrick Calhoun, and interestingly, it bore his name at the top of the monument, not hers, such was the status husbands had over their wives then.

The inscription read:

"PATK CALHOUN ESQ. IN MEMORY OF MRS CATHERINE CALHOUN, AGED 78 YEARS, WHO WITH 22 OTHERS, WAS HERE MURDERED BY THE INDIANS, THE FIRST OF FEBRUARY, 1760."

In the several days after the massacre, children were found wandering in the woods, some of them wounded by tomahawks and left for dead. Others lay on the ground, scalped but still living. It was a bloody massacre, too awful to contemplate and, tragically, part of the inevitable dangers which white settlers faced on the 18th century frontier.

The Calhouns were leading citizens of Long Cane/Abbeville, enjoying a deference and respect from the wider community. Patrick and his wife Catherine were given places of honour on public associations such as Presbyterian church services, weddings and burials.

Rebecca Calhoun, the 15-year-old daughter of Ezekiel and Jean Ewing Calhoun, was found hiding in the woods after the massacre of Long Cane on February 1. She later became the wife of Andrew Pickens, an illustrious South Carolina patriot general in the Revolutionary War.

Pickens was, like the Calhouns, Scots-Irish, and Rebecca was the mother and grandmother of governors of South Carolina—Andrew Pickens (1816-18) and Francis W. Pickens (1860-1862).

Being married to a senior American patriot soldier during the Revolutionary War brought grave danger for Rebecca Calhoun Pickens from the pro-British Tory forces and hostile Indian tribes. On many occasions, with her husband away on military service, she and her children were forced to abandon their home in Abbeville and move to a secret location.

It was said that Rebecca endured all "with a fortitude that never failed and true to her country, she never forgot that she was a soldier's wife."

In the Long Cane massacre, two other of the Calhoun children Anne (Ann), four, and Mary, two, were captured and taken away to be raised by Indian squaws, but Anne was allowed to return to her family 14 years later after treaty negotiations.

Anne Calhoun learned to speak English again, but she never was able to read or write. She maintained the character of an Indian woman and wore moccasins made from the inside bark of trees. She married Isaac Matthews, a farmer, when she was 29 and they raised six children

Three weeks after the massacre, the *South Carolina Gazette* in Charlestown reported: "Mr. Patrick Calhoun, one of the unfortunate settlers at Long-Canes, who were attacked by the Cherokees on 1st instant, as they were removing their wives, children and best effects to safety, is just come to town and informs us—'that the whole of those settlers might be about 250 souls, 55 or 60 of them fighting men; that their loss in that affair amounted to about 50 persons, chiefly women and children with 13 loaded wagons and carts; that he had been at the place where the action happened, in order to bury the dead; and that he believes all the fighting men would return to and fortify the Long Canes settlement, were part of the rangers so stationed as to give some assistance and protection."

The Long Cane attack and other Indian raids in 1760 temporarily halted the flow of settlers to the Abbeville (South Carolina) and Augusta (Georgia) regions. Two days after the massacre, several hundred Cherokee Indians attacked the fort at Ninety Six in another part of the South Carolina Piedmont. The fort's surrounding building were burned, but the white settlers withheld the attack.

In another assault, a Cherokees attacked the Stevens Creek settlement in the Carolina Piedmont, killing twenty settlers. About 170 survivors were forced to flee to the neighbouring Fort Moore.

The barbarity at Long Cane, and other violent attacks in South Carolina, was a fall-out from the French/Indian War of 1754-63. Cherokee Indians of the upper part of South Carolina became allies of the British forces and went north with them to fight the French in Canada.

Family involvement in this tragedy and the traumas which the Calhouns faced on the Carolina frontier may explain why John C. Calhoun was such a tough conservative politician.

Cateechee, the young Indian women who alerted the Calhoun settlement of the Long Cane attack, was originally a Choctaw squaw who was adopted by a Cherokee chief. Through trading contacts between the Cherokees and white settlers at Ninety Six fort in South Carolina, Cateechee became friendly with a young man called Allen David Francis and, although divided by race and culture, they pledged a life together.

However, their relationship faced obvious difficulties through the outbreak of the French-Indian War with Cherokee plans to attack Long Cane and Ninety Six settlements.

Cateechee learned of these after a council of war was held by the tribal leaders at Keowee Indian township and immediately she set her mind on alerting both Allen Francis and leaders of the white settlements.

Her journey on horseback on the Keowee Path towards Ninety Six and Long Cane was a highly significant event which undoubtedly saved lives, but, unfortunately, it could not prevent the massacre of the Calhoun wagon train members.

Cateechee and Allen Francis later married, building a cabin at Ninety Six, but they were captured and held hostage for a time at Keowee by the Cherokees for upwards a year. They managed to escape towards the Savannah River and spent a considerable time on the run from their captors, living rough in the wooded wilderness.

They eventually reached the safety of the Augusta fort and, after lying low for a period, the couple returned to Ninety Six, and there they spent the rest of their lives, raising a family at a cabin known as Poplar Hill.

The legend of Cateechee and her part in alerting the white settlers at Long Cane and Ninety Six is part of South Carolina-Georgian folklore. Proof of the gallant role that she adopted is contained in a letter dated January 31, 1760, the day before the long Cane Massacre, signed by James Francis, father of Allen Francis, at Ninety Six.

The letter related to a deposition given to him by an Indian woman which described in detail the war council at Keowee and the Cherokee intentions to attack.

KATHARINE (FISHER) STEEL—"KATY OF THE FORT" ON THE CATAWBE RIVER

Some women were called to give stout leadership at times of hardship and perils on the American frontier, and brave Katharine (Fisher) Steel certainly was in that category. Katharine was born in Pennsylvania of a Scots-Irish family who had emigrated from Ulster in the early 18th century, and when she married Thomas Steel from the same region the couple headed for a new settlement in South Carolina.

This was about 1745, with Katharine in the early twenties, and their new home at Fishing Creek was on the eastern side of the Catawba River, which runs close to the Waxhaws and to Charlotte in Mecklenburg County.

Katharine quickly became accustomed to the ways of the frontier, labouring in the fields and in the woods with her husband to provide food and hearth for the home and learning to shoot from a rifle which she accomplished with expertise.

Other settlers moved into the region from Pennsylvania and Virginia, mainly of Scots-Irish diaspora, and for survival from the elements and from attack by hostile Cherokee Indian tribes they had to co-operate closely in a tight network surrounding their log cabin homes.

The Steel home was heavily fortified as a block house, where the settlers could congregate when danger arose, and several other similar structures were erected nearby to compliment the defences.

The women's role when the men folk were away from their homes either fighting the Cherokees or working in the fields was to maintain continued vigilance and raise the alarm when a threat emerged.

Katharine Steel took full responsibility for organising the women and her firmness, courage and commonsense approach provided re-assurance and real security for those who had fled their homes in a hurry to find safety in the fort houses.

Young girls were trained in the use of the rifle, for this was a life or death situation, especially if the husbands and fathers were not available in the event of a surprise Cherokee attack.

The women came together too in public worship at the nearby Waxhaws Presbyterian Church, which later became a target for the rampaging Redcoat soldiers during the Revolutionary War and where young Andrew Jackson, American president to be, and his family belonged.

Even during Sunday services a vigilant watch had to be kept in case Indians attacked suddenly, and in alerts the women were always directed to the block-houses, where they would remain for days until the all-clear was given.

Thomas Steel, effectively the leader of the settlement at Fishing Creek, gained a reputation as an Indian trader who was familiar with the language of the Cherokees. On one occasion, he led a party of a dozen men to rescue seven children, who were captured by Indians after their parents (John McDaniel and his wife) were killed in a Cherokee attack on their Rocky Creek home.

At the end of a long chase, Steel's party encountered the Indians on the borders of the Cherokee territory and, after killing nearly all of one them, they recovered the seven children, the eldest of whom was fifteen, and took them back to the fort houses. The children's uncle Hugh McDaniel was there to take the children into his care.

Katharine Steel kept a constant check on how the women fared, and she even maintained contact with other settlements into North Carolina towards the Yadkin River. Katharine was an accomplished horsewoman and she was prepared to travel 100 miles at a time through remote and highly dangerous territory.

In 1764, Thomas Steel lost his life when he and two associates James Hemphill and Stephen White were returning from a trading expedition with the Indians. They had been away for more than a year west of the Mississippi River in the direction of New Orleans and on the way home they were way-laid by a party of Indians who stripped them of everything they had including their clothes.

Somehow, they managed to piece together some garb, and one morning when they were about to resume their journey, Thomas Steel suddenly disappeared into the woods. He did not return, and after some time his companions heard a gun discharged from a distance. A search was mounted, but Steel's body was never found and he was presumed dead, almost certainly murdered by Indians.

Katharine Steel was informed and tragically left alone in a bleak wilderness with five children—three daughters and two sons—she gave not only sound motherly advice, but "fatherly" counsel and instruction to her children and wider settlement.

By 1780, Katharine's three daughters Margaret, Mary and Nancy had married, leaving the sons John and Thomas still at home with her. In the distribution of her husband's estate, Katharine divided the land and chattels equally among the children, giving each of the daughters a valuable plantation.

Katharine was admired as a high-spirited mother and a concerned community leader who gave great personal sacrifices for the safety and the prosperity of the settlers on this part of the frontier.

"Katy" encouraged her sons to take up arms in the Revolutionary War. John fought against the Cherokees in several campaigns, and he was also involved as a patriot militia captain at the sieges of Savannah and Charleston, and at Kings Mountain.

Thomas, the younger lad still only seventeen, was advised by his mother: "You must go now and fight the battles of our country with John." He promptly heeded the call and joined his brother at the front.

Katharine Steel, very proud of her eldest son's military exploits, died at the old Fishing Creek fort in 1785, in her early sixties. Captain John Steel was killed in the War of 1812, by a fall from his horse.

ELIZABETH (HUTCHINSON) JACKSON—DOUGHTY MOTHER OF A PRESIDENT

The natural responsibilities of motherhood mixed with the sense of adventure as an immigrant traveller and frontier settler and experience of real tragedy characterised the life and times of Elizabeth (Hutchinson) Jackson, mother of American President Andrew Jackson.

Elizabeth Jackson, described as an extraordinary woman, of great courage, high purpose and enormous inner strength, survived her husband Andrew's death and the loss of two sons as a result of action in the Revolutionary War. Unfortunately, she did not live to see her youngest son Andrew rise to become a successful lawyer, soldier and national statesman.

Andrew and Elizabeth Jackson, both of lowland Scottish Presbyterian families who had settled in Ulster in the 17th century, lived for a few years of their marriage in the tiny Co Antrim hamlet of Boneybefore, a mile from Carrickfergus on the shores of Belfast Lough.

The Jacksons were linen weavers, a productive occupation in the north of Ireland at the time, but, while they would have enjoyed a reasonable existence, they were not considered affluent.

They lived through a period of great movement from Ulster to the American colonies, and in the 1760-70 decade tens of thousands of people left the main ports of Belfast, Londonderry, Larne and Newry, bound for Philadelphia, New York, New Castle (Delaware) and Charleston. Andrew and Elizabeth, with their sons Hugh (aged two) and Robert (six months) made the 12-mile journey from their home to the port of Larne, where they set sail for Charleston, South Carolina.

Within a short time of their arrival they had made it to the Carolina Piedmont and settled on a small plot of land at Waxhaw Creek in South Carolina, an area that was also inhabited by the Catawba Indians, considered one of the more friendly native American tribes.

Scots-Irish Presbyterians had built a church at the Waxhaw and the Jackson family was assured of a welcome as family connections (the Crawfords and McCamies) and former neighbours from Ulster had settled there. Branches of the Hutchinson family had also settled at the Waxhaw and at Long Cane (near Abbeville in South Carolina). William Hutchinson was one of the earliest frontier settlers, and the family married into the Mecklins or McLins.

Andrew Jackson Sr. had little means to feed his family, although in the less than two years of his life in America he managed to build a log cabin and produce enough crops to see them through. The hard work took its toll and he died suddenly, of unknown causes, in March 1767, just before Elizabeth give birth to Andrew Jr.

Following a sparse funeral for her husband, Elizabeth moved to the home of her sister Jane Crawford and her husband Robert at nearby Lancaster, and on March 15, the child who was to become president was born, appropriately named Andrew after his just buried father.

Elizabeth had grand ambitions for Andrew and, indeed, for her other two sons Hugh and Robert. But life was very tough in this part of the American frontier with war clouds looming; the small holding was abandoned and she took up permanent residence with the Crawfords, as a housekeeper and nurse to her ailing sister.

Described as a woman very conversive and industrious, Elizabeth Jackson was said to spin flax beautifully, her heddie yarn spinning was "the best and finest ever seen."

The boy Andrew taught by his mother could read at five, and at eight he was able to write a neat legible hand." In later years, Andrew Jackson recalled long winter evenings when his mother told him and his brothers stirring tales from the Ulster homeland, of their grandfather Hugh Jackson's exploits in battle there and the oppression by the nobility of the labouring poor. These were tales celebrating courage, pride and independence. Andrew was reported to have received a £400 inheritance from the Hugh Jackson estate back in Ulster.

Young Andrew became a hot-tempered young man, even with the saintly influences of his mother who wanted him to become a Presbyterian minister, and growing up for the first 12 years of his life in a household (the

Crawfords) that was not his own, he became somewhat impatient, unsettled, and even rebellious.

Indeed, as a youth Andrew had a reputation as being wild, frolicsome, wilful, mischievous and daring. His mother, pre-occupied and wearied with work in the Crawford home, did her best to keep him on the straight and narrow, but without the guiding hand of a father young Andrew was hard to handle.

The Revolutionary War was in progress and the Jackson brothers got caught up in the struggle as the Scots-Irish settler people in the Waxhaw region virtually to a man backed the American patriot movement against British Redcoat forces.

When Elizabeth Jackson and other women of the Waxhaw used their log cabin Presbyterian church (established by the region's first Scots-Irish settlers in 1755!) as a hospital for patriot soldiers, it was attacked by revengeful Redcoat forces, who, because of the fierce patriot opposition they faced from the local settler community, saw Presbyterian meeting houses as legitimate targets.

Elizabeth's eldest son Hugh, then barely 16, joined the South Carolina militia and after engaging at the battle of Stone Ferry, he died from the excessive heat of the weather and the fatigues of battle.

It was a second tragedy for Elizabeth, and her concerns were increased with other sons Robert and Andrew, a mere boy of 13, also in the militia ranks. The Jackson boys were at the Battle of Hanging Rock and, on return to the Waxhaw, they were among forty local militiamen gathered at Waxhaw Presbyterian Church on April 9, 1781 when a company of British dragoons attacked them with sabres drawn. Eleven of the forty were captured and the church was burned down by the British.

The Jacksons were arrested by the dragoons while attempting to escape with their cousin Lieutenant Thomas Crawford, and during the initial detention, Andrew was ordered by one of the Redcoat officers to clean his boots. The impetuous teenager bluntly refused, declaring he was a prisoner of war and required to be treated as such.

Incensed at this insubordination, the British officer promptly lifted his sword and aimed it at Andrew's head. Andrew ducked, but he still caught the force of the weapon on his head and fingers and was physically scared for the rest of his life.

With twenty other young patriot prisoners, Robert and Andrew Jackson were taken to Camden, forty miles away, and thrown into jail with 250 other prisoners.

Their prison was a hell hole of a detention centre, with no beds, no medicines and no dressing for their wounds. They contracted smallpox, much to the alarm of their mother who had followed their long trail to Camden, and Elizabeth successfully pleaded with the authorities for the boys' release, as part of the normal war-time exchange between American and British prisoners.

Robert was in very poor shape; he could not stand nor sit on horseback without support. Elizabeth managed to obtain two horses for the arduous journey back to Waxhaw, with the strapped Robert on one mount and herself on the other. The sickly Andrew, barefooted and inadequately clothed for the atrocious weather conditions, walked the arduous and dangerous path home.

Tragically, Robert died within two days. Andrew was in a delirious state and it took all of Elizabeth's devotion and nursing skills, developed from years of looking after her sister Jane Crawford, to pull him through. Indeed, it was months before Andrew fully recovered.

Elizabeth, absolutely committed to a life of care, decided that Andrew was well enough for her to leave home for Charleston, 160 miles away, to nurse American prisoners of war held in prison ships in the harbour. Her main concern was two nephews, but, poignantly, Elizabeth contracted cholera fever herself while tending to the sick patriot soldiers on the ships, and she died after a short illness.

It was a tragic ending for such a courageous woman and, pitifully, her remains were buried in an unmarked grave in the small suburbs of Charleston. The small bundle of Elizabeth's possessions were returned to 14-year-old Andrew, only surviving member of the family. He was distraught, an orphan and sole survivor of his family.

But Andrew remembered words his mother had imparted to him: "Make friends by being honest, keep them by being steadfast; Andy... never tell a lie, nor take what is not your own, no sue... for slander... settle these cases yourself."

For a time, Andrew Jackson lived at the homes of relatives Thomas Crawford and Joseph White before he was able to decide on his future. He was a victim of the Revolutionary War, losing his mother and two brothers in the conflict.

Their memory and the sad circumstances of their deaths were to live with Andrew Jackson for the rest of his life, right through his military career and two Presidential terms. He was determined to fulfill the high hopes that his strong-willed mother had for him, and his remarkable achievement in reaching the American presidency was in many ways attributable to the true grit and character which he had inherited from Elizabeth Jackson.

A granite monument at Waxhaw Presbyterian Church erected and looked after by Waxhaw Chapter of the Daughters of the Revolution pays fulsome tribute to Elizabeth Jackson for her extraordinary tenacity and determination in overcoming the many problems which beset the family in this part of the Carolinas during the defining period in the establishment of the American nation.

This is one of the few monuments to Scots-Irish women in the United States, which gives it a very special resonance, and the simple inscription bears testimony to the legacy to one of the outstanding women of the American frontier. Poignantly, the gravestones of Elizabeth Jackson's two sons Hugh and Robert lie alongside the granite monument.

THE OUTSTANDING CONTRIBUTION JACKSON AND
HIS MEN MADE AT CHANCELLORSVILLE INSURED
VICTORY FOR ROBERT E. LEE

·⌒12⌒·

AMERICAN CIVIL WAR HEROES

GENERAL THOMAS JONATHAN "STONEWALL" JACKSON

Thomas Jonathan "Stonewall" Jackson figures high in the list of Scots-Irish heroes whose outstanding courage and military prowess gave him an honoured place in the annals of American history. "Stonewall" Jackson may have fought and died on the losing Confederate side during the Civil War of 1861-65, but he was a soldier of special quality, and his upright Christian ideals marked him down as a true leader of men.

Jackson was given the nickname "Stonewall" at the battle of Bull Run in Virginia in July 1861 after it was said of him: "This is Jackson, standing a stone wall." The highly significant role that he played for the Confederates in this decisive battle earned him promotion to major general.

The Civil War hero was the great-grandson of an Ulsterman John Jackson, who at the age of 33, emigrated to America in 1748 as "a respectable and prosperous tradesman," settling in Maryland, and then putting down his roots in the Shenandoah Valley after passing through West Virginia.

John Jackson's family were lowland Presbyterian Scots who settled in the north of Ireland during the 17th century Scottish Plantation years and defended Londonderry during the Siege of 1688-89. The Jacksons were scattered across Ulster, some located in the north-west of the province around Londonderry and Coleraine, while others lived in counties Armagh, Down, and Antrim.

Varying claims are made about exactly where in Ulster John Jackson was born. In the biography of "Stonewall" Jackson by English writer Colonel G. F. R. Henderson, a letter is referred to which states that the ancestors of the great Confederate general had lived in the parish of Londonderry.

The letter, according to Henderson, was in the possession of Thomas Jackson Arnold, of Beverly, West Virginia, a nephew of General Jackson. Another report, of American origin, gives John Jackson's birthplace as near Coleraine in Co Londonderry.

Residents, however, in the Birches-Tartaraghan area of Co Armagh close to the shores of Lough Neagh in the centre of Ulster are adamant that John Jackson was one of their kin. Their belief is reinforced by a plaque unveiled on July 22, 1968 in Ballinary, a section of the Birches, which states that this was the reputed birthplace of John Jackson, great grandfather of Thomas Jonathan "Stonewall" Jackson (1824-1863). The then United States Consul General in Northern Ireland unveiled the plaque at the Ballinary site, located about 70 miles from Londonderry-Coleraine.

Today, there are reportedly more Jacksons living in this part of Co Armagh than in any other region of Northern Ireland, and they are convinced of the local connection with "Stonewall" Jackson's family. John Jackson is traced by the Co Armagh Jacksons as a son of John Jackson, who is buried in Tartaraghan Parish Churchyard.

Another John Jackson, from this area, fought with King William III at the Battle of the Boyne in 1690, and his sword and cutlass used in the battle have been displayed at Carrickfergus Castle in Co Antrim

The Jacksons of Co Armagh have always been strong supporters of the Orange-Protestant cause in Ireland and today that tradition is manifested in their membership of various Orange lodges in a region, where the Orange Order was founded in 1795. These Jacksons primarily belong to the Church of Ireland (Episcopal) and, if the American link is authentic, it would have meant that the emigrant John Jackson and his family almost certainly converted to Presbyterianism when they reached America.

John Jackson had a brief sojourn in London before he reached Maryland in 1748. It was there that he met the girl he was to marry, Elizabeth Cummins, the daughter of a London hotelier, who, when her father died and her mother remarried, decided to emigrate. Elizabeth was a highly educated woman of a large stature, and it was said she was "as remarkable for her strength of intellect as for beauty and physical vigour." John Jackson was a "spare diminutive man, of quiet but determined character, sound judgment and excellent morals."

The pair married in 1755, and within two years they headed to the Shenandoah Valley of Virginia with the great flow of Scots-Irish families, who had moved from Ulster. They settled at Moorefield in Hardy County, West Virginia, but after the French-Indian war of 1754-63, they moved 150 miles westwards to find a home at Buckhannon in Randolph County, Virginia.

In his exploits as an Indian fighter and scout, John Jackson amassed sizeable land holdings in the Shenandoah Valley and these he distributed to his eight children. The Jacksons in time became one of the leading families in the Valley. In terms of wealth and influence, Jackson was a Randolph County justice and, in 1779, at the age of 74, he served as a captain of a frontier militia regiment.

Elizabeth Jackson, who had possession of 3,000 acres of land in her own right at Buckhannon, survived her husband, and she lived until she was 105. She also showed tenacity and courage in fending off Indian attacks on their home and family records show that even in the most dangerous situations, she never wilted.

Two sons rose to high office. Edward (1759-1828), grandfather of "Stonewall," was Randolph County surveyor, militia colonel, commissioner of revenue and high sheriff. He represented Lewis County in the Virginia Assembly and was "a citizen who acquired some knowledge of medicine, was an expert millwright, and a farmer of more than usual ability."

George, his older brother, after service as a colonel in the Revolutionary War, completed three terms in the American Congress and was a close associate of General Andrew Jackson, later to become President. George and Andrew Jackson were not related, but they frequently talked about their first generation Ulster connections who had moved to America several decades earlier. George Jackson's son, John George Jackson replaced his father in

Congress and, as lawyer, he was an articulate spokesman in Washington for the Shanendoah Valley dwellers.

Jonathan Jackson , father of "Stonewall," studied law at the Clarksburg office of his uncle and, although married to the daughter of a merchant from Parslbury, West Virginia, Julie Beeleith Neale, he was never a man of great wealth. He died when his son Jonathan was only three.

John George Jackson married Mary Payne, of Philadelphia, a sister of Dolly Madison, wife of James Madison, the fourth president of the United States. This increased the influence of the Jackson clan to the highest level, and John George was appointed by Madison's successor in the White House, James Monroe, as the first federal judge for the western part of Virginia. A brother, Edward Burke Jackson, was the army surgeon during the Creek Indian War of 1812, a Clarksburg doctor and a member of the American Congress for four years.

It was from this noble family tradition of soldiering and public service that Thomas Jonathan "Stonewall" Jackson emerged and in 1842, at the age of 18, he was given a Congressional appointment to the top American military academy at West Point.

With his father leaving little property on his death and his mother forced to seek the help of her relatives, and the Free Masons to rear the family, before she died four years later, it was a rough upbringing for Thomas Jonathan and his brother Warren and sister Laura. When orphaned they went to live with their father's half-brother on a western Virginia farm.

"Stonewall" was a youth of "exemplary habits, of indomitable will and undoubted courage," and in the rough and tumble of frontier society he demonstrated an integrity and a determination to succeed in life.

Before he enrolled at West Point, "Stonewall" was a constable in his Virginia county executing court decrees, serving warrants, summoning witnesses and collecting debts. The West Point training was far removed from the law-enforcement duties of his frontier homeland, but "Stonewall" adapted well, and in 1846 he graduated 17th in a class of 70 which contained men who were to serve as the leading generals in the Civil War, in both the Union and Confederate armies.

"Stonewall" was first assigned as a lieutenant in the Mexican War, under General Zachary Taylor, a fellow Virginian who later became American President in 1849. He also fought in the Seminole Indian War in Florida and was elevated to major. However, Jackson moved away from the front line of battle in 1851 when he accepted a teaching position at the Virginia Military Institute in Lexington, and although still technically in soldiering, this brought him back into civilian life. The 10 years in Lexington was perhaps the most crucial period of his life, and there he was to build a solid base for the later affray at the head of the Virginia Confederate troops in the Civil War.

Thomas Jonathan, although born into a Presbyterian family, had very little religious grounding as a youth and during his early military career. This changed when he met Colonel Francis Taylor, a commandant of his regiment in Mexico and a committed Christian. "Stonewall" studied the Bible for himself, and curiosity about various religions even led him to the Roman Catholic archbishop of Mexico for advice. But he was not convinced of the validity of Roman Catholic doctrine and in 1849 he was baptised at the age of 25 into the Episcopal Church, the American branch of Anglicanism.

In Lexington, however, it was the Presbyterian Church—the creed of the pioneering Ulster settlers, which provided him with a spiritual satisfaction and he made his profession of faith as a dissenting Calvinist in November 1851. Soon after he became a Presbyterian elder and a lay preacher with intent to win souls for Christ.

"Stonewall" married Eleanor Junkin, daughter of the Rev. George Junkin, president of Washington College in Virginia, in 1854, but she died 14 months into the marriage. His second marriage in 1857 was to Mary Anna Morrison, daughter of the Rev. Dr. R. H. Morrison, president of Davidson College in North Carolina. They had one daughter.

Religion was the main pre-occupation for "Stonewall" in those Lexington years, and he daily took the Bible as his guide, literally interpreting every word on its pages. He was strict Sabbatarian—never reading on that day, nor posting a letter; he believed that the U.S. federal government in carrying the mail on Sundays was violating a divine law.

To the church, Jackson gave one-tenth of his income, established a Sunday school from his own means and was particularly compassionate about the plight of the black slave children in the area. Jackson's faith transcended every action of his life. He started the day with a blessing and always ended it with thanks to God. His watchword was: "I have long cultivated the most trivial and customary acts of life with a silent prayer."

His two wives, during their marriages, were of similar fundamental Christian outlook, both daughters of the Presbyterian manse. Eleanor Junkin's father was of Scottish Covenanting stock, who had come from Ulster in the late 18th century. The Morrisons were also of Scots-Irish extraction.

Jackson was not a wealthy man, notwithstanding his senior position at Lexington Military College. He depended solely on his salary and both his wives were also of limited means. But he still managed to extend traditional Virginian hospitality to all who came in contact with him.

When the Civil War broke out in April 1861 and Virginia was seceded from the Union, "Stonewall" Jackson answered the Confederate call to action and was commissioned a colonel. He led a detachment of Virginia Military Institute cadets from Lexington to Richmond to defend the Confederate flank there. This led to the command of the Virginia forces at Harper's Ferry, a posting that placed him in the front line.

Jackson distinguished himself at the Battle of Bull Run at Manassas in July 1861, when he inflicted a crushing defeat on the Union Army. The bravery was such that General Bernard E. Bee, commander of the South Carolina Confederacy, cried out to his men to look to Jackson, stating: "There he stands like a stone wall. Rally behind the Virginians." Bee, Jackson's classmate from West Point, died in the battle, but the "Stonewall" tribute became a legend.

At the second Battle of Bull Run in August 1862, "Stonewall" further distinguished himself by his valour. After marching 51 miles in two days, his "foot cavalry" smashed the Union depot at Manassas, went underground for another two days, and then held off superior forces until Confederate reinforcements could be called. He also had notable battle success at Harper's Valley, Antietam-Sharpsbury and Frederickburg.

"Stonewall" Jackson sadly had his last stand at the Battle of Chancellorsville on May 2, 1863, and the outstanding contribution he and his men made there ensured victory for General Robert E. Lee. However, the advantage from the victory was not to last as the tide gradually turned against the Confederates, due to lack of money and resources.

After his heroics at Bull Run, Jackson, was upgraded to Major-General and placed in charge of the Confederate Army in the lower Shenandoah Valley. His soldiers referred to him as "Old Jack," and his tall, thin frame and long beard belied his barely 40 years. He remained a man of puritan tastes, a non-smoker, non-drinker and non-gambler and he ate sparingly. His commitment to the Confederate cause was total and in uniform he was a stern disciplinarian, but he looked on war as "the sum of all evil."

Jackson moved to attack the Union forces in the Valley, and while they had reversals, they managed to hold the line and send the enemy retreating back to Washington. It was at Chancellorsville that Jackson was a victim of mistaken fire by one of his own men. He lost an arm after being struck three times and had to retire from the battle-field. Death followed quickly when he contacted pneumonia, but in a final order, Jackson called out: "pass the infantry to the front."

His last words underlined his abiding Christian faith: "Let us cross over the river and rest under the shade of the trees." Thomas Jonathan "Stonewall" Jackson was only 39 when he died on May 10, 1863. General Robert E. Lee, who had lost his finest soldier, said: "I know not how to replace him." Jackson was much respected even by enemy officers on the Union side for his heroism, bravery, devotion to duty and purity of character.

He was the true Christian patriot, and President Abraham Lincoln, who died within two years, described him as "a very brave soldier."

Jackson's death two years into the Civil War had fuelled debate as to what might have happened if he had lived. Serious reversals in the Shenandoah Valley and at Gettysburg sealed the fate of the Confederacy, for without the sterling leadership qualities of the redoubtable "Stonewall," the Johnny Rebs were never the same potent force again. Economic factors also negated their war effort.

The heroics in battle of the gallant "Stonewall" Jackson were in the best Scots-Irish tradition. He was a soldier of a very special quality.

JAMES EWELL BROWN (JEB) STUART

James Ewell Brown ("JEB") Stuart was another distinguished Confederate general in the American Civil War whose 18th century family descendants were Ulster Presbyterians. The gallant Stuart was the great, great, grandson of Archibald Stuart, who emigrated from Londonderry to Pennsylvania in 1726 and was one of the earliest settlers in the Shenandoah Valley of Virginia.

JEB Stuart was described by General Robert E. Lee as "the eyes of the Confederacy," and in the Virginia campaign he became a real thorn in the flesh for the Union command, leading raid after raid on their posts and taking hundreds of prisoners back to the South.

When "Stonewall" Jackson was killed at Chancellorsville in May, 1863, the imposing Stuart took over temporary command, but General Lee maintained he was irreplacable as the Confederates' chief of cavalry, and he kept him in that position.

Stuart, a graduate of West Point military college and a soldier who served with the U.S. Cavalry in Texas and Kansas, resigned his commission to join the Confederate army at the start of the Civil War, and he rose from second lieutenant to major general. He was a strongly religious man in the Calvinist tradition and a strong advocate of temperance, but he was of a fiery disposition which brought him into occasional conflict with his peers at West Point and which he harnessed to good effect in the various Civil War battles.

Stuart inherited his undoubted fighting qualities from stout Presbyterian kinsfolk who fought at the Siege of Londonderry in 1688-89 after they had settled arrived from lowland Scotland during the 17th century Scottish plantation of Ulster. Archibald Stuart was followed to America by his wife Janet Brown and two young children, Thomas and Eleanor. Two other children Alexander and Benjamin were born in Pennsylvania, and in 1737 the family set up home in Augusta County in the Shenandoah Valley.

Janet's Brown's brother was Rev. John Brown, minister of Providence Presbyterian Church in Rockbridge County, Virginia for 44 years and the second rector of Liberty Hall Academy, now Washington and Lee University in Lexington.

Alexander Stuart was a major in the Virginia militia during the Revolutionary War, and he later acquired extensive properties throughout the Shenandoah Valley. This land was distributed among the 11 children of his three marriages when he died in 1824, aged 90.

Thomas Stuart inherited his father's main estate in Rockbridge County and with it, the large family Bible, which had been taken from Londonderry in 1726. Eleanor, Archibald's only daughter, married Edward Hall, who was also born in Ulster and had moved to the Shenandoah Valley with his family. She and her brother Benjamin were also given farms from the prosperous estate of their father.

Judge Alexander Stuart, a son of Major Alexander Stuart and Mary Moore Paxton (Stuart's second marriage) was a lawyer, a member of the executive council of Virginia and a United States judge in Illinois and Missouri. He is buried beside his half-brother Judge Archibald Stuart. From the marriage of Major Stuart and Mary Patterson, Judge Alexander Stuart married Anne Dabney, from a family of French immigrants, and they had a son Archibald and daughter Anne.

This Archibald Stuart was the father of James Ewell Brown Stuart, and his other six sons and four daughters were prominent in business, church, civic and political life in Virginia and surrounding states.

JEB Stuart as a colonel of the First Virginia Cavalry, fought at Fort Manassas-Bull Run, leading his troops in the charge which secured a significant Confederate victory. He set out detailed plans for the Virginia campaign and got behind enemy lines for an assessment of Union Army strengths. This took him to the Potomac region, and he returned to the Shenandoah Valley base with 165 prisoners and 260 captured horses.

His promotion to major general placed Stuart in charge of all the cavalry in Northern Virginia and, in another ambitious foray into Union territory with 1,800 troopers, he returned with 500 captured horses. JEB's daring exploits became the talk of the South, and his men took inspiration from his fearlessness and willingness to take on any assignment for the Confederate cause.

This huge frame of a man with a flowing beard, invariably led from the front, nearly always astride a magnificent charger. His dashing demeanour manifested itself in his long grey Confederate coat, trimmed in red and a cavalier's cocked hat with a gilt star and a long peacock's plume. JEB enjoyed music and dancing, and, socially, he was the life and soul of the party. But he had a strong aversion to alcohol and discouraged his men against its consumption.

Stuart and his Virginia cavalry continued to act as a buffer and intelligence unit for Lee's main army, but they had their set-backs, particularly at the Battle of Gettysburg, the real turning point in the Civil War.

Stuart's cavalry covered Lee's movements during the Wilderness campaign of May, 1864, and he led 4,500 troopers in pursuit of the 12,000 Federal Cavalry Corps, commanded by Co Cavan (Ireland)-born general Philip Henry Sheridan. The Confederate cavalry reached Yellow Station on the Richmond Road and, while they succeeded in moving the Union troops off the main route to Washington, Stuart was a casualty. He was shot in the abdomen and died from his injuries in Richmond the following day, aged only 31.

General Robert E. Lee, in a tribute, said: "JEB Stuart never brought me a false piece of information. He was a gallant soldier and a fine Southerner."

JEB Stuart was married to Flora Cooke, daughter of Philip George Cooke, a general in the United States army, but a native of Virginia and a Confederate sympathiser. They had two children JEB (James Elwell Brown) and Virginia Pelham.

Other American Civil War generals of note who had Scots-Irish family and Ulster connections included George Brinton McClellan, Irvin McDowell, Ambrose Everett Burnside, David McMurtrie Gregg, Philip Henry Sheridan, Charles Graham Halpine and James Shields in the Union Army and Joseph Eggleston Johnston, Albert Sidney Johnston, Daniel Smith Donelson and Leonidas Polk in the Confederacy.

McClellan, son of a Philadelphia surgeon and a class associate of Thomas Jonathan "Stonewall" Jackson at West Point, had Ulster-Scots ancestors who fought alongside George Washington in the Revolutionary War.

Burnside's family roots can be traced back to the Ballymoney area of Co Antrim and to a migration of Ulster Presbyterians to Londonderry in New Hampshire in 1718. Burnside, a commanding figure with flamboyant whiskers, gave the word "sideburns" to the language.

CHURCH LIFE WAS A DEFINING CHARACTERISTIC ON
THE AMERICAN FRONTIER.

·⟨ 13 ⟩·

RELIGION ON THE
AMERICAN FRONTIER

THE PRESBYTERIANISM TRADITION

Ulster characteristics in early American church life were marked after Presbyterianism was introduced to the American colonies in the latter part of the 17th century, with first congregations set up in Maryland, Pennsylvania and New Jersey.

A pioneering spirit in American Presbyterianism was the Rev Francis Makemie, a pastor from the Laggan presbytery, Co Donegal who emigrated from Londonderry in 1683 after graduating from Glasgow University.

Makemie was an itinerant minister with exceptional organising abilities which earned him the reputation of being "the father of American Presbyterianism." He was a scholarly man who wrote a catechism on Calvinist doctrines and Westminster standards of the church.

Significantly, as a Presbyterian founding father, Francis Makemie was a strong advocate of religious freedom in America, and in 1707 he was imprisoned for six weeks by Lord Cornbury, Anglican Governor of New York, for preaching without a licence.

Makemie was Moderator of the first American presbytery, formed in 1706, and the firm foundations which he laid allowed Presbyterianism to establish itself as arguably the most influential denomination in America in the latter half of the 18th century.

By 1740, the American Presbyterian Church had established 95 congregations, primarily in the eastern seaboard region. By 1775, when the United States was a fledgling nation, the number of congregations had reached 588, with a total membership of 63,063, clustered overwhelmingly in the Delaware Valley around Pennsylvania, central New Jersey, Chesapeake Bay of Maryland and Virginia. Presbyterians were then the second-largest denomination in America, next to the Congregationalists.

The Rev Francis Allison, like Makemie a son of Donegal, born at Leck near Letterkenny, was an educator who championed the twin-track Presbyterian church and school system in the American colonies and on the frontier. He arrived in Pennsylvania in 1735 and pastored at New London church, where he formed an academy.

Allison felt there was a need for the education of ministerial candidates, and his teaching prowess was recognised when he became rector of the Academy of Philadelphia. His pupils included Declaration of Independence signers Thomas McKean and George Read and Charles Thomson, Maghera-born secretary of the American Continental Congress. During the War years, Allison emerged as the favoured preacher to members of Congress.

Leading Philadelphia statesman Benjamin Franklin described Francis Allison as "a person of great ingenuity and learning, a Catholic divine and an honest man."

Much of the language and aspiration contained in the Declaration of Independence of July 4, 1776 is widely acknowledged to carry the distinctive stamp of non-conformist Calvinism and radical Presbyterianism, as espoused by the likes of Ulster-born Charles Thomson and Francis Allison.

There was even an organised Presbyterian group clamouring for political and social change in Pennsylvania in the years leading up to the Revolutionary War.

Scots-Irish Presbyterians, more than any other religious group, were firmly identified with the revolutionary cause in America and, as a denomination, they invested much of their identity in the war for independence. This proved costly in many instances, with more Presbyterian frontier churches burnt to the ground by British Crown loyalists during the War than buildings belonging to any other religious denomination.

Hawkins Historical Notices of the period recount that the Presbyterian Church suffered severely during the War of Independence—"Its ministers and elders went into the struggle for constitutional liberty with all their strength. Churches were destroyed, ministers and elders slain, congregations scattered."

However, whatever the competitions, set-backs and challenges they faced in 18th century America, Scots-Irish Presbyterians remained a potent political, social and cultural force well into the 19th century, and the Calvinist legacy remains an integral part of American religion today.

With their insistence upon college-educated clergy, the Scots-Irish produced highly articulate and vocal clergy who made sure the interests of the church and their people were best served in the cities, towns and backcountry where they ministered.

Legislation enacted from the War of Independence had the initial effect of making Presbyterian colleges more restricted in enrolment, and with less influence in state affairs. However, by 1800, the Presbyterians were the single largest non-English sector of the white population in most Appalachian states, a confident people buoyed by the witness of their Calvinist beliefs and strength of numbers.

Religion was an important ingredient in the lives of frontier people, especially the Ulster-Scots immigrants, back to the very first settlements in the 1720s. The church was the central core of the community in early townships of Pennsylvania, New Hampshire, Virginia, Tennessee, Kentucky, Georgia and the Carolinas, and its influence impacted on the cultural and social life of these regions.

The Rev. Charles Beatty, the first Presbyterian minister west of the Allegheny Mountains, was born in Co Antrim in 1715 and pastored in western Pennsylvania from 1758 at the outpost of Fort Pitt (Fort Duquesne), site of present-day Pittsburgh.

Beatty was followed by another Scots-Irish cleric, the Rev. Dr. James McMillan, who founded the first school in this section of western Pennsylvania in 1780 and by the Rev. Samuel Barr, from Londonderry, and another Ulsterman, the Rev. James Steele.

Thomas Dungan, who also came from the north of Ireland, was the first Baptist preacher in Pennsylvania, while the Rev John Black, from Co Antrim, was pastoring at First Reformed Presbyterian Church (Covenanting) in Pittsburgh in 1800. Dr. James McMillan founded in his log cabin home in 1787 the Washington Academy, which later became the Washington and Jefferson College.

The Scots-Irish influence at the University of Pittsburgh from its inception in 1787 was very pronounced. By the mid-19th century there were three Presbyterian theological seminaries in western Pennsylvania—Western (started in 1825); Allegheny (1825) and Reformed (1856). The significance of this can be measured by the fact that there were no Roman Catholic theological colleges in the region until 1870.

The one-room log cabin schools founded on the American frontier by diligent 18th century Scots-Irish Presbyterian pastors in time became academies and colleges.

Some even progressed to university status, such as Liberty Hall Academy, Virginia to Washington and Lee University; Blount College to the University of Tennessee and Cumberland College.

The University of Georgia, University of North Carolina and Transylvania University in Lexington, Kentucky were also cradled from a Presbyterian ethos.

Princeton theological college in New Jersey emerged from the Log College, founded in 1735 by Armagh-born Church of Ireland cleric the Rev William Tennant, who converted to Presbyterianism when he moved to Philadelphia. Noted early frontier preachers, the Revs Samuel and John Blair and Samuel Finlay, graduated from Princeton. Woodrow Wilson, American president and second generation Ulster-Scot, was also educated there and later became a college professor.

The Presbyterian community who moved from the Bann Valley in Ulster to New Hampshire in 1718, under the leadership of the Rev. James MacGregor, had a meeting house erected within a year of their arrival, and within six years, had established four schools in the Londonderry township.

Augusta Academy, which progressed to Washington and Lee University at Lexington in the Shenandoah Valley of Virginia, was the earliest educational institution west of the Blue Ridge Mountains in Virginia.

The Academy was founded in 1749 by Ulster-Scot Robert Alexander, a member of the Presbyterian congregation at Timber Ridge, where early 19th century Tennessee-Texas statesman Sam Houston worshipped as a child. Presbyterians from east Co Antrim laid the foundations at Timber Ridge.

Maryville College—fourth oldest educational institution in Tennessee—was established on the initiative of the Rev. Dr. Isaac Anderson, grandson of a Co Down Presbyterian and a descendant of family members who fought at the Siege of Londonderry in 1688-89. One of Dr. Anderson's pupils at Maryville College was Sam Houston after the Houston family had moved from Lexington to the Great Smoky Mountain region of East Tennessee.

Presbyterians on the American frontier were intensely proud of their church system of education which prepared young men for ministry. They propounded the theory that "the most ignorant College learnt man could open the true meaning of the Scriptures better than the best and wisest of God's children that had not College education."

One of the earliest Presbyterian clerics to reach the outer frontier region was the Rev. Charles Cummings and his arrival in western Virginia-North Carolina region in the mid-1770s was hailed with joy by the Scots-Irish settlers, who, it was reported, were "hungering and thirsting for spiritual nourishment" in the wooded wilderness they then inhabited.

Cummings was in the traditional mould of the frontier settlers he preached to: tough and direct, with a message which was fundamental to the spiritual needs of those who inhabited this wild and desolate countryside.

Travelling through a parish which extended over hundreds of miles, Cummings always had a long rifle at his side in case of Cherokee Indian attack. And when he preached, members of his congregation stood guard with long rifles in hand.

Another pioneering cleric who made an indelible mark on the American frontier was the Rev. Samuel Doak, whose parents left Co Antrim in 1740. Doak was chaplain to the Scots-Irish militiamen who fought in the decisive Revolutionary War battles of Kings Mountain and Cowpens, and he was the founder of Washington and Tusculum (Greeneville) colleges in East Tennessee.

The mid-18th century parish of Ulster-born Rev. John Craig, pioneering Presbyterian cleric in the Shenandoah Valley of Virginia, extended over a vast area of 10,000 square miles and, in a 27-year active ministry, Craig established several dozen congregations. John Craig, it is said, prepared the seed-bed for permanent Presbyterianism in Virginia, from which the church expanded west and south into the regions of North Carolina, Tennessee, Kentucky and Georgia, and beyond to Mississippi and Texas.

Charlotte in North Carolina was an 18th century town settled largely by Ulster-Scots families, with the message from the area's seven Presbyterian churches, then providing the main spiritual outreach. The surrounding Mecklenburg County was an Ulster-Scots (Scots-Irish) stronghold with a radicalism and sustained patriot involvement during the Revolutionary War years which was influenced to a large degree by Presbyterian ministers Rev. Alexander Craighead, Rev. David Caldwell and Rev Hezekiah Balch.

The Mecklenburg Declaration of May 20, 1775, which was seen as the forerunner to the Declaration of Independence of July 4, 1776, was Presbyterian-inspired with 18 of the 27 signatories of Ulster origins.

In the Charlotte of today, as in many other cities and towns in the eastern and south eastern American states, strong Presbyterian influences still play a big part in local community life.

The Faith and Freedom legacy passed on by the Ulster settlers who made America their home 200-250 years ago still has much relevance today across the states of this mighty nation.

The poet Van Dyke pays this tribute to the Rev Francis Makemie, the founding father of Ulster Presbyterianism in America:

THE CHURCH

"OH, WHO CAN TELL HOW MUCH WE OWE TO THEE
MAKEMIE, AND TO LABOURS SUCH AS THINE,
FOR ALL THAT MAKES AMERICA THE SHRINE,
OF FAITH UNTRAMMELLED AND OF CONSCIENCE FREE?
STAND HERE, GRAY STONE, AND CONSECRATE THE SOD,
WHERE SLEEPS THE BRAVE SCOTS-IRISH MAN OF GOD."

"We see every day travelling to Carolina, some on foot with packs, and some in large covered wagons. The road here is much frequented," said a Presbyterian minister in the Shenandoah Valley of Virginia in 1775, describing the westward migration.

REV JOSEPH RHEA, PIONEERING PASTOR:

Disagreement over his annual stipend with Fahan and Inch congregations in Co Donegal led the Rev. Joseph Rhea to seek a new life in America, and to become only the second Presbyterian cleric to minister in the frontier territory that became the state of Tennessee.

For 20 years, from 1749 to 1769, Joseph Rhea was the faithful pastor of Fahan and Inch Presbyterian churches on the Innishowen Peninsula. But there reached a stage where he could no longer exist and maintain his family on the very small amount paid in annual stipend.

Rhea resigned his post on August 16, 1769 with the following letter: "As I received the congregation of Fahan from the Presbytery of Londonderry, I have laboured in the work of the ministry above twenty years in that place and as the congregation has fallen into very long areas and has been deficient in the original promise to me which was 24 pounds yearly I am unable to subsist any longer among them and I do hereby demit my charge of them and deliver them into the hand of them from whom I received them."

Joseph Rhea, descended from the Campbell clan in Scotland, was born and grew up in Kennecalley near St Johnston, East Donegal, and his grandfather Matthew Campbell Rhea had a prominent role in the Siege of Londonderry in 1688-89.

After graduating in 1742 with an MA degree from Glasgow University, Joseph Rhea was ordained by Londonderry presbytery, and he first preached at the little church of Barracanaugh or Bun Cranaugh (now Buncrana) near the shores of Lough Foyle.

He was described as a scholarly man, well versed in philosophy, theology and the classic Hebrew and Latin languages, and he was spoken off as one of the most eminent clerics in Ulster and later in the frontier lands of America. Large in stature—six feet tall—with cheerful disposition, he was pleasant in manner, kind and charitable to a fault.

In September, 1769, Rhea sailed from Londonderry to America with his wife Elizabeth McIlwaine, and seven children—John, Matthew, Margaret, William, Joseph, Elizabeth and Samuel. Elizabeth McIlwaine came from Lisfannin, Co Donegal and another son James was born in America.

Rhea preached at Piney Creek near Taneytown in Maryland for four years on an annual salary of £112, and in 1775 he took a call to the Appalachian frontier region of the Holston River settlement in North Carolina (today North East Tennessee).

The Rev Charles Cummings, another Ulster-Scots cleric, had pioneered the settlement, and together they witnessed for Christ in this heavily forested wilderness that brought constant danger from hostile Indian tribes.

During his time on the Holston, Joseph Rhea joined up as chaplain to the militia patriot troops of Colonel William Christian (another of Ulster-Scots tradition) for a four-week engagement against the Cherokees on the Little Tennessee River.

Rhea, a gifted preacher, and by then a man of 60, took every opportunity to preach to the settlers in their frontier homes and forts, and to the soldiers during his short time with them.

Accompanied by his eldest son John, he purchased land at Beaver Creek in the Holston in 1777 and decided that he must return to Maryland to prepare other members of the family for the long wagon train trek to the new home on the frontier.

Sadly, after selling his property in Maryland, Joseph Rhea became ill with pneumonia and died, aged 62. He was buried at Piney Creek cemetery, Maryland.

Widow Elizabeth, son John and the rest of the family carried out his wish of removing to the Holston area and, after a hazardous six-week journey, they reached their new home in the middle of a snowstorm in February, 1778.

The Rheas were followed to the Holston and Watauga regions of North Carolina by other Scots-Irish settlers who had been members of Joseph Rhea's congregation in Piney Creek. They were joined by others from the Shenandoah Valley of Virginia, and together they formed a settlement at Holston Fork with a church called New Bethel, where they were ministered by a contemporary of Joseph Rhea, the Rev Samuel Doak, whose parents emigrated from Co Antrim in 1749.

Allison, Anderson, Breden, Hodges, Dysart, McAllister, McCorkle and Lynn Ulster families were enlisted in the congregation..

The 2,000-acre Rhea farm on the Holston near the present-day town of Blountville in the Great Smoky Mountain region of East Tennessee was the scene of some of the earliest religious services in Tennessee. Joseph Rhea and Samuel Doak preached from a pulpit stone on the farm, and portions of the old rock remain to this day.

The large field behind the Rhea house served as training grounds for the militia before the Revolutionary War and Presidents Andrew Jackson and Andrew Johnson were frequent family guests.

Of the direct descendants of the Rev. Joseph Rhea, 21 became church ministers—Presbyterians, with a single exception—and 54 were soldiers in the Confederate Army during the American Civil War.

John Rhea, born at Langhorn near Londonderry in 1753, was like his father a leader in the frontier community, and he served with the patriot army in the Revolutionary War at the battles of Kings Mountain and Brandywine. He was a Democratic member of the United States Congress for 18 years and was a commissioner in the 1816 peace talks with the Choctaw Indians. He was a strict Calvinist and had planned to become a Presbyterian minister, but although taken on trial by the Hanover Presbytery in Tennessee, he was never licensed nor ordained.

John's brother Matthew, born in Co Donegal in 1755, was a lieutenant in the Virginia regiment in the Revolutionary War and was recognised for his gallantry. A son Robert P. became a teacher in Virginia and he taught General Thomas Jonathan "Stonewall" Jackson, the great Confederate Army general of Ulster stock.

Matthew Rhea, son of Matthew Sr. and grandson of Rev. Joseph, published in 1832 the first map of the state of Tennessee, based on actual land surveys. This was considered a major contribution to early Tennessee life.

Hill McAllister, the governor of Tennessee in 1933-37, was a direct descendant of the Rhea-Breden-Dysart families of the Holston settlement and many other Tennessee luminaries of the 19th and 29th centuries originated from this illustrious Ulster-Scots Presbyterian line.

Fahan and Inch Presbyterian churches in Co Donegal today belong to Derry and Strabane Presbytery of the Presbyterian Church in Ireland.

EARLY CHURCH AT DONEGAL SPRINGS

Donegal Presbyterian Church near Lancaster in eastern Pennsylvania was the focal point for one of the earliest Scots-Irish settlements on American soil, the congregation being established in 1721. Co Donegal in northwest Ireland was the homeland of the first families who moved inland from Philadelphia to set up homes on the Indian-titled territory of Chiquesalunga, fertile but largely wilderness lands highest only inhabited by the native American tribes.

Presbyterianism was taken to America by Donegal pastor, the Rev. Francis Makemie in 1683 and in 1706 he founded the Philadelphia Presbytery, the first independent church body of any kind in the "New World" colonies.

The earliest documented evidence of a Presbyterian congregation at Donegal Springs was contained in a letter dated August 1, 1721, dispatched by Andrew Galbraith to the presbytery of New Castle, Delaware. In the letter, Galbraith asked that a minister be sent to support the people at "Chickens Longus" (his spelling version of the word Chiquesalunga). Supply ministers were sent, but without adequate guides, and in the rugged frontier terrain they lost their way and never appeared.

The first full-time pastor appointed was Scottish-born Rev. James Anderson, who had worked in America since 1709 and supplied a New York city pulpit before the call in August 1727 to the log cabin meeting house at Donegal Springs , alongside the Susquehanna River and bountiful springs.

A stone church was erected in 1730 to replace the log cabin, the stone gathered by the men and women of the congregation from the quarries and fields nearby. Tradition in the area relates that the women drove the wagons which carried the stones to the site of the building and that the old horse which pulled the wagon died just as the last stone was placed at the peak of the chip-roofed structure. As a gesture of gratitude for faithful service, the horse's head was buried in the pulpit.

The first Donegal stone was erected similar to the church at Rathneedy near Donegal town in Ireland, the first Presbyterian meeting house built for and by the people of that county in 1674. A cemetery was started soon after Donegal Springs Church became established, and a school was up and running within a short period.

The first gravestone in the cemetery belongs to Thomas Jamison, who died in 1732. The Rev. Colin McFarquhar, church minister during the Revolutionary War, is buried there beside his wife as is Colonel Alexander Lowrey, who led a battalion of militia from the church to the battle of Brandywine in 1777. Colonel Lowery was one of the first in the region to advocate independence.

It was Lurgan-born James Logan, agent for Governor William Penn, who reserved all of Donegal township for the Scots-Irish. The township was later divided into Rapho, Mount Joy, East and West Donegal and Convoy townships, all named after localities in Co Donegal back in Ireland. It included what are now the boroughs of Elizabethtown, Marietta and Mount Joy.

FRONTIER WORSHIP AT TIMBER RIDGE CHURCH

Timber Ridge Presbyterian Church in Rockbridge County, Virginia was founded by Ulster-Scots who moved to this part of the Shenandoah Valley during the 1730-40s from Co Antrim. This is the oldest community in Rockbridge County (main town Lexington), and the church was the earliest in the area.

It was Ulsterman Ephraim McDowell who led his family and friends in 1737 on to the border lands they were to call Timber Ridge and, being strong Presbyterians, they continued to worship in the traditional manner they had been taught back in their former homeland.

McDowell and his compatriots set about erecting log cabin homes, but it was not until 1746 that they had a proper church meeting house—services, until then, were held in the various homes.

Worshippers of Timber Ridge and the adjoining New Providence congregation were "put into church order" during a missionary visit by the Rev. John Blair, from Donegal Presbytery in Pennsylvania, and the first minister the Rev. William Dean, was called in 1748.

He died before assuming the charge, and it was not until 1755 that a replacement arrived—the Rev. John Brown, another of Ulster extraction. At this time, the settlers were under constant threat of Indian attacks, and one of John Brown's first duties as pastor of Timber Ridge was to organise a day of fasting and prayer on account of the French-Indian War and the many murders by the Indians in the region.

The call to the Rev. John Brown was signed by 116 persons, with the first signature that of Co Antrim man John Houston, grandfather of General Sam Houston, governor of Tennessee and Texas. Sam was born a few yards from Timber Ridge Church. The list of signatures included the McDowells, Lyles, Davidsons, McClungs, Campbells, Paxtons, Thomsons, Mackeys and Alexanders—all families who had moved a few years earlier from Ulster. A stone church was erected in 1755-56 with John Lyle and James McClung heading the building committee.

A marble tablet, bearing the date 1756, was erected on the front wall of the simple limestone structure, which sat on an acre of land deeded by Robert Houston. The families donated generously to buy the building materials, but work was carried out by voluntary labour, with the bare hands of the most able-bodied members. The sand used for "lyme" in the construction was carried by the women on horseback from South River, a distance of five miles. The women rode under protection of the men, who walked with rifles at the ready through forests inhabited by hostile Indian tribes.

The building of stone and lyme is the nave of the present church. Daniel Lyle was the stonemason, and his building has been in use for 240 years, and is one of two such colonial structures west of the Blue Ridge Mountains, the other being the Augusta Old Stone Presbyterian Church.

The Timber Ridge structure was designed as a fortress during the period of the French-Indian War. There was an earthen floor with split logs for seats. The pulpit was at the northeastern corner of the church. Each family had their own log, a tradition which was continued through the benches and the pews, and even exists to some extent today.

Dr. James G. Leyburn, in his book *The Scotch-Irish*, A Social History, tells about the all-day service they would have been accustomed to in churches like Timber Ridge. Two sermons were preached each Sunday, with twelve points, compared to today's three-point sermons. The people would stand up and stretch when they needed to. During lunch, young couples would court (talk to each other!) under the watchful eye of their parents and other members of the congregation.

Fathers would talk crops and weather, or perhaps politics. Mothers would compare stories of children or news of those who had moved westward. The church provided the opportunity to socialise. The Presbyterians of Timber Ridge were not always united, and doctrinal differences led to splits between those who adhered to the more evangelical "New Lights" movement and the more traditional and formal "Old Lights."

In the 19th century there were three different Presbyterian factions operating at Timber Ridge. One faction, the Seceders, later attached to the Associate Reformed Presbyterian Church. They confined themselves to singing metrical translations of the Psalms, a tradition dating back to the Covenanters on the Scottish hillsides.

A grammar school was founded in 1749 by Robert Alexander, one of the Timber Ridge congregation, and this eventually became Washington and Lee University at Lexington. Timber Ridge congregation generously funded the school and maintained it during the Revolutionary War years. The University is the oldest American institution of learning off the Atlantic seaboard and the fifth oldest U.S. university. In 1798, President George Washington granted the University the largest grant up to that time in the history of American education—$50,000.

COVENANTING PREACHER THE REV WILLIAM MARTIN

Many Ulster Presbyterian clerics created an unfavourable impression with British colonial interests in America at the time of the Revolutionary War. They were seen as "turbulent priests," unwilling to conform or move their congregations away from the dissenting path that was leading to independence from the Crown.

Covenanting pastor Rev. William Martin was a thorn in the flesh of the British authorities in his South Carolina Piedmont parish, and so strong was the revolutionary tone of his sermons to his people that he was arrested and his church burned down by British forces.

Martin, a Presbyterian of the Reformed code, was born at Ballyspollum near Ballykelly in Co Londonderry in 1729. When minister of the church at Ballymoney in Co Antrim, his uncompromising advocacy of the gospel was matched by his fearless out-spokeness against the Anglican-influenced British authorities, who had been discriminating against the Ulster Presbyterians on the matter of civil rights.

After a sustained period of excessive rent demands and eviction of tenants from their homesteads in rural parts of Ulster like Ballymoney, William Martin declared from his pulpit that "enough was enough."

"Anyone who knows anything about the Ulster countryside realises that the rents are so high that the land does not bring in enough to pay them. Many of us are beggared and in time all would be," he told his congregation in 1772, adding that as a minister he could not stand idly by and await the violence and ruin that would come.

"Steps should be taken now to see that such situations did not develop," Martin advised and suggested that they all pool their limited resources and send to Belfast to charter ships for emigration to South Carolina, where they would "obtain free land and live free men."

With other Covenanting families, the Rev. William Martin and his congregation left for Charleston in five ships during the autumn of 1772—the

James and Mary and Lord Dunluce sailing from Larne; the *Pennsylvania Farmer* and the *Hopewell* from Belfast and the *Free Mason* from Newry. In all, 467 families, representing more than 1,000 people, set sail.

Many Ulster immigrants arrived in South Carolina under the "bounty" scheme. This entitlement of £4 was being offered to "poor Protestants" from Europe to settle in the region, with small amounts paid to children. The Scots-Irish took advantage of the bounty, and when the offer was abolished in 1768 the South Carolina authorities ruled that the settlers should be given the lands free.

William Martin and his Ballymoney congregation settled on the free Carolina lands, alongside Seceders, a splinter Presbyterian group from neighbouring Ballyrashane, Derrykeghan and Kilraughts in North Antrim.

They initially combined in a Reformed union church at Rocky Mountain Road, about 15 miles from the South Carolina town of Chester, appropriately called "Catholic," but later Martin moved to their own log church two miles further along.

The Revolutionary War had just broken out and it provided William Martin with the opportunity to remind his congregation of why they had to leave their Ulster homeland, and he bluntly denounced the British colonial rulers.

Recalling the hardships their fathers had endured in religion and in their possessions, Martin pointed out: "They had been forced out of Ireland, had come over to America and cleared their lands and homes and their church and were free men."

Martin warned that the British were coming into the region and soldiers would again be depriving them of the fruits of their labours and would be driving them out. They should not stand, he said, meekly and idly by while all they had wrought was taken from them.

"There was a time to pray and a time to fight and the time to fight had come," he implored.

Two companies of militiamen were formed from the congregation, and the next day they set off with arms and horses to join the American revolutionary army. Martin's sermon, had reached the ears of British commanders in the region, and his church was burned down.

Martin was even brought before Lord Charles Cornwallis to give an account of his activities, such was in his reputation with the British. When he was released, he lived for a period in the strong Presbyterian dissenting community of Mecklenburg County in North Carolina, but after the British surrender at Yorktown, he returned to Chester County and resumed charge of his congregation.

The Revolutionary War service of William Martin and 64 of his congregation from the Catholic Presbyterian Church at Chester County, South Carolina is recorded in a memorial at the church, unveiled in 1933. Almost all were first generation Ulster-Scots.

It was common for most of the male members of Presbyterian congregations in the backwoods territories to join the militia units involved in the independence struggle. Historical accounts of the Nazareth congregation in another part of the South Carolina Piedmont show that every able-bodied man fought for the patriot cause.

They were at the battles of Kings Mountain, Cowpens, Charleston, Yorktown, Valley Forge, and Ninety Six, significant encounters on the frontier. Between battles, these farmers were allowed to return to their homes for the protection of their families against Indian attack, and when they were needed, the word was spread quickly from neighbour to neighbour.

The Nazareth Presbyterians formed the Spartan regiment, from which the town of Spartanburg got its name, and it was said their womenfolk showed "as much fortitude in suffering and hardship as the men displayed in fighting."

Pioneering Ulster-American links

Boston, Massachusetts was the set destination port for the first ship to set sail from Ulster shores for America, but its 1636 voyage from the Co Down coastal resort of Groomsport was aborted after heavy storms in mid-Atlantic.

Some 140 Presbyterians from congregations on both sides of Belfast Lough in North Co Down and East Co Antrim sailed from Groomsport on September 9, Boston-bound. The journey ended back in Carrickfergus Bay on November 3 with the ships shrouds asunder, mainsail in ribbons and rudder badly damaged.

It had been a traumatic experience for the voyagers who had completed three-quarters of the journey when one of the Presbyterian ministers on board, Rev. John Livingstone, advised, in the face of the continuing storm, that it was God's will that they should return home. The ship's captain was of similar mind, and the 150-tonne vessel was turned around. The *Eagle Wing* journey, notwithstanding its apparent failure, is remarkable in that it took place only 16 years after the Puritan Pilgrim fathers landed at Plymouth Rock after crossing the Atlantic on the Mayflower.

The first recorded sailing of an immigrant ship from the north of Ireland to America was that of the Friend's *Goodwill* from Larne in Co Antrim in April 1717. Five thousand people, mostly of Presbyterian stock, left Ulster that year, laying the foundations for future immigration and settlement.

Massachusetts was the American colony which the Scots-Irish first focused on as an immigrant point and before the trek from Ulster began in earnest in 1717, a significant number came to Boston as indentured servants.

In the summer and autumn of 1718, an estimated 600 Presbyterians from the Bann Valley region around Coleraine, Aghadowey, Macosquin and Ballymoney arrived in Boston, then a strong English Puritan settlement. Their passage had earlier been sounded out by the Rev. William Boyd of Macosquin, who was sent ahead to view out the land of their adoption.

William Boyd presented a petition to the Massachusetts Governor Samuel Shute, calling for a portion of land to be allocated to the would-be Bann Valley emigrants and Boyd's report of the land and climate was highly favourable. The reasons given for the emigration by the Bann Valley Presbyterians were not founded on materialism, but on matters of faith—"to avoid oppression, to shun persecution, to cease from communications with idolaters and to secure freedom of worship."

Assurances of support were given by Governor Shute, who was to be a steadfast friend of the Ulster immigrants. On October 31, 1718, a petition for a grant was presented to the House of Representatives of Massachusetts by the Rev. James MacGregor and Archibald Boyd on behalf of themselves and 26 others just arrived in Boston and 40 families who, were on their way. Sailing ships which took them were the *William and Elizabeth, William and Mary, McCallom,* and *Mary and Elizabeth.*

MacGregor had been Presbyterian minister of Aghadowey, and he was leader of the 1718 exodus from the Bann Valley. He was the son of Captain MacGregor, of Co Londonderry, and as a youth had been at the Siege of Londonderry in 1688-89. His text on the eve-of-departure sermon in Aghadowey Presbyterian Church was: "If Thy presence go not with me, carry us up not hence."

The first of the ships carrying the Bann Valley Presbyterians arrived in Boston harbour on August 4, 1718. The initial reception in Boston for the Ulster families was grudging. Massachusetts Puritans were opposed to all "Irish immigrants," which certainly applied to the Ulster influx. In 1700, leading New England Puritan Cotton Mather denounced proposals to bring "Irish" to the colony as "formidable attempts by Satan and his sons to unsettle us."

Shortly after arrival the Presbyterians were informed that citizenship would not be granted in any Puritan colony only by membership of the established Congregational church. But only a few of the immigrants were prepared to forsake the Presbyterian Church.

Governor Shute granted the Presbyterians township rights, which permitted them to occupy any suitable area, twelve miles square on the frontier. Shute recommended to them the region around Casco Bay, near the present city of Portland, Maine. This region verged on Indian land and in the early years the Presbyterian settlers had an "unenviable time" from the hostile tribes.

However, on the frontier away from the Puritans, the Bann Valley Presbyterians founded a church and a school, and managed to develop a thriving community.

Later, the Massachusetts governor referred to his assembly the heavy charge falling on the New England authorities because of immigration of "poor people from abroad, especially those that come from Ireland."

The Bann Valley Presbyterians introduced two commodities into New England that had never before been seen there—the small flax spinning wheel and the Irish potato, which was different from the American-grown sweet potato and looked upon as good staple food by the Ulster folk. The settlers complemented the potato with the bean porridge and barley broth they brewed from the health ingredients of the New World. The Ulster-

Scots were well versed in supplanting cottage industry and the means of providing very necessary food supplies.

In April, 1719, sixteen Presbyterian families were settled in two rows of cabins along West Running Brook to the east of Beaver Brook. Initially known as Nuffield, the New Hampshire settlement became Londonderry in 1723 and a field was planted known as the Common Field, where the first Irish potato was grown in North America.

Fifty Presbyterian families were settled in the New Hampshire township of Worcester, from which a nearby town of Coleraine emerged.

MISSION REVIVAL IN KENTUCKY AND TENNESSEE

Religious revivals were a common event in the Appalachian states during the early 19th century, and one of the most famous of these mass inspirational witnesses occurred in Kentucky in 1800, amongst a population predominantly Scots-Irish. The Kentucky spiritual movement has been likened to the 1859 Revival which took place in Ulster, mainly among the Presbyterian stock of counties Antrim and Down.

The centre of the 1800 revival was Logan County, in southwest Kentucky close to the Tennessee border and what was then known as Cumberland County. This is a beautiful region, with a salubrious climate and fertile soil, a place where the Scots-Irish settlers who moved from Virginia and the Carolinas had no hesitation in making their home.

The Presbyterian segment of the population was the most numerous in Logan County, and the revival that was initiated by pioneer preachers came within the bounds of the Transylvania presbytery and synod of Kentucky.

The tendency to revivalism which got to the roots of fundamentalist Calvinism was strongly opposed by the leaders of the synod, and some of those who initiated the movement were disciplined for alleged laxity and practice of religion.

The Rev. James McGready, son of Ulster-born parents, was the man who ignited the spark of revivalism when he arrived in Logan County from North Carolina in 1796. This doughty Scots-Irishman preached a modified Calvinism, dwelling on the necessity of the new birth and the importance of knowing the time when and the place where the conversion occurred.

McGready was one of the founding fathers of the Cumberland Presbyterian Church, which has its origins in the Cumberland region of Tennessee and quickly spread into Kentucky and Virginia in the early 1800s.

The theology was similar in style to that practiced by the Revs. John Wesley and George Whitefield, the 18th century English preachers who spread the word of God through the eastern colonies of America. The message was clear and strong with impenitent sinners urged to seek immediate salvation in Jesus Christ.

McGready became minister of three small Presbyterian congregations—Gasper River, Muddy River and Red River. Logan County, like other frontier communities in the late 18th century, was a turbulent, rumbustious society where so lax was the enforcement of justice that many law-breakers prevailed. Even among the law-abiding people in what was classed as a Presbyterian settlement there was a significant degree of irreligion, with drunkenness a common trait. But when James McGready arrived the mood changed, and a greater spirituality transcended the county.

From the preaching they heard folk speak increasingly of the need of the soul's salvation, and news was noised abroad of the evangelical zeal of James McGready. In the summer of 1799, two McGee brothers—William, a Presbyterian, and John, a Methodist, arrived at Red River and from James McGready's gospel meetings they found the inspiration to develop a ministry which extended into neighbouring states. Other pastors who joined were William Hodge, Samuel McAdoo and John Rankin.

The Rev. William Henry Foote, in his history of North Carolina and Virginia, recounts how the revival fires were lit by people who returned from McGready's meetings. From distances of up to 200 miles families came in covered wagons, equipped with food and bedding to listen to the preaching at Red River, Gasper River and Muddy River settlements. The Gasper River gathering of 1800 was the first known religious camp meeting in America.

The Ulster Revival of 1859 had remarkable parallels with the Kentucky experience of 1800, more than just the Presbyterian kin which bonded the communities on both sides of the Atlantic. It began in the Connor district of Co Antrim close to the town of Ballymena as the result of a fellowship meeting in a butcher's shop. The Revival extended across Co Antrim and into neighbouring counties of Down and Armagh with congregations of several thousand people gathering in the open air, remaining all day in prayer and praise.

THE FEARLESS EXPLOITS OF DARING SCOTS-IRISH
FRONTIERSMEN

14

ROBERT ROGERS OF THE NORTHWEST FRONTIER

Major Robert Rogers, who led the Rogers Rangers in the French-Indian War of 1756-63, was the son of an Ulster Presbyterian couple and was born in Methuen, Massachusetts after the family emigrated from Co Londonderry around 1730.

As a soldier, Rogers used unconventional tactics in warfare, which spawned the concept of light infantry, and he later became governor of Michilimackinac (northern Michigan).

His father, James Rogers, came from Montelony, in the Sperrin Mountains near to the present-day Northern Ireland town of Dungiven, Co Londonderry, and he married Mary McFatridge several years before they emigrated. They had four children born in Ireland (Daniel, Samuel, Martha and James) and six in America (Robert, Richard, Mary, John, Catherine and Amy).

On arrival in America, they settled at Methuen, Massachusetts, an area inhabited by a Puritan community, but moved to the Merrimack River territory in 1736 and finally settled in New Hampshire, at Rumford, which is present-day Concord.

New England was not a particularly welcoming place for Ulster-Scots Presbyterians. The Puritans, whose ancestors crossed the Atlantic on the Mayflower from Plymouth in England in 1620, eyed them coldly as "a parcel of Irish" and some even damned them as "black Papists."

Methuen, however, was a Puritan township which showed some degree of tolerance for the Scots-Irish families who settled there, and with no Presbyterian church in the region, James and Mary Rogers had their children baptised by a local Puritan pastor and attended services regularly.

In Massachusetts, James and Mary Rogers became good friends of Joseph Putney and his family, and they acquired land in a nearby region known as the "Great Meadows," with 365 acres allocated to each family. This was a virtual wilderness way off the recognised frontier boundary, and in the spring of 1739, the two families loaded all their possessions on to two ox carts for the movement to the new lands.

James Rogers named his farm Montelony after the townland in the north of Ireland from which they had come and after five years of toil the farms were in a prosperous state, with 100 acres fenced in for hay-meadow and animal pasture, with as many more sown to grain, and a sizeable apple orchard.

From 1745 the upsurge in violence as a result of French-backed Indian attacks raised serious concerns for families on the outer reaches of the frontier. In May, 1746, the Rogers and Putney families had to make a hasty retreat when scouts arrived to alert them about an Indian war party dispatched by the French from Fort St. Frederick on Lake Champlain.

When James Rogers and Joseph Putney returned the next day to retrieve belongings they found the ruins of their log cabin homes still smouldering, cattle slaughtered and the orchard of apple trees—some already in fruit—destroyed except for one tree.

Both families made several attempts to return to their land and rebuild their homes, and James Rogers even petitioned the governor of New Hampshire "praying for assistance against the savages." By 1748, they joined with a group of settlers from Londonderry, New Hampshire, whose families had moved from the Lower Bann Valley region in Ulster in 1718, and formed the town of Starkstown, named after Ulsterman, Archibald Stark, along the Massachusetts state line.

Each shareholder in Starkstown received 200 acres, but tragedy struck in 1753 when James Rogers was accidentally shot dead by an old hunter friend who mistook him for a bear. It was dusk, and folk tradition says Rogers was wearing a bearskin coat.

James Rogers was buried at East Derry, New Hampshire, and he left real estate valued at £1,500 and personal property of £444, a considerable amount in those days. Evidently, he prospered when Starkstown was established.

Robert Rogers was born in 1731, and he grew up in a typical frontier farming community. His soldiering began with the New Hampshire regiment and, after showing exceptional skills as a leader of raids and scouting expeditions in the Merrimack and Contoocook Rivers, he was appointed captain of an independent ranger company supported by British government funds and consisting of frontiersmen of similar robust stock.

The companies were used by the British colonists mainly for reconnaissance against the French and Indians, and in Rogers commanded nine such units. He fought in the battles of Halifax (1757), Ticonderoga (1758) and Crown Point (1759), and in 1760 took part in final operations against Montreal and went west to receive the surrender of Detroit and fought engagements from Scioto River to Sonioto (Shawneetown) on the Ohio River.

Robert Rogers, six feet tall, always felt the urge to know and what was beyond the distant hills. He constantly talked with hunters and Indians about the uncultivated desert, listening and questioning about the mountains, valleys, rivers, lakes and passes. He became not only inured to the hardships faced in the frontier wilderness, but singularly prepared for service in the great beyond.

Robert Rogers, who married Elizabeth Browne, daughter of Presbyterian minister Rev. Arthur Browne, also led an independent company of rangers in operations against the Cherokee Indians in 1761, and he commanded a New York company in the relief and defence of Detroit.

For his brave exploits in soldiering, Rogers received wide acclaim, but his business and financial affairs were not in good shape and he moved to England to escape creditors. During the stay in London in 1765, he published his journals as a hero in the wild and rugged American frontier: Concise Account of North America and Ponteach—The Savages of America, a Tragedy.

In the years leading up to the American Revolutionary War, Rogers courted both the American patriots and the British, and in 1776—at the height of hostilities—he was imprisoned by George Washington "as a spy." He strongly denied the charge, declaring: "I love America and I intend to spend the evening of my days in it." He was eventually released.

His political leanings, however, were as a Tory, and he escaped and was commissioned to raise the Queen's American Rangers. But this last military charge was short-lived and in 1780, Rogers made it back to England where he died 15 years later, a largely anonymous and impoverished hero.

The story of the exploits of Major Robert Rogers is related in a hollywood movie, titles "Northwest Passage" and starring actor Spencer Tracey.

Boston Tea Party: Two Co Down brothers Robert and James Maxwell took part in the infamous Boston Tea Party in December 16, 1773, dressed as Indians. The Maxwells were part of a radical group called "The Sons of Liberty" campaigning for American independence.

SAMUEL LANGHORN CLEMENS,
THE AUTHOR MARK TWAIN

$\cdot\!\sim\!\mathbf{15}\!\sim\!\cdot$

ULSTER-SCOTS LUMINARIES
ACROSS SOCIETY

Americans from an Ulster-Scots family background contributed much to the social, economic and literary life of the United States over the past 200 years. Their initiative, foresight and energy ensure that they enjoy and deserve a proud and lasting place on the pages of American history.

These luminaries, who played a key role in making America great, included:

SAMUEL LANGHORN CLEMENS, the world-acclaimed author Mark Twain, had direct Ulster links on both sides of his family.

Clemens, under the pseudonym of Mark Twain, became a novelist, short story writer and humourist. His childhood growing up in the wilds of Missouri were recalled in classic books *The Adventures of Tom Sawyer* (1876) and *The Adventures of Huckleberry Finn* (1884). He worked as a printer and journalist and as a pilot on the Mississippi River steamers. His literary pen name was taken from the riverboat term, meaning safe water of two fathoms.

Revolutionary War hero Colonel William Casey and his wife Jane Montgomery Casey were grandparents of Jane Lampton Clemens, Samuel

Langhorn's mother, and both belonged to families who emigrated from Ulster in the mid-18th century. Colonel Casey was a prominent landowner after the War in Virginia, Tennessee and Kentucky.

John Marshall Clemens, Mark Twain's father, was born at Bedford county in the Shenandoah Valley of Virginia into a family with Co Antrim roots. The family moved to Adair County in Kentucky, where John was a lawyer and he married Jane Lampton, daughter of Benjamin and Peggy Casey Lampton, a couple who had pioneered a wild and remote region at Cherry Creek, deep in the Cumberland mountains of Tennessee. They later moved to Missouri where their son Samuel Langhorn was born in 1835.

CYRUS HALL MCCORMICK: This mid-19th century inventor of the agricultural reaping machine which revolutionised grain harvesting in the United States came of an Ulster Presbyterian family who settled in the Shenandoah Valley of Virginia.

McCormick, born in 1809 on a farm in Rockbridge County close to Lexington, was obsessed with experimenting on the tools of the land, and in 1831 he built his first reaper which he tested on the wheat and oats of his father Robert's farm.

By 1840 Cyrus, with the help of his brothers, had perfected the reaper as a saleable commodity in Virginia, and within a few years, he had expanded his business to other parts of the United States.

The horse-drawn reaper enabled farmers to harvest more than 10 acres of grain a day, quite an advance from the two or three acres achieved via the hand-scythe methods.

It was an invention which really caught the imagination of farmers across America, and when his business expanded, McCormick moved to Chicago in 1847. There he used the Great Lakes of the Mid-West to transport the reapers to the eastern states and the Mississippi River to the territories of the South, and into Canada.

The advent of the railways boosted trade, and by the early 1850s, McCormick Harvesting Machine Company was listed as the largest farm implement factory in the world. McCormick remained president of the multi-million dollar company until his death in 1884, and by 1902 the concern had merged to become the International Harvester Company under his son Cyrus Jr.

The enterprising Cyrus McCormick was a man possessed with enthusiasm, inventive genius and commercial ability. He also established the McCormick Presbyterian theological seminary and was also engaged in real estate, mining and railroading interests.

McCormick's humble ancestors had moved to the Shenandoah Valley from the north of Ireland in the mid-18th century and prospered at Rockbridge County. In Northern Ireland today the McCormick or McCormack family link is very strong, right across the Province.

Cyrus McCormick is remembered at an exhibition in the ancestral home of President Ulysses Simpson Grant's great grandfather John Simpson, at Dergenagh near Dungannon, Co Tyrone. The McCormick family lived near the Simpsons in this rural locality.

THOMAS ANDREW MELLON, founder of a vast industrial and commercial enterprise in the United States during the 19th century, was born outside Omagh in Co Tyrone and emigrated with his family to Pennsylvania as a five-year-old in 1818.

Mellon, a lawyer and later a judge, became one of the leaders of the Pittsburgh Bar, and he was legal adviser of wealthy business and financial entrepreneurs in the city.

In 1870, Thomas Mellon established the banking house of T. Mellon and Sons, with his sons Thomas Alexander and James Ross as partners. The highly successful Mellon family business dynasty was expanded with the purchase of the Ligonier Valley railway, and Thomas Sr. also became the owner of an iron foundry and was a major share-holder in traction lines in Pittsburgh.

Andrew William Mellon, a son of Thomas Mellon, served as secretary of the United States treasury under three presidents—Warren G. Harding, Calvin Coolidge and Herbert Hoover. In 1932, he became American Ambassador to Britain.

The Mellons were descended from Archibald Mellon and his wife Elizabeth, lowland Scottish Presbyterians who arrived in Ulster in 1660 to settle on an Omagh farm, which today forms the site of the Ulster-American Folk Park.

WILLIAM CLARK, who with Meriwether Lewis led the celebrated overland expedition to the north-west Pacific coast region of America in

1804-06, was a second generation Ulster-Scot whose family moved from the north of Ireland to Pennsylvania and into the Shenandoah Valley of Virginia during the mid-18th century.

Clark's family settled at Charlottesville, Virginia and a brother General George Rogers Clark was a distinguished Revolutionary War soldier in frontier battles in Virginia and Kentucky.

The Clark-Lewis expedition over thousands of miles, through rough mountainous terrain and during the hot and cold extremes of weather, was undertaken at the behest of President Thomas Jefferson, who had purchased the Louisiana territory in 1803 from the French Goverment for 15 million dollars. The territory, stretching more than 800,000 square miles from the Mississippi River to the Rocky Mountains, doubled the country's size.

Main objectives of the expedition were to determine how easily the American continent could be crossed and, along the way, the William Clark-Meriwether Lewis-led party studied the various aspects of the land—the soil, climate, plant and animal life. They also offered friendship, trade, education and even vaccination to the native American people and studied every aspect of Indian life—tribal names, numbers, languages, laws and traditions. William Clark was the first governor of Missouri in the 1813-21 period.

CHRISTOPHER "KIT" CARSON, a Kentuckian of a Scots-Irish family who had moved from Ulster to America in the mid-18th century, was an Indian fighter, scout, and frontiersman who explored the far west and the south into Mexican territory for upwards of 50 years.

Carson was born in Madison County, Kentucky, where his family was close associates of Daniel Boone, and Kit grew up in Missouri. He gained his apprenticeship as a saddle-maker, and after leaving home at the age of 17, teamed up with a band of traders moving in the direction of the Rocky Mountains.

For most of a decade Carson was involved in the lucrative business of beaver trapping, and he was also a driver on the wagon-hauling freight trains across the Santa Fe Trail which opened up in the 1820s.

Carson guided a U.S. government-funded expedition to California and in 1842-46, and he assisted the noted explorer John Charles Fremont in making an accurate map of the Oregon Train, which detailed such things as campsites and estimates of possible daily travel.

Kit was also a guide to the force which captured California during the Mexican War, and in 1853 he became the Indian agent at Taos, New Mexico.

During the Gold Rush of 1849, Carson was involved in the delivery of a half a million sheep from New Mexico to California. The gold miners were prepared to pay a good price for the sheep.

When the Civil War began, Carson joined the Union Army, serving as colonel in the New Mexico Volunteers, and a for a short time he commanded Fort Union, the U.S. Army's largest post at the strategic point of the mountain branch and the Cimarron Cutoff of the Santa Fe Trail.

Kit Carson, of diminutive stature, was a man of extraordinary courage and daring, and his exploits were legendary in the rapid expansion of American interests in the southern and western frontiers during the mid-19th century. In one daring escapade, the colourful Carson and a lone companion took on and defeated 30 outlaw Indians.

For a century and a half dozens of books and comic strips have covered his remarkable frontier exploits.

ROBERT WORTH BINGHAM, whose family roots are traced back 200 years to Kilmore near Crossgar, Co Down, was a leading Kentucky politician and newspaper proprietor of the early 20th century. Bingham, a Democratic Mayor of Louisville and publisher of the Louisville Courier-Journal, was British ambassador in 1933-37.

WILLIAM RANDOLPH HEARST, founder of the great American publishing dynasty, was a direct descendant of John Hearst, a Ballybay, Co Monaghan Presbyterian who emigrated to America with 300 co-religionists, sailing from Newry, Co Down in 1764.

JAMES CLARK MCREYNOLDS: This great, grandson of 18th century immigrants from Killyman, Co Tyrone was attorney-general in the administration of President Woodrow Wilson, and he also served in the administrations of Presidents Theodore Roosevelt and William Howard Taft.

SAMUEL DAVID MCREYNOLDS, a distant cousin of James Clark McReynolds, was a Tennessee lawyer and criminal court judge, who, during the White House administration of President Franklin D. Roosevelt in the 1930s, was leader of the House Foreign Affairs (Representatives) Committee. McReynolds was a member for Tennessee in the U.S. House of Representatives.

JOHN BELL, a candidate for the American Presidency against Abraham Lincoln in 1860 on the Whig ticket, is descended from Shenandoah Valley settler Joseph Bell, one of three brothers whose father emigrated from the north of Ireland in the 1730s. Bell, a Tennessee lawyer, served 14 years in the U.S. House of Representatives, one year as speaker; as war secretary in 1841 and a senator for 12 years.

JOHN ADAIR, eighth governor of Kentucky, was the son of Ulster-born parents William and Mary Moore Adair, who lived in Chester County, South Carolina and Charlotte, North Carolina after emigrating from Ireland. John Adair was a political activist, who distinguished himself as a militiaman and in state and national office. He was state representative and speaker of the Kentucky House and was a United States senator and congressman over different periods. He was elected governor of Kentucky in 1820 and, during his term of office, was instrumental in passing stringent anti-gambling laws and abolishing imprisonment for debt. He fought in the Revolutionary War, and during the War of 1812 he was commander of the Kentucky rifle brigade at the Battle of New Orleans.

THE ULSTERMAN WAS THERE

HI! UNCLE SAM!
WHEN FREEDOM WAS DENIED YOU,
AND IMPERIAL MIGHT DEFIED YOU,
WHO WAS IT STOOD BESIDE YOU,
AT QUEBEC AND BRANDYWINE?
AND DARED RETREATS AND DANGERS
REDCOATS AND HESSIAN STRANGERS
IN THE LEAN, LONG-RIFLED RANGERS,
AND THE PENNSYLVANIA LINE!

HI! UNCLE SAM!
WHEREVER THERE WAS FIGHTING,
OR WRONG THAT NEEDED RIGHTING,
AN ULSTERMAN WAS SIGHTING,
HIS KENTUCKY GUN WITH CARE:
ALL THE ROAD TO YORKTOWN,
FROM LEXINGTON TO YORKTOWN,
FROM VALLEY FORGE TO YORKTOWN,
THAT ULSTERMAN WAS THERE!

HI! UNCLE SAM!
VIRGINIA SENT HER BRAVE MEN,
THE NORTH PARADED GRAVE MEN,
THAT THEY MIGHT NOT BE SLAVE MEN,
BUT PONDER THIS WITH CALM:
THE FIRST TO FACE THE TORY
AND THE FIRST TO LIFT OLD GLORY,
MADE YOUR WAR AN ULSTER STORY,
THINK IT OVER, UNCLE SAM!

W. F. MARSHALL (REV),
CO TYRONE.

"It is Scotch-Irish in substantial origin, in complexion and history - Scotch Irish in the countenance of the living and the records of the dead" - report to the American Congress in the late 18th century about Western Pennsylvania and Pittsburgh.

FROM DONEGAL TO THE SHENANDOAH VALLEY, TO TEXAS, TO OUTER SPACE…!

16

Frontiersmen in Virginia and Kentucky

John Lewis—Shenandoah Valley's First Scots-Irish Settler

Donegal couple John and Margaret Lewis and their six children are widely acknowledged to be the first immigrants to settle at the southern end of the Shenandoah Valley of Virginia. In 1732 the Lewises arrived in the region that today is Augusta County with its main town of Staunton, and they established a family settlement which more than 270 years on is still very firmly rooted in the fertile soil of Virginia.

John Lewis, a Presbyterian, was descended from French Huguenots, who had moved to Ulster during the 17th century. He was born in Donegal in 1678, son of Andrew and Mary Calhoun Lewis and his wife Margaret was of the Lynn connection, also a Presbyterian family and from East Donegal close to Londonderry and Lough Foyle.

Margaret's brother, Dr. William Lynn, also emigrated to Virginia, settling in Fredericksburg, and in his will he refers to brothers and sisters living in Strabane, Co Tyrone and Letterkenny (Co Donegal). The Lynns were related to the Pattons, of Limavady, who also moved to the American colonies.

Members of the Lewis and Lynn families are believed to have figured on the Protestant Willamette side at the Siege of Londonderry in 1688-89. John Lewis was a child during this period.

Historical reports relate that John, a tenant farmer of some substance, left Ireland under a cloud after an affray with a landlord who had threatened to dispossess many of his land tenants, including Lewis. In the sharp exchange, the landlord was killed and Lewis hurriedly fled to America arriving in Pennsylvania in 1731.

Agatha Towels, a grand-daughter of John Lewis, in a memoir in 1837, stated that after his encounter with the landlord, Lewis took refuge and as soon as a ship was ready, he left for America. Margaret Lewis and her children came on a vessel with 300 passengers, all Presbyterians, and after a journey of three months landed on the Delaware River.

Within a year, John Lewis was joined by his wife and young family— four sons and Samuel, Thomas, Andrew and William and two daughters Margaret and Anne. A fifth son, Charles, was born in Augusta County four years after their arrival. The Lewises came to the Shenandoah Valley as an isolated family before careful attempts were made to settle the region as part of the Beverley Manor. They had trudged most of the journey on foot, trekking along an old buffalo trail used by Indians.

There are no reports that John Lewis was ever charged for the alleged misdemeanour in Ireland although he must have received some form of pardon. He never returned to his Donegal homeland and stories about involvement in the killing of a landlord have been given various slants by historians in America down the years.

Whatever the true nature of the incident, John Lewis and his family prospered in America after a few tough years acclimatising to the wilds of the frontier. He built his Irish-style Fort Lewis home—a half stone, half log cabin structure—at Bellefonte about a mile east of present-day Staunton, and with his four sons immediately set about tilling the lush Shenandoah lands. The Lewises were assisted in the settlement by an aristocrat of English stock, Sir William Beverly, who was heavily involved in land speculation in Virginia.

Beverley, in 1736, acquired 118,491 acres of land in the shadow of the Blue Ridge Mountains close to the Shenandoah River, and in the several years from the arrival of the Lewises, about 50 families of Scots-Irish vintage moved into the region. These settlers squatted at first in clearings they had opened up with their bare hands, but they eventually bought the holdings from Beverley.

Additional settlers were attracted to Staunton along the Great Wagon Road, while Beverley circulated notices in Pennsylvania and hired an Ulster sea captain, James Patton from Limavady, Co Londonderry, to entice the ever-increasing flow of emigrants and indentures from the north of Ireland. Within a decade, so many Scots-Irish families had settled on Beverley's lands that it became widely known as the Irish tract, with Staunton a town of much Scots-Irish influence.

Patton, who served in the Royal Navy, used his own ship and is reported to have crossed the Atlantic 25 times, carrying cargoes of goods and hundreds of Ulsterman and women. Patton was related to John and Margaret Lewis by way of his mother's Lynn connections.

August County was formally organised in 1745, with Thomas Lewis, son of the first settlers, appointed county surveyor and Captain James Patton sheriff. With Orange County, which had been organised in 1734, Augusta County stretched from the Blue Ridge Mountains, to the frontier limits of Virginia, bordering on so-far largely unpopulated territory.

Until the Scots-Irish settlers and German moved in, the Valley of Virginia had lain largely uninhabited. The native Indian tribes passed through the region and hunted there , but they had not settled villages. Relationships between the settlers and Indians in the early years were friendly but guarded. Tensions, however, surfaced after 1750 when the pioneers began crossing the Allegheny Mountains to take up Indian lands, and hostilities started that were to become known as the French-Indian wars. Andrew and Charles Lewis, son of the first settler, participated in this conflict.

John Lewis, for the bargain price of fourteen pounds, acquired the title for 2,071 acres of Beverley Manor land in 1739. But William Beverley explained "the favour was bestowed on Lewis for the extraordinary trouble of his house and charges in entertaining those who had come to settle on Beverley Manor." It was located in the vicinity of the twin hills "Betsy Bell" and "Mary Gray," which were named after two similar hills in the Sperrin mountain region of Co Tyrone.

The Lewis home was a meeting place and social centre for the new settlers. It was there was that the Rev. James Anderson, who had been sent to Virginia by the Presbyterian Synod of Philadelphia, preached in 1738 in what was the first regular sermon ever delivered in this part of the American frontier.

The new settlers were arriving daily, some on horseback or by mule-drawn carts along what were nothing more than dirt tracks. Much later, settlers came in the horse-drawn Conestoga covered wagons which were a familiar sight in the opening up of the West in the early 19th century. From 1750 to 1776, it was said that the south-bound settlers heading along the Great Wagon Road were numbered in tens of thousands.

John Lewis was a highly ambitious pioneer and not only did he enjoy the reputation of being the first settler in the southwest Shenandoah Valley, but he was the most influential during the middle part of the 18th century.

His five sons and two daughters sustained the family influences. Thomas surveyed the Fairfax Line, which forms the northern boundary of Rockingham County and part of Virginia's borders with West Virginia. He also laid out the formal plan of the town of Staunton in 1746-48, and by the end of his life was the largest land-owner in Rockingham County. Thomas was also a member of the Virginia Convention; Andrew, a close associate of George Washington, became the region's most prominent military leader, defeating the Indians at Point Pleasant on the Ohio River, becoming a brigadier-general in the Continental Army and commanding the Virginian troops at the defence of Williamsburg.

William, a pious Covenanting Presbyterian and church elder, moved to West Virginia, where his family developed the region's valuable mineral deposits; while American-born Charles died at the Battle of Point Pleasant, after heroics as a frontiersman and militia soldier. William Irvine Lewis, a grandson of William, died with Davy Crockett at The Alamo in 1836, while many of the Lewises lost their lives on both sides of the American Civil War.

Margaret Lewis, John's elder daughter, settled at Kentucky, while Anne moved back to Pennsylvania. Members of the Lewis family were among the first to settle Georgia, Tennessee, Kentucky, Texas and Utah, and astronaut Edward H. White II, a descendent of Andrew Lewis, became the first American to walk in space.

Other descendants were John Francis Lewis, United States Senator for Virginia and twice lieutenant governor of Virginia; George Rockingham Gilmer, first lieutenant in the war against the Creek Indians in 1813 and Governor of Georgia and Charles Spittal Robb, governor of Virginia in the 1980s.

John Lewis, the first southern Shenandoah Valley settler, died at Bellefonte on February 1, 1762, aged 84. His wife Margaret died 11 years later, aged 80. Both were exceptional people who courageously blazed a trail along the American frontier that was to be a shining inspiration to thousands of their kinsfolk who headed along a similar path.

The epitaph on the grave of John Lewis at Staunton reads: "Here lies the remains of John Lewis, born in Donegal County, Ireland in 1668, who slew the Irish lord, settled Augusta County, located the town of Staunton, and furnished five sons to fight the battle of the America Revolution. He was a brave man, a true patriot and a friend of liberty throughout the world."

BENJAMIN LOGAN

Next to Daniel Boone, Benjamin Logan was the leading pioneer soldier and politician in the settlement of Kentucky during the late 18th century. In very difficult circumstances in "the dark and bloody land," Logan's distinctive Scots-Irish characteristics of courage and dogged determination stood out.

Logan was born in Augusta County in the Shenandoah Valley of Virginia, son of an Ulster-born couple David and Jane (McKinley) Logan, who had moved from the north of Ireland in the early 1840s.

Benjamin and his younger brother John were baptised in the New Providence Church by the Rev. John Craig, from Co Antrim, the first Presbyterian minister in the Shenandoah Valley.

Their father David and uncle James served as a members of the Virginia militia in the French-Indian War of 1754-63, and Benjamin was a militia recruit at 16. He inherited his father's estate in 1757, but, instead of taking it for himself, sold it and divided the proceeds among other members of the family. This led to further land speculations, which made Benjamin one of the wealthiest men in the region.

Benjamin moved to the Holston River area of south-western Virginia, marrying Ann Montgomery and settling at Black's Station, site of the present-day town of Abingdon near the Tennessee state border. There, he was closely involved with Colonel John Donelson, leader of the Watauga movement, and James Knox, a surveyor and a hunter widely acknowledged as "leader of the Long Hunters."

Logan participated in the Governor Dunmore war campaign against Indian tribes in 1774 which opened up the Kentucky lands to white settlers and, within a year, had set up a frontier stockade at St. Asaph in eastern Kentucky. He became the first sheriff of Kentucky County, and in 1781 led militia attacks on Shawnee Indian tribes along the Ohio River.

His experience as a Republican legislator on the Virginia assembly equipped Logan for service on the various conventions which resulted in the establishment of Kentucky as a state in 1792. The first Governor Isaac Shelby appointed him major-general in the state militia, with a full division of soldiers under his command.

In 1796, Logan, along with three others, sought the nomination to succeed Governor Shelby, but, although a highly popular figure in the Kentucky frontier communities, he was pipped for the post by a fellow Republican James Garrard.

Logan's leadership of the essentially Scots-Irish community in the early formative years of the new settlements of Kentucky was totally practical and meaningful. Like his kinsfolk, he worked from dawn to dusk, both in farming the lands and providing defence against Indian attacks.

St Asaph stockade was highly vulnerable to Cherokee Indian attack, and defences had to be maintained at all times. In one attack on May 23, 1777, the fort was besieged by 100 Indians, and the womenfolk weighed in behind the men to resist the attack. Frontier woman needed to be handy with a rifle when danger presented itself.

There were fatalities in this attack, including a William Hudson, who was struck down while rounding up the livestock. Burr Harrison, a close associate of Logan, was injured and died later from his wounds and most of the livestock was targeted, a favoured ploy for the Indians.

Another attack was imminent and, with food supplies and gun powder low, Logan left the fort for the Holston settlements in western Virginia to seek reinforcements.

While he was away, a second Indian attack came in late August. Ambrose Grayson, one of Logan's men, was killed and two companions wounded as they ventured out for corn supplies. On Grayson's body, the Indians left several copies of a British proclamation, signed by a Colonel Henry Hamilton, which detailed instructions from London about deploying Indians against the white settlers, mostly of Scots-Irish origin, who were in revolt against the Crown in the Revolutionary War.

The proclamation offered food, lodging and humane treatment to all who deserted the American cause and presented themselves to any British post. Those who would take up arms against the Americans and continue "until the extinction of the rebellion" were promised "pay adequate to their former stations in the rebel service."

"All common men who shall serve during that period shall receive Her Majesty's bounty of 200 acres," the proclamation added.

When Benjamin Logan was shown copies of the proclamation he realised the implications for the morale of his men, and he quietly hid them. The British had forged an alliance with the Indians, and a bid was made to buy off wavering white settlers, but it did not work.

For several decades, St Asaph's or Logan's Fort was a dangerous outpost on the Kentucky frontier, and it needed raw courage from Benjamin Logan and the brave clutch of men and womenfolk, who surrounded him. Logan and his wife Ann had nine children (five sons and four daughters) and Benjamin died in 1802 after spending the last years of his life unconstitutional politics.

John Logan, Benjamin's bother, was also a militia officer and was the first state treasurer of Kentucky for five years from 1792. John had been on various expeditions against the Indians, was a Virginia legislator and was involved in Kentucky statehood conventions. He married Jane McClure, and they had six daughters and a son.

In 1795, John Logan, acting on authority from Kentucky Governor Isaac Shelby joined James Knox, at a wage of two shillings and sixpence daily, to improve the Wilderness Road route through the Cumberland Gap for the many migrant families trekking into the region from eastern states.

The McAfee family were Scots-Irish associates of the Logans in Kentucky, with Robert Breckinridge McAfee, a leading state legislator of the early 19th century, the grandson of Ulster pioneers James and Jane McAfee who emigrated to Pennsylvania about 1740.

The couple's three sons—Robert, James Jr. and George—and son-in-law James McCoun set up McAfee's station in Mercer County, Kentucky. Robert McAfee was known as "first Commodore of western rivers" for his operation of the first flatboats to New Orleans via the Ohio and Mississippi rivers. Robert was murdered in New Orleans during one of these expeditions.

His son Robert Breckinridge McAfee, became a guardian on the death of his parents to John Breckinridge McAfee, later to become the attorney-general of the United States in the cabinet of President Thomas Jefferson. He was elected to the Kentucky state legislature and senate from Mercer County, was the state's first lieutenant and was an influential figure in Andrew Jackson's Democratic Party.

He served for five years as charge affairs to the republic of Columbia in South America and he fought under Andrew Jackson in the War of 1812.

The three McAfee brothers founded the New Providence Church at Mercer County, naming it for what they saw as the work of God's providence during dark and dangerous days in Kentucky. New Providence was one of the first churches established in the territory.

Robert Fulton, the man who first applied steam to water navigation, was born in Lancaster County, Pennsylvania, of Scots-Irish parents, who emigrated from Ulster around 1730. His father was a founder of Lancaster Presbyterian Church.

FRONTIER REVOLT OVER FEDERAL INTERFERENCE

·✌ 17 ✌·

WHISKEY REBELLION

The Scots-Irish of western Pennsylvania were largely instrumental in the whiskey insurrection of 1794 against government tariffs imposed on the frontier people. The Scots-Irish were in revolt over taxes levied on whiskey, their principal product and virtually their only source of income.

The rebellion was a watershed in American politics and one result of the Scots-Irish mutiny was that it motivated federal officials to pay more heed to the needs of those who had settled in the far-flung western frontier.

The troubles about the whiskey excise first emerged when Congress adopted the tax in 1791. The federal government was badly in need of finance, to put the nation's economy in order and so that the debts incurred with the states during the Revolutionary War could be repaid. When the United States constitution was first adopted the nation's debt was 54 million dollars. Of this sum 12 million was owed to France and Holland, while the rest was owed internally.

Alexander Hamilton, the first Secretary of the Treasury, pleaded for both the payment of the national debt and the assumption by the Government of indebtedness which the various states had incurred during the Revolution and which amounted to more than 20 million dollars. To meet the interest on such a vast sum, an annual revenue of 4.5 million dollars was needed, and to raise this Congress placed an excise on distilled liquors and a tariff on imported goods.

The whiskey tax alarmed the Scots-Irish farm communities in eastern Pennsylvania and in the western region around Pittsburgh. There, about one in four had a still which produced whiskey (poteen) and other alcoholic substances, and the farmers argued the tax was not only unjust, but impossible to meet.

In their situation on the frontier, far removed from the corridors of power in Philadelphia, New York and Boston, whiskey was "not only a commodity, not only a drink, not only a medicine for all ills, not only a source of nourishment, but also a bartering agent in lieu of money."

In the years after the Revolutionary War money was scarce and the frontiersmen saw very little of it. A farmer of the period recalled that beside his axes he never laid out "more than 10 dollars a year, which was for salt, nails, and the like; nothing to wear, eat or drink, was purchased as my farm provided all."

Money may have been in short supply, but whiskey was certainly not and, in western Pennsylvania, rye, from which whiskey was made, grew abundantly. On its own a bushel of rye fetched only 40 cents in 1794. But if it was distilled into whiskey the price soured. A bushel and a half of rye produced a gallon of whiskey, and when sold in the east this fetched a dollar.

Another problem for the frontier farmers was that the payment for the whiskey sales was strictly a paper transaction. Cash was rarely paid out, with contra arrangements between the eastern merchants and the farmers in the purchase of essential goods for life in the western outposts. Without cash, the farmers could not pay the excise demanded by government.

The Whiskey Rebellion was effectively quelled in 1794, but the ill-feeling over it simmered well into the 19th century with the Scots-Irish settlements in Pennsylvania and in the Appalachian states. The measure was highly unpopular in Virginia, North Carolina, Kentucky and Tennessee and excise officers sent to the frontier to enforce the law were violently treated, with some federal officials publicly humiliated with tarring and feathering.

President George Washington warned those who campaigned against the excise demands "to desist from all unlawful combinations and proceeding whatsoever having for object or tendering to obstruct the operation of the laws."

The Whiskey Rebellion cost the Government 1.5 million dollars and 15,000 federal troops sent by President Washington into western Pennsylvania were needed to restore order.

In his book '*The Making of Pennsylvania*, Sidney George Fisher wrote: "The western Presbyterians were almost exclusively Scotch-Irish; always sought the frontier and advanced with it westwards. In religion, there was but little difference between the two divisions of Scottish settlers, but in character and temperament the Scotch-Irish were more excitable and violent."

The making of poteen illicit whisky, originated in Scotland and Ulster and was brought to America by the Scot's-Irish.

LEARNING THE CULTURE AND CUSTOMS OF
THE INDIAN TRIBES.

18

Co Antrim—Born James Adair: Friend of the Indian Tribes

The Scots-Irish and the native American Indian tribes were for the most part during the early pioneering years of the American frontier not friendly disposed to one another, and much blood was spilled on both sides, mainly over land rights.

One Ulsterman who did cultivate peaceful co-existence with the Indian tribes was James Adair, who went further than most in the white settler community to try to understand the varying cultures and traditions of the tribes.

Adair, born in Co Antrim in 1709, carved a niche as a peace-maker among the Indian tribes of the American southeast, which included the Cherokees, Siouans, Catawbas, Creeks, Shawnees, Choctaws and Chickasaws. His book, *History of the American Indians*, published in London in 1775, was regarded at the time as the most authoritative work on the native American tribes.

On the book, Adair theorised that the Indians were descended from the lost tribes of Israel, and his detailed observations provided valuable insights for ethnologists and students of 18th century literature.

The "Lost Tribes" theory may not have been universally shared, although some writers and commentators at the time did propound the view in books and pamphlets. One early 17th century writer Garcia claimed to have found many Hebrew features in the native American languages, declaring that the lost tribes passed Behring Strait and made their way southwards on to the American continent.

James Adair emigrated to America in 1735 and, from his tavern at Cherokee Creek in South Carolina, he traded with the Indians, and from years of close-hand working managed to penetrate their society, from a position of mutual trust.

He recorded Indian manners, customs, and language from a standpoint that had not been seen by a white man. Adair lived for seven years with the Overhill (or Western) Cherokees Indians in the Tennessee River territory and in 1754 he moved to the Mississippi to reside with the Chickasaw tribes, whose influence extended into North Carolina and South Carolina.

James Adair looked on the "Chikkasah" as cheerful and brave people. He was impressed by their independence and bravery, and they reciprocated the friendship. The Chickasaws disliked the French, and Adair even joined them in encounters against the Shawnee, who were then aligned with the French and came to grief into the French-Indian War.

Accounts of Adair describe him as a man of liberal education, with a sound knowledge of the Hebrew language. His diplomacy was a strong point, but his acridity of speech, an unsmooth temper and vain spirit brought him into conflict with his white contemporaries.

James Adair recognised in the Chickasaws "love of the lands, constancy in hatred and friendship, sagacity, alertness and consummate intrepidity."

A manuscript of his book, published in 1775, came to light in the *South Carolina Gazette* of September 7, 1769. This stated: "An account of the origin of the primitive inhabitants and a history of those numerous warlike tribes of Indians situated to the westward of Charleston, and subjects hitherto unattempted by any pen.

"Such an attempt had been made by Mr. James Adair, a gentleman who has been conversant among the Cherokees, Chickasaws, Choctaws etc, for thirty-odd years past; and who, by the assistance of a liberal education, has written essays on their origin, language, religion, customary methods of making war and peace etc."

The report announced that Adair was planning a trip to England to publish a book. A month later, both the *South Carolina Gazette* and the *Savannah Georgia Gazette* published Adair's prospectus of the book, for sale by subscription.

Essays were published on the origin, history, language, religion, customs, civil policy, methods of declaring and carrying out war and of making peace, military laws, agriculture, buildings exercise, sports, marriage, and funeral ceremonies, habits, diets, temper, manners etc of the Indian tribes of the continent of North America, particularly of the several nations of tribes of the Catawbas, Cherokees, Creeks, Chickasaws, and Choctaws, inhabiting the western parts of the colonies of Virginia, North and South Carolina, Georgia and the Tennessee territory.

In Winsor's *Narrative and Critical History of America,* James Adair's book is described as a work of great value, of much importance to students of Indian customs.

Logan, in his *Native of History of South Carolina,* said that from Adair's book the world had derived most that is known of the manners and customs of the southern Indians.

"The book's style is exceedingly figurative and characteristic and partakes much of the idiom of the Indian dialects to which the author was so accustomed," he said.

MOVEMENT TO THE FRONTIER
LANDS OF THE MISSISSIPPI.

·⌐⌐**19**⌐⌐·

SCOTS-IRISH IN THE
MISSISSIPPI LANDS

Natchez region of Mississippi was settled by Scots-Irish and Scottish highland settlers from 1773, and on hilly poor farmland they became "a border people" living on the highly dangerous edge of civilisation alongside Choctaw Indian settlements. The Scots-Irish acted as a buffer to the Choctaw and Chickasaw Indians along the banks of the Mississippi and in townships known as the "Scotch Settlements".

They were expanded in 1780 when Scots-Irish families were encouraged to move from Kentucky and Tennessee. Early records show the settlers grew tobacco and indigo for shipment from Natchez to New Orleans and then to Cuba and Spain. Records also confirm some Presbyterian and Methodist church services were conducted in Scottish Gallic language until after the Civil War, and the Psalms and Shorter Catechism were written in the old dialect.

When hostilities with the Indians ended and treaties were drawn up, the Choctaw and Chickasaw tribes were moved into Oklahoma as part of President Andrew Jackson's ill-fated "Trail of Tears" in the 1830s. Much of their land was taken over by some of the Scots-Irish families.

The old Scotch settlement at Union and Ebenezer Presbyterian churches in the Natchez was a mixture of Ulster-Scots and Scottish highlanders who had moved via North Carolina and Tennessee.

The first settlers here in 1805 were George Torrey, his son Dongold, Laughlin Currie and Robert Willis. They were soon followed by the Gilchrists, Galbreaths and Camerons. These families were noted for the simplicity of their manners; they were not wealthy, but were plain, unpretending, honest God-fearing people. The settlement is mainly a history of the two churches, organised soon after the arrival of the first families and, through Presbyterian and Methodist influences, the region was prosperous and highly civilised.

The countryside was rich in game and rivers in fish, and land was extremely fertile for farming, with hills and lowlands covered in canebrake. Settlers used the traditional Indian method of burning away the brake and planting the corn. Some Scots-Irish were not averse to strong drink, and an over-indulgence of whisky brought stern rebuke from elders in the church, even excommunication.

Records of Union-Ebenezer churches confirm firm dealings of the elders with their brethren: "Let a man be overtaken in a fault, such as violating the Sabbath Day, or taking God's name in vain, or becoming intoxicated, and he was certain of discipline by the church."

The Dragoons militia company from Jefferson County, Mississippi, comprising many Scots-Irish lads, won distinction in the New Orleans campaign of 1813-15, routing a British division. This brought a glowing commendation from General Andrew Jackson, who said: "You have been the astonishment of one army, the admiration of another."

The Culbertsons, Bradys and Stephensons were among scores of Ulster Presbyterian families who migrated from Kentucky to the Natchez region. The Bradys were in Pennsylvania from 1720 and later in the Carolinas, while the Culbertsons, a family of three brothers—Alexander, Joseph and Samuel—from Ballygan near Ballymoney in North Antrim, settled at Lurgan town in Franklin County, Pennsylvania before moving to Virginia and South Carolina. These families were related through marriage and members were distinguished Indian fighters and soldiers in the Revolutionary War.

BONDING FOR THE SCOTS-IRISH WITH
THE NATIVE AMERICAN TRIBES.

·❧ 20 ❧·

COMMON CURRENCY
WITH THE INDIANS

Ulster-Scots settlers endured many violent run-ins with the native American Indian tribes through the 18th century, but they shared a common currency in things like farming and reconnoitering the Appalachian mountains and forests to eke out a living. Indians, particularly Cherokees, normally grew several hundred acres of crops in each of their villages.

By tradition, corn and beans were the staple crops, planted in trees four feet apart in four-foot rows. In between the corn hills were planted May apples. Indians also grew potatoes, peas, pumpkins and gourds. The slash, burn and plant Indian method of productivity in working the land was copied to good effect by the very adaptable Scots-Irish farmers as they set down their roots and meticulously staked out territory they could call their own.

For instance, in the Shenandoah Valley of Virginia, the Ulster-Scots settlers found hitherto uninhabited lands which they must have looked upon as a paradise, compared to the bleak desolate countryside they had left behind. Indians used the Valley only as hunting grounds and, at the end of each season, they set fire to open ground on the prairie, which ensured it did not develop as woodland. Indians had their sights on buffalo, which lived on grassland and avoided forest.

By their ritual firings, Indian tribes maintained the Shenandoah grassland and all its flowering beauty: dogwood, azalia, rhododendron and laurels. Herds of buffalo, elk and deer roamed freely. The Scots-Irish adopted Indian ways of farming, hunting and fighting. The slash, burn and plant method of toiling land was used to advantage by the settlers as they dug deep into Shenandoah soil.

Their pattern of life in the backwoods grew closer to that of the native Americans, and some historians believe this is what led ultimately to confrontations as more and more land was seized up. Apart from horses, dogs and turkeys were the only domesticated animals found on an Indian reservation, and most of the meat was supplied by hunting wild animals like buffalo in the plains and deer and bear in the forests they roamed.

When the white settlers arrived into regions like Virginia, North Carolina, Tennessee and Kentucky in the late 18th century, they first erected a log cabin in a forest clearing before planting corn and raising a crop. In most cases, the men initially came in advance along rough pathways opened up for them by scouts and surveyors, and, after setting up a home on an allotted space, they returned for their families and settled usually the following year.

FAMILY TRADITION WAS A FEATURE
OF THE ULSTER EMIGRANTS.

·❧ *21* ❧·

THE MCKINNEYS OF COLERAINE AND TENNESSEE

One of the foremost families in the early frontier settlements of the American state of Tennesseee were the McKinneys from Coleraine in Ulster, Family members are listed in Tennesseee historical records as leaders in the civic, religious, educational and social life, and their contribution to public life in the eastern part of the state in the early 19th century was significant.

Lawyer John Augustine McKinney, who left Coleraine for America as a 19-year-old in 1800, was considered the top legal man of his day on the Tennessee frontier, and in public affairs, he was a contemporary of President Andrew Jackson.

McKinney, the youngest of five brothers, received a university education in both Ireland and Edinburgh, and the taking of a medical degree after landing in the United States gave him added stature on the rapidly evolving American social scene.

McKinney began a law practice in 1807 in the Knoxville area and his influence was extended by acquiring large tracts of land in East Tennessee. He was United States District Attorney when John Quincy Adams was

President in the 1820s and was chosen as a representative to the Tennessee state constitutional convention in 1832-34.

A 'History of Tennessee' records this tribute: "John A. McKinney's great success was due to his thorough knowledge of the law, his untiring perseverance and his incorruptible integrity."

John Augustine McKinney was said to be a man who was interested in building up the religious, educational and material welfare of the country. This obviously came from his strict Presbyterian Church upbringing—he was a ruling elder in the First Presbyterian Church at Rogersville in East Tennessee—and his home was open-house for ministers, teachers and others who found there a hearty welcome and a generous sympathiser.

Although a black slave owner himself, as many men of his position in the Tennessee of the early 19th century were, John A. McKinney considered slavery to be "an evil we must be rid of as soon as possible."

"We can't get rid of it overnight, but we must do it as soon as possible or there will be a real calamity," said McKinney, who saw the solution to slavery a form of share cropping. He did not live long to enough to see the practice abolished, but in his will he decreed that he did not want to see the slave families on his estate broken up.

It was in 1806 that John A. McKinney first came to Rogersville, a town founded by a Cookstown, Co Tyrone man, Joseph Rogers, and where the Ulster-Scots family of frontiersman Davy Crockett farmed. McKinney was there for a law hearing representing a client from Philadelphia, and so impressed was he by the beauty of the wooded, hilly landscape, that he decided to seek a home in the town.

By 1810, McKinney had built an impressive white brick mansion with green shutters, along the lines of the big houses he had known in his Ulster homeland.

The house, at McKinney Avenue/Colonial Road, facing Crockett Creek and beside an oak tree 500 years old, is still standing and inhabited. McKinney lived there with his wife Eliza and seven children.

Before he settled in Rogersville, McKinney had been in correspondence with Joseph Rogers and, in one letter (postmarked Philadelphia January 16, 1805), he talked of a most severe winter where some of the poorer frontier settlers had perished from cold and hunger.

Rogersville became an important legal staging post for the East Tennessee region and it was an area highly influential in the politics of the state. Nearly everyone who was anyone in Tennessee at the time visited Rogersville regularly, including Andrew Jackson and two other Tennesseans of Ulster-Scots roots with presidential ambitions—James Knox Polk and Andrew Johnson, and, of course, Davy Crockett.

John A. McKinney felt that that town needed an elegant dwelling house for its important visitors and in 1824 he ordered the building of a large three-storey building, to be known as the McKinney Tavern House. It was run by members of the McKinney family and rapidly became a main stopping-off point for the stage coach trade of the day. Andrew Jackson, "Old Hickory" to his many admirers in Tennessee, visited the Tavern House many times—the last in 1832 after his first term as president.

John A. McKinney, described as the best friend Upper East Tennessee and Rogersville ever had, died suddenly in 1845, aged 64. His Coleraine-born four brothers and a sister had also come to America and made their mark.

The eldest brother, the Rev. James McKinney was an eminent minister of the Reformed Presbyterian Church in America, having graduated from Glasgow University in 1778 in medicine and theology. Two brothers were doctors—Samuel practiced in Philadelphia and Rogersville and Archibald in Philadelphia and Cincinnati. Robert McKinney settled in Pittsburgh and sister Sarah lived at Chester, South Carolina.

In 1867, the McKinney Tavern, used as the headquarters and hospital for the Confederate Army in the American Civil War of 1861-65, passed out of the family hands. By 1884, the Tavern was re-named Hale Springs Inn in keeping with the increasing popularity of mineral springs in the area, and it has remained an East Tennessee landmark since.

Robert McKinney, son of Dr. Samuel McKinney and a nephew of John Augustine McKinney, was a very distinguished Tennessee lawyer and judge. He too was born in Coleraine and moved with his family to America in 1809. After passing through Philadelphia, they settled at Rogersville and young Robert combined his law studies with the tasks on the family farm.

He was licensed in 1824 and soon became circuit lawyer for three counties in East Tennessee. His legal skills were acclaimed throughout Tennessee, and in 1847 he was elevated as a judge of the state's Supreme Court. McKinney held this position until 1861 when the courts were closed because of the

Civil War, and he was subsequently dispatched to Washington as a peace commissioner. Judge McKinney opposed the War, but when Tennessee seceded from the Union, he remained loyal to his state.

Described as man of sound judgment and good business ability, he was thorough and accurate as a lawyer; sedate and dignified in manner; strict in business matters, but kind and generous. He was married twice, to the daughters of the Rev. Charles Coffin—Margaret, who died two years after their marriage in 1843, and Mary, who he wed in 1851.

Robert McKinney was a loyal member of First Knoxville Presbyterian Church and he is buried in the city's Greenwood Cemetery, in the McKinney family plot.

THE RICH CULTURE OF SETTLERS
ON THE AMERICAN OUTPOSTS.

·◦22◦·

FRONTIER TRADITIONS

Routines and superstitions of frontier life endured with the seasons, with Sunday (The Sabbath) strictly set aside for worship and rest. The remainder of the week was for getting things done, materially and socially, although some thought Fridays and Saturdays were unlucky for tackling fresh enterprises.

President Andrew Jackson, a frontiersman in the traditional mould, never liked to begin anything of consequence on a Friday. He believed in leaving things off until the beginning of the week, which perhaps says more for the slower pace of life in those days.

Life was far from easy in the bleak wilderness landscape of the white frontier settlements, but the Scots-Irish, alongside Germans, English, Scottish highlanders, French Huguenots, Welsh and Scandinavians persevered and together, as diverse peoples in a great melting pot, they left a rich cultural and social legacy that was to form the backbone of the American nation in the several hundred years that followed.

In the Carolina rural up-country, the superstitions and folk beliefs of the Scots-Irish people were many and varied:

- For every August fog, there will be snow in winter.
- Eat the last biscuit on the plate so that it will be fair weather tomorrow.
- If your right hand itches, you will meet a stranger; if your left hand itches, you will come into some money.
- A cricket in the house is good luck; to kill on is bad luck.
- If you sweep under a person's feet, he (she) will never marry.
- If you dream of snow, someone you know will die soon.
- Heavy amounts of red berries on piracantha bushes mean an unusually hard winter.
- Kiss a red-haired person to cure fever blisters.
- Dig post holes by the light of the moon and the posts will set in as if in concrete.
- To enter one door and exit another is bad luck.
- To stop a chain of infant deaths, name the next male child Adam, next female Eve.

Medical remedies still practiced in the Waxhaws region of North Carolina, a Scots-Irish stronghold, are:

- For kidney trouble, boil some stag-horn in a pot and drink the tea or just chew up the sour red berries of the plant.
- For earache, take a piece of hair from another race, place it in your ear and the pain will disappear.
- To cure warts, take a half of an Irish potato, rub on the warts, bury the potato and when it rots the warts will be gone.
- For a sprain, take a dirt dobber's nest and mix with vinegar and place this around the sprain, secured with an old rag.
- Use soot and spider webs to stop bleeding.
- Catch the first snow of the year, melt this and use on burns throughout the year. Helps in heakling and prevents scars.
- To cure sores on the hand, let a dog lick the wound.
- To cure a bad cold, boil green pine straw and put in a little sugar. Drink this as a tea.
- An axe under the bed will cure labour pains.

THE SCOTS-IRISH CHRONICLES
BY BILLY KENNEDY

THE SCOTS-IRISH IN THE HILLS OF TENNESSEE

(First published 1995)

This book centered in Tennessee is the definite story of how the American frontier of the late 18th century was advanced, and the indomitable spirit of the Scots-Irish shines though on every page. From the Great Smoky Mountain region to the Cumberland Plateau and the Mississippi delta region, the Scots-Irish created a civilisation out of a wilderness. The inheritance they left was hard-won, but something to cherish. The careers of Tennessean Presidents Andrew Jackson, James Knox Polk and Andrew Johnson and state luminaries Davy Crockett and Sam Houston are catalogued in the book.

313

THE SCOTS-IRISH IN THE SHENANDOAH VALLEY

(First published 1996)

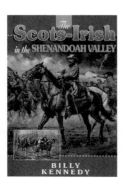

The beautiful Shenandoah Valley alongside the majestic backdrop of the Blue Ridge Mountains of Virginia is the idyllic setting for the intriguing story of a brave resolute people who tamed the frontier. The Ulster-Scots (Scots-Irish) were a breed of people who could move mountains. They did this literally with their bare hands in regions like the Shenandoah Valley, winning the day for freedom and liberty of conscience in the United States. In the Shenandoah Valley, the Scots-Irish led the charge for the American patriots in the Revolutionary War and for the Confederates in the Civil War a century later.

THE SCOTS-IRISH IN THE CAROLINAS

(First published 1997)

The Piedmont areas of the Carolinas, North and South, were settled by tens of thousands of Scots-Irish Presbyterians in the second half of the 18th century. Some moved down the Great Wagon Road from Pennsylvania, others headed to the up-country after arriving at the port of Charleston. The culture, political heritage and legacy of the Scots-Irish so richly adorned the fabric of American life, and the Carolinas was an important homeland for many of these people. It was also the launching pad for the long trek westwards to new lands and the fresh challenge of the expanding frontier.

THE SCOTS-IRISH IN PENNSYLVANIA & KENTUCKY

(First published 1998)

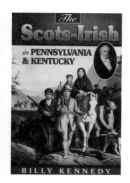

Pennsylvania and Kentucky are two American states settled primarily at opposite ends of the 18th century by Ulster-Scots Presbyterians, yet this book details how the immigrant trail blended in such diverse regions. William Penn and the Quaker community encouraged the European settlers to move in large numbers to the colonial lands of Pennsylvania from the beginning of the 18th century. The Scots-Irish were the earliest settlers to set up homes in cities like Philadelphia and Pittsburgh. Kentucky, established as a state in 1792, was pioneered by Ulster-Scots families who moved through the Cumberland Gap and down the Wilderness Road with explorer Daniel Boone.

FAITH AND FREEDOM: THE SCOTS-IRISH IN AMERICA

(First published 1999)

A common thread runs through Pennsylvania, Virginia, North Carolina, South Carolina, Tennessee, West Virginia, Georgia, Kentucky, Alabama and other neighbouring states—that of a settlement of people who had firmly set their faces on securing for all time—their faith and freedom. This inspirational journey of the Scots-Irish Presbyterian settlers details how they moved the American frontier to its outer limits, founding log cabin churches that were to spiral the message of the gospel and establishing schools, which were to expand into some of the foremost educational institutions in the United States.

315

HEROES OF THE SCOTS-IRISH IN AMERICA

(First published 2000)

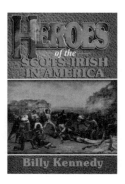

Heroism was a distinct characteristic of the 18th century Scots-Irish immigrants, and the raw courage shown by these dogged determined people in very difficult circumstance helped make the United States great. Forging a civilisation out of a wilderness was a real challenge for the Ulster settlers and how well they succeeded in moulding a decent law-abiding society, from the eastern seaboard states, through the Appalachian region into the south to Texas and beyond. The Scots-Irish heroes and heroines have become enshrined in American history, not just as presidents, statesmen, soldiers and churchmen, but many plain ordinary citizens whose quiet, unselfish deeds were worthy of note, and a shining example to others.

THE MAKING OF AMERICA: HOW THE SCOTS-IRISH SHAPED A NATION

(First published 2001)

In establishing of the United States, the Scots-Irish were one of the most highly influential groups, both in the signing of the American Declaration of Independence on July 4, 1776, and in the Revolutionary War which followed. This group of dedicated stalwarts, whose families emigrated to America from the Irish province of Ulster throughout the 18th century, were resolute and uncompromising champions of the movement for American independence. Bitter experience of religious discrimination and economic deprivation in their Scottish and Ulster homelands gave impetus to the Scots-Irish throwing off the shackles of the old order when they moved to the American colonies and opened up the great frontier lands. The Scots-Irish were in the vanguard of American patriot involvement on all fronts of the Revolutionary War, but it was on the frontier that they made their most significant contribution. Quite uniquely as a people, they rose to the awesome challenge of the American frontier—its danger, its inaccessibility and its sheer enormity.

WOMEN OF THE FRONTIER

(First published 2004)

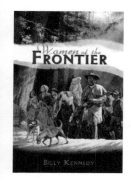

American frontier women of the 19th century were an extraordinary people whose contribution to the creation of the United States is one of most enduring stories in history. The gallant women of the frontier have never been given the full credit which they deserve for settling, with their families, in an uninhabited wilderness. This book places on record the notable achievements of these heroines. The book gives recognition to the women whose lot was far from glamorous in the bleak and lonely frontier territories. They faced personal hardships and tragedies in hazardous conditions. While the men toiled arduously from dawn to dusk to lay down a stake in the New World, the women were the cornerstone of the home the church and the wider community. Women had to be strong, self-reliant, resourceful and loyal to their families. Through their honest and dedicated endeavours on the frontier, a democratic and decent civilisation emerged which now extends across the great American expanse from the Atlantic to the Pacific. Indeed the women of the American frontier deserve our honour and admiration.

These books are available from authorised booksellers in the United Kingdom, the United States and the Republic of Ireland or direct from the publishers in Belfast (Northern Ireland) and Greenville (South Carolina).

Author's Acknowledgements:

Dr. Samuel Lowry, Ambassador International, Greenville and Belfast.

David Wright, Nashville, Tennessee.

Cherel Henderson, East Tennessee Historical Society, Knoxville, Tennessee.

Gregory Campbell MP, Londonderry.

Bobby F. Edmunds, McCormick, South Carolina.

Dr. David Hume, Larne, Co Antrim.

Councillor Dr. Ian Adamson, Belfast.

Dr. Bobby Moss, Blacksburg, South Carolina.

Larry Crabtree, Huntsville, Alabama.

Andy Croston, Greenville, South Carolina.

John Rice Irwin, Museum of Appalachia, Norris, Tennessee.

Tennessee State Library and Archives, Nashville, Tennessee.

Tony Guzzi, Curator, The Hermitage, Nashville, Tennessee.

Stephen Graham, Tandragee, Co Armagh.

Barbara Parker, Gallatin, Tennessee.

Rev Dr. Charles L. and Sara Moffatt, Gallatin, Tennessee.

Fred Brown, Knoxville, Tennessee.

Caneta Hankins, Historic Preservation Center, Middle Tennessee State University, Murfreesboro, Tennessee.

Captain Carl Netherland-Brown, Rogersville, Tennessee.

George Patton, chief executive, Ulster-Scots- Agency, Belfast.

George Holmes, cultural director, Ulster-Scots-Agency, Belfast.

Lord Laird of Artigarvan, Belfast.

DR. KATHARINE BROWN, STAUNTON, VIRGINIA.

ALISTER MCREYNOLDS, PRINCIPAL, LISBURN COLLEGE, CO ANTRIM.

LINDA PATTERSON, AMBASSADOR PUBLICATIONS, BELFAST.

CHRIS MCIVOR, LIBRARIAN, ULSTER-AMERICAN FOLK PARK, OMAGH, CO TYRONE.

CHRISTINE JOHNSTON, ULSTER-AMERICAN FOLK PARK, OMAGH, CO TYRONE.

PRESIDENT JIMMY CARTER, ATLANTA, GEORGIA.

THE LATE JANE WILSON, DONALDS HISTORICAL SOCIETY, SOUTH CAROLINA.

THE LATE TOMMY RYE, MARYVILLE, TENNESSEE.

PROFESSOR MICHAEL MONTGOMERY, UNIVERSITY OF SOUTH CAROLINA.

DR. RICHARD MCMASTER, FLORIDA.

JOHN AND CAROLE LEBERT, KNOXVILLE, TENNESSEE.

CHERITH CALDWELL, BELFAST.

SAM WYLY, DALLAS, TEXAS.

WALLACE CLARK, UPPERLANDS, CO LONDONDERRY.

ROY A. JACK, NEWTOWNSTEWART, CO TYRONE.

FRANCIS TRIMBLE, HOUSTON, TEXAS.

MARYLIN BELL HUGHES, TENNESSEE STATE LIBRARY AND ARCHIVES, NASHVILLE, TENNESSEE.

ROBERT O. KING, GREENVILLE, SOUTH CAROLINA.

KENT REDGRAVE, NASHVILLE, TENNESSEE.

EMILY YARBOROUGH, MARYVILLE COLLEGE, TENNESSEE.

GLENN M. BRADY, ZACHARY, LOUISIANA.

GERALD ROBERTS, SHANNON WILSON, SIDNEY FARR AND HARRY RICE, SPECIAL COLLECTIONS DEPARTMENT, BEREA COLLEGE, KENTUCKY.

LOYAL JONES, BEREA, KENTUCKY.

BRENTON COOK, AMBASSADOR INTERNATIONAL, GREENVILLE, SOUTH CAROLINA.

TIMOTHY LOWRY, AMBASSADOR INTERNATIONAL, GREENVILLE, SOUTH CAROLINA.

ANDREW RAMOS, AMBASSADOR INTERNATIONAL, GREENVILLE, SOUTH CAROLINA.

DANIELLE BOOMERSHINE, AMBASSADOR INTERNATIONAL, GREENVILLE, SOUTH CAROLINA.

GILLIAN LOWRY, AMBASSADOR INTERNATIONAL, BELFAST.

LINDA PATTERSON, AMBASSADOR INTERNATIONAL, BELFAST.

ROBERT ANDERSON (PRINTER), RICHHILL, CO ARMAGH.

GEORGE HAMILTOIN 1V, FRANKLIN, TENNESSEE.

THE LATE DAVID BABELEY, KNOXVILLE, TENNESSEE.

THOMAS MOORE CRAIG JR., ROEBUCK, SPARTANBURG, SOUTH CAROLINA.

STAFF AT CALVIN M. MCCLUNG MUSEUM HISTORICAL COLLECTIONS, KNOXVILLE, TENNESSEE.

PROFESSOR GEORGE SCHWEITZER, TENNESSEE STATE UNIVERSITY, KNOXVILLE.

PETER MCKITTERICK, US CONSULATE GENERAL OFFICE, BELFAST.

CAROL BORNEMAN, CUMBERLAND GAP NATIONAL HISTORICAL PARK, KENTUCKY.

MARCIA MULLINS, CURATOR, THE HERMITAGE, NASHVILLE, TENNESSEE.

ANN TOPLOVICH, DIRECTOR, TENNESSEE HISTORICAL SOCIETY, NASHVILLE.

KELLY WILKERSON, TENNESSEE HISTORICAL SOCIETY, NASHVILLE.

CAPTAIN R. LYNN MCR. HAWKINS, BLUFF CITY, TENNESSEE.

TOM CAMPBELL, ELIZABETHTOWN, PENNSYLVANIA.

321

Bibliography:

Stories of the Great West—Theodore Roosevelt.

Liberty's Women—edited by Robert McHenry.

Log Cabin Pioneers—Wayne Erb Sr.

America's First Western Frontier: East Tennessee—Brenda C. Calloway.

The American Heritage: Encyclopedia of American History—edited by John Mack Faragher.

The Encyclopedia of the South—Robert O'Brien.

Woodrow Wilson, Life and Letters—Ray Stannard Baker.

Woodrow Wilson, The Early Years—George C. Osborne.

Woodrow Wilson—August Heckscher.

History of Augusta County (Virginia).

Thomas Jefferson and his World—Henry Moscow (American Heritage).

Timber Ridge Presbyterian Church (The Old Stone Church).

Lexington—Religion and Marriage.

Two South Rivers of the Shenandoah and James Rivers—Bobby Sue B. Henry.

President Woodrow Wilson's Irish and Scottish Heritage—Edward and Elizabeth Hardy.

Old Farm Tools and Machinery, An Illustrated History—Percy C. Blandford.

Frontier Preacher (the Rev Samuel Black) -Natalie K. Black

Annals of a Scotch-Irish Family—William G. Whitsett.

Six Months of an American Adventure—Senator Lamar Alexander.

The Scotch-Irish of Augusta.

GOD'S FRONTIERSMEN, THE SCOTS-IRISH EPIC—RORY FITZPATRICK.

SAMUEL DOAK—EARLE W. CRAWFORD.

HISTORIC SUILLIVAN COUNTY, TENNESSEE—OLIVER TAYLOR

SAMUEL DOAK (1749-1830)—WILLIAM GUNN CALHOUN

THE WATAUGANS—MATT DIXON.

THE SCOTCH-IRISH, A SOCIAL HISTORY—JAMES G. LEYBURN.

ULSTER SAILS WEST—W. F. MARSHALL.

ONE HEROIC HOUR AT KINGS MOUNTAIN- PAT ALDERMAN.

THE OVERMOUNTAIN MEN—PAT ALDERMAN.

THE SCOTCH-IRISH LETTERS IN THE VALLEY OF VIRGINIA—BOLIVAR CHRISTIAN.

THE LEXINGTON PRESBYTERIAN HERITAGE—HOWARD McKNIGHT WILSON.

WHO WAS WHO IN THE CIVIL WAR—JOHN S. BOWMAN.

'STONEWALL' JACKSON, PORTRAIT OF A SOLDIER—JOHN BOWERS.

'STONEWALL' JACKSON—LIEUT. COL. G. F. R. HENDERSON.

FOLKS FROM LARNE—GEORGE WEST DIEHL.

THE FAMILY OF JOHN LEWIS, PIONEER—IRWIN FRAZIER.

WITH FIRE AND SWORD—WILMA DYKEMAN.

THE PEOPLING OF VIRGINIA—BEAN R. BENNETT.

THE SCOTCH-IRISH IN WESTERN PENNSYLVANIA—ROBERT GARLAND

PITTSBURGH—THE STORY OF AN AMERICAN CITY—STEFAN LORANT.

THE MELLONS—BY DAVID E., KOSNOFF.

THOMAS MELLON AND HIS TIMES (CENTRE FOR EMIGRATION STUDIES, UNIVERSITY OF PITTSBURGH).

THE PLANTING OF CIVILISATION IN WESTERN PENNSYLVANIA—SOLON J. BUCK AND ELIZABETH HAWTHORN BUCK

BIOGRAPHICAL ALBUM OF PROMINENT PENNSYLVANIANS.

HISTORY OF DAUPHIN COUNTY, PENNSYLVANIA.

THE FAIR PLAY SETTLERS OF WEST BRANCH SETTLERS (1769-84)—GEORGE D. WOLF.

KENTUCKY BIOGRAPHICAL DICTIONARY.

Pioneer Outline History of North Western Pennsylvania—W. J. McKnight.

The Growth of Democracy—(1740-1776)—Theodore Taylor.

History of Pennsylvania—William H. Egle.

Pennsylvania: The Colonial Years (1681-1776) by Joseph J. Kelley Jr.

From Ulster to Carolina Tyler Blethen and Curtis Wood Jr.

Kentucky: A Guide to the Bluegrass State.

The Kentucky Encyclopedia—John E. Kleber.

Kentucky Settlements and Statehood (1750-1800)—George Morgan.

Historic Families of Kentucky—Thomas Marshall Green.

Early Families of Eastern and South-Eastern Kentucky.

A History of Kentucky—Thomas D. Clark

John Adair's History of the American Indians.

Pioneers of Destiny—W. D. Weatherford.

Princetonians (1769-1775)—Richard A. Harrison.

Kentucky Descendants of James Bingham of Co Down—James Barry Bingham

Colonialists from Scotland—Ian Charles Cargill Graham.

The Scotch-Irish of Colonial Pennsylvania.

The Pioneers of Mifflin County, Pennsylvania.

Donegal Presbyterians—Richard K. McMaster.

Conestoga Wagon: Masterpiece of the Blacksmith—Arthur L. Reist.

History of the Sesquhanna River and Paxtang Church.

The Southern Highlander and his Homeland—John C. Campbell.

Land of the Free, Ulster and the American Revolution—Ronnie Hanna

The Life of Andrew Jackson—Robert V. Remini.

Young Hickory by Hendrik Booraem.

Robert Rogers of The Rangers—John R. Cuneo.

Rising Above Circumstances—The Rogers Family in Colonial America—Robert J. Rogers.

DAVID CROCKETT: THE MAN BEHIND THE MYTH—JAMES WAKEFIELD BURKE.

DAVY CROCKETT—THE MAN , THE LEGEND, THE LEGACY—MICHAEL A. LOFARO.

TWO HUNDRED AND FIFTY YEARS AT UPPER OCTORARA.

PATHS OF THE PAST: TENNESSEE (1770-1970)—PAUL H. BERGERON.

TENNESSEE MUSIC: ITS PEOPLE AND ITS PLACES—PETER COATS ZINNERMAN.

TENNESSEANS AT WAR—JAMES A. CRUTCHFIELD.

HISTORY OF NEW PROVIDENCE PRESBYTERIAN CHURCH, MARYVILLE TENNESSEE— WILL A. MCTEER.

SKETCH OF THE OLD SCOTCH SETTLEMENT AT UNION CHURCH, NATCHEZ, MISSISSIPPI.

THE GREAT WAGON ROAD—FREDERICK AND MAXINE NEWBRAUGH.

FIRST FAMILIES OF TENNESSEE (PUBLISHED BY EAST TENNESSEE HISTORICAL SOCIETY)

PRESIDENTS OF THE UNITED STATES—COFFMAN PUBLICATIONS, MARYLAND.

JAMES BUCHANAN AND HIS FAMILY AT WHEATFIELD, LANCASTER, PENNSYLVANIA— SALLY SMITH CAHALAN.

MOUNTAIN MEN OF THE AMERICAN WEST—JAMES A. CRUTCHFIELD.

SAM HOUSTON: THE LIFE AND TIMES OF THE LIBERATOR OF TEXAS—JOHN HOYT WILLIAMS.

FIRST PITTSBURGH PRESBYTERIAN CHURCH—REV ERNEST E. LOGAN.

ALAMO DEFENDERS—A GENEALOGY: THE PEOPLE AND THEIR WORDS—BILL GRONEMAN.

THE STORY OF THE ALAMO (THIRTEEN FATEFUL DAYS IN 1836).

THE ALAMO HEROES AND THEIR REVOLUTIONARY ANCESTORS, SAN ANTONIO, TEXAS.

THREE ROADS TO THE ALAMO—WILLIAM C. DAVIS.

NEW HISTORY OF THE CIVIL WAR—BRUCE CATTON AND JAMES M. MCPHERSON.

CUSTER: CONTROVERSIAL LIFE OF GEORGE ARMSTRONG CUSTER BY JEFFRY D. WERT.

HISTORIC SULLIVAN, TENNESSEE—OLIVER TAYLOR.

ANDREW JOHNSON—HANS L. TREFOUSSE.

SCOTCH-IRISH WOMEN—REV HENRY C. MCCOOK.

JAMES BUCHANAN—BATCHELOR AND FAMILY MAN—PHILIP STRIVER KLEIN.

Religion in Tennessee 1777-1945—Herman A. Norton.

History of the Lost State of Franklin—Samuel Cole Williams.

Three Roads to the Alamo—William C. Davis.

An Amiable Woman: Rachel Jackson—Katherine W. Cruise.

Ulster Emigration to Colonial America—R. J. Dickson.

Mary Patton: Powder Maker of the Revolution—Robert A. Howard and E. Alvin Gerhardt Jr.

Tennesseans at War—James A. Crutchfield.

Tennessee During the Revolution—Williams.

The American President—Philip B. Kunhardt Jr., Philip B. Kunhardt III and Peter W. Kunhardt.

Encyclopedia of the American Revolution—Mark M. Boatner III and McPherson.

A Few Bloody Noses (The American War of Independence)—Robert Harvey.

History of Rhea County, Tennessee by Betty J. Broyles.

Hitch Hiking Along the Holston River—Mayme Parrot Wood.

History's Women—The Unsung Heroines (Deborah Sampson: A Soldier of the Revolution)—Renie Burghardt.

Appalachian Frontiers—Robert D. Mitchell.

Tennesseans and their History—Paul H. Bergeron, Stephen V. Ash and Jeannette Keith.

Knox County, Tennessee—Betsey Beeler Creekmore.

For Christ in the Heart of Knoxville (History of Knoxville's First Presbyterian Church)—Ashley Mack.

Heart of the Valley—A History of Knoxville, Tennessee—edited by Lucile Deaderick.

The French Broad-Holston Country: A History of Knox County, Tennessee - edited by Mary U. Rothrock.

Women's History in Wyoming by Carl Hallberg, Wyoming State Archives.

Irish Immigration in the Land of Canaan—edited by Kerby A. Millar. Arnold Schrier, Bruce D. Boling and David N. Doyle.

THE GRANDFATHER OF JOHN C. CALHOUN—A. S. SALLEY.

THE WOMEN OF THE AMERICAN REVOLUTION—ELIZABETH F. ELLET.

CAROLINA CRADLE—SETTLEMENT OF THE NORTHWEST CAROLINA FRONTIER (1747-62)—ROBERT W. RAMSEY.

BOONESBOROUGH TOWNSHIP—C. NEWELL BOWIE.

SOUTH CAROLINA NATURALIZATIONS 1783-1853—BRENT H. HOLCOMB.

HISTORY OF THE LOST STATE OF FRANKLIN—SAMUEL COLE-WILLIAMS.

THE HIGHLAND SCOTS OF NORTH CAROLINA 1732-1776—DUANE MEYER.

THE FRONTIER RIFLEMAN—RICHARD B. LACROSSE JR.

SCOTCH -IRISH MIGRATION TO SOUTH CAROLINA—JEAN STEPHENSON.

HISTORY OF PRESBYTERIAN CHURCH IN SOUTH CAROLINA—GEORGE HOWE.

THE ROAD TO GUILFORD COURTHOUSE (AMERICAN REVOLUTION IN THE CAROLINAS) - JOHN BUCHANAN.

CHARLES THOMSON—'PRIME MINISTER' OF THE UNITED STATES—FRED S. ROLATER.

CHARLES THOMSON, SECRETARY OF CONGRESS 1774-1789—KENNETH R. BOWLING.

THE GREAT SEAL OF AMERICA (PUBLISHED BY U.S. DEPARTMENT OF STATE 1980).

HISTORY OF NAZARETH PRESBYTERIAN CHURCH, MOORE, SOUTH CAROLINA.

HAND-ME-DOWN SONGS (TRADITIONAL MUSIC OF NORTH CAROLINA)—KAREN G. HELMS.

THE MECKLENBURG DECLARATION OF INDEPENDENCE—GEORGE W. GRAHAM.

THE CAROLINA BACKCOUNTRY—CHARLES WOODMASON.

KATE BARRY—MARY MONTGOMERY MILLER.

LEAVE-TAKING: THE SCOTCH IRISH COME TO WESTERN NORTH CAROLINA —H. TYLER BLETHEN AND CURTIS WOOD JR.

THE HEARST FAMILY—THE EARLY YEARS.

HISTORY OF FAIRVIEW PRESBYTERIAN CHURCH—MARY LOU STEWART GARRETT.

HISTORIC WALNUT GROVE PLANTATION 1765.

DANIEL BOONE, MASTER OF THE WILDERNESS—JOHN BAKELESS.

KINGS MOUNTAIN AND ITS HEROES—LYMAN C. DRAPER.

THE CAREER OF ARTHUR DOBBS OF CARRICKFERGUS (1689-1765).

THE PATRIOTS OF COWPENS BY DR. BOBBY GILMER MOSS.

WESTERING MAN, THE LIFE OF JOSEPH WALKER—BIL GILBERT.

THE HERITAGE OF ROWAN COUNTY, NORTH CAROLINA—JAMES S. BRAWLEY.

THE ROWAN STORY (NORTH CAROLINA) 1753/1953—JAMES S. BRAWLEY.

NINETY SIX—THE STRUGGLE FOR THE SOUTH CAROLINA BACK COUNTRY
   - ROBERT D. BASS.

SOUTH CAROLINA—A SYNOPTIC HISTORY FOR LAYMEN—LEWIS P. JONES.

HISTORY OF SPARTANBURG COUNTY—DR. J. B. O. LANDRUM.

LONG RIFLES OF NORTH CAROLINA—JOHN BIVION JR.

SOUTH CAROLINA—A SHORT HISTORY BY DAVID DUNCAN WALLACE.

PATRIOTS, PISTOLS AND PETTICOATS—WALTER J. FRASER JR.

A HISTORY OF ROWAN COUNTY, NORTH CAROLINA—REV JETHRO RUMPLE.

HISTORY OF DAVIE COUNTY, NORTH CAROLINA—JAMES W. WALL.

THE GREAT WAGON ROAD BY PARKE ROUSE JR.

THE WILD WEST. PUBLISHED BY WARNER BOOKS.

THE AMERICAN FRONTIER: PIONEERS, SETTLERS AND COWBOYS 1800-1899
   —WILLIAM C. DAVIS.

HISTORY OF THE LOST STATE OF FRANKLIN—SAMUEL COLE WILLIAMS.

BOUND AWAY: VIRGINIA AND THE WESTWARD MOVEMENT—DAVID HACKETT FISCHER
   AND JAMES C. KELLY.

SKETCH OF THE LIFE AND IMPRISONMENT OF MARY (NEELY) SPEARS. TENNESSEE STATE
   LIBRARY AND ARCHIVES, NASHVILLE.

FROM SEA TO SHINING SEA—JAMES ALEXANDER THOM.

HOUSTON AND CROCKETT, HEROES OF TENNESSEE AND TEXAS—AN ANTHOLOGY.

THE AMERICAN HERITAGE: ENCYCLOPEDIA OF AMERICAN HISTORY—EDITED BY JOHN
   MACK FARAGHER.

DANIEL BOONE: MASTER OF THE WILDERNESS—JOHN BAKELESS.

DANIEL BOONE AND THE WILDERNESS ROAD—BRUCE H. ADDINGTON.

Colonial Heroines of Tennessee, Kentucky and Virgini—David J. Harkness. Tennessee.

Escape from Indian Captivity: The Story of Mary Draper Ingles and son Thomas Ingles—Edited by Roberta Ingles Steele and Andrew Lewis Ingles.

Appalachian Frontiers: Settlements, Society and Development in the Pre-Historic Era. Edited by Robert D. Mitchell.

Women in the American Revolution—Edited by Jeanne Munn Bracken.

American Scripture: How America Declared Its Independence From Britain - Pauline Maier.

Tennessee: A History—Wilma Dykeman.

The Mammoth Book of the Wild West—Jon E. Lewis.

Sketch on the Life and Imprisonment of Mary (Neely) Spears. Tennessee State Library and Archives, Nashville.

The Making of McCormick County (South Carolina)—Bobby F. Edmonds.

Albion's Seed: Four British Folkways in America—David Hackett Fischer.

South Carolina Gazette February 23, 1760 and March 1-8, 1760 (South Carolina State Archives, Columbia).

The South Carolina Up-Country—E. Don Hurd Jr..

The Life of Anne Calhoun Matthews—Hobert W. Burns.

The Fighting Elder: Andrew Pickens—Alice Noble Waring.

The Grandfather of John C. Calhoun—A. S. Salley.

The Women of the American Revolution—Elizabeth F. Ellet.

The Patriots of Kings Mountain—Bobby Gilmer Moss.

Alex Stewart, Portrait of a Pioneer—John Rice Irwin.

Knox County, Tennessee—Betsey Beeler Creekmore.

Belfast News Letter—250 Years (1737-1987).

Andrew Jackson's Hermitage.

Zion Presbyterian Church, Columbia, Tennessee.

Knoxville's First Graveyard 1800-1970 (East Tennessee Historical Society).

A Precarious Belonging, Presbyterians and the Conflict in Ireland - Rev Dr. John Dunlop.

The Cousins War—Kevin Philips.

The Pursuit of Equal Liberty: George Bryan and the Revolution in North Ccarolina—E. R. R. Green.

The Friersons of Zion Church—Theodore Frierson Stephenson.

For Christ in the Heart of Knoxville (History of Knoxville's First Presbyterian Church)—Ashley Mack

The Women of the American Revolution—Elizabeth F. Ellet.

The Life of Andrew Jackson—Robert V. Remini.

Young Hickory: The Making of Andrew Jackson—Hendrik Booraem.

To the Best of My Ability: The American Presidents—edited by James M. McPherson.

Tennessee Encyclopedia of History and Culture—edited by Carroll Van West.

The Scotch-Irish and Ulster—Eric Montgomery.

The Tinkling Spring (Headwater of Freedom).

PICTURES AND ILLUSTRATIONS:

DAVID WRIGHT, NASHVILLE, TENNESSEE.

GRAY STONE PRESS, NASHVILLE, TENNESSEE.

LARRY CRABTREE, HUNTSVILLE, ALABAMA.

BOBBY F. EDMONDS, MCCORMICK, SOUTH CAROLINA.

DR. DAVID HUME, LARNE, CO ANTRIM.

EAST TENNESSEE HISTORICAL SOCIETY, KNOXVILLE.

TONY GUZZI, CURATOR, THE HERMITAGE, NASHVILLE, TENNESSEE.

MUSEUM OF APPALACHIA, NORRIS, TENNESSEE.

MUSEUM OF AMERICAN FRONTIER CULTURE, STAUNTON, VIRGINA.

IMAGE OF SAM HOUSTON, TENNESSEE STATE MUSEUM, TENNESSEE HISTORICAL COLLEGE, NASHVILLE.

FILSON HISTORICAL CLUB, LOUISVILLE, KENTUCKY.

FRIENDS OF THE GOVERNOR'S MANSION, AUSTIN, TEXAS.

DAUGHTERS OF THE REPUBLIC OF TEXAS, SAN ANTONIO, TEXAS.

DOVER PUBLICATIONS INC., MINEOLA, NEW YORK.

UNITED STATES SENATE PHOTOGRAPHIC STUDIO, WASHINGTON DC.

NATIONAL PORTRAIT GALLERY, SMITHSONIAN INSTITUTION, WASHINGTON DC.

ROBERT WINDSOR WILSON (ARTIST), WOODRUFF, SOUTH CAROLINA.

INDEX